Andrew C. Isaak

Row Houses and Cluster Houses

An International Survey

Hubert Hoffmann

Row Houses and Cluster Houses

An International Survey

Frederick A. Praeger, Publishers
New York · Washington

BOOKS THAT MATTER

Published in the United States of America in 1967
by Frederick A. Praeger, Publishers
111 Fourth Avenue, New York, N.Y. 10003
All rights reserved
Copyright in Stuttgart in 1967 by Verlag Gerd Hatje, Stuttgart, Germany
Library of Congress Catalog Card Number: 66-18903
Translation into English: E. Rockwell
Printed in Germany

Preface

A man's dwelling is among the most important factors that affect his being. His home should provide a congenial environment offering the most favourable conditions under which both the individual and the family can develop and grow. However most contemporary dwellings are anything but congenial—too often they are souless boxes bearing the stamp of meanness and stupidity. However our achievements in other fields have now given us the practical means to improve this state of affairs so discreditable to our culture; and increased leisure is only one of the factors that make this a matter of vital importance.

There have been innumerable projects as well as a few actual examples which suggest the directions in which residential housing should move. But the most essential consideration is that individual dwelling and the urban or rural structure that provides its setting should once again be meaningfully related to each other and that this relationship should be reflected in appropriate architectural and environmental forms.

Among all the possibilities available, it seems to me that it is through low-rise housing that good living standards can be most readily achieved.

Graz, January 1967   Hubert Hoffmann

Vorwort

Als einer der bedeutendsten Umweltfaktoren prägt die Wohnung den Menschen in seinem Wesen. Daher sollte Wohnen ein »Habitat« sein, das heißt sich in einem Raum vollziehen, welcher die günstigsten Bedingungen für das Wachsen und Gedeihen des einzelnen und der Familie bietet. Jene Wohnungen, in denen der Mensch unserer Epoche überwiegend wohnen muß, sind aber alles andere als ein Habitat; es sind lieblose Behälter, geboren aus Geiz und Dummheit.

Wir haben, nachdem unsere Welt auf anderen Gebieten grundlegend verändert wird, die Mittel, diesen für unsere Kultur so beschämenden Zustand zu ändern. — Nicht nur durch vermehrte Freizeit gewinnt das Wohnen wieder eine zentrale Bedeutung.

Es gibt mannigfache Vorschläge und einige wenige Realisierungen, welche die Richtung weisen, in der sich unser Wohnungsbau vollziehen sollte. Eines wird dabei jedoch stets notwendig sein: Die Wohnung als Einzelzelle und die Stadt als gemeinschaftlicher Rahmen müssen wieder sinnvoll aufeinander bezogen werden und diese Beziehung muß in einer entsprechenden räumlichen Gliederung und Vielseitigkeit ihren Ausdruck finden. Unter den hierfür gegebenen Möglichkeiten erscheint mir die Realisierung eines qualitativen Wohnens am ehesten im verdichteten Flachbau erreichbar zu sein.

Graz, Januar 1967   Hubert Hoffmann

Contents

Inhalt

1. Nördlingen as example of a medieval European town structure. The incipient desintegration outside the walls is clearly recognizable.

1. Nördlingen als Beispiel einer mittelalterlichen europäischen Stadtstruktur. Deutlich ist die außerhalb der Stadtmauer beginnende Zersiedlung zu erkennen.

2. City on a Greek Island as an example of urban low-rise housing. Single-storey and two-storey units of a similar type are grouped around a centre, in this case the church, and convey a lively space effect combined with economy in size.

2. Griechische Inselstadt als Beispiel für urbanen Flachbau. Ein- und zweigeschossige ähnliche Elemente um ein Zentrum, die Kirche gruppiert, ergeben lebendige Raumbildungen bei ökonomischer Bebauung.

Loosening-up or Greater Concentration?

The population of the world increases by 2 per cent every year, i.e., it will double in about 40 years. This alarming fact and, on the other hand, the planless and uninhibited residential sprawl so often encountered in modern urban practice, have given rise to the demand for greater concentration. In view of the spoiling of entire regions by urban sprawl and of all the aesthetic, social and economic drawbacks resulting from this process, such a demand must no doubt be welcomed. More concentrated low-rise housing has also been advocated in the book "Die gegliederte und aufgelockerte Stadt," written by J. Göderitz and R. Rainer in association with the present author (Second Edition, 1964). This book also deals with the limits to which concentration and deconcentration can be taken and draws the relevant conclusions as to an appropriate type of housing. In a somewhat similar manner, British town planners are aiming at a kind of levelling process, i.e. a greater concentration of low-rise housing concomitant with a reduction in the density of over-populated districts of industrial cities. On a theoretical plane, opposing ideals have led different authors to postulate, or at least to try and justify, certain extreme solutions–extreme concentration on the one hand, e.g. William H. White in "The Exploding Metropolis" (New York, 1958), and extreme decentralisation on the other hand, e.g. Lloyd Rodwin in "The Future Metropolis" (London, 1962), Kevin Lynch in "The Image of the City" (Cambridge, 1960), and Lowdon Wingo, go in "Cities and Space–The Future Use of Urban Land" (Baltimore, 1963). In our opinion, "density" should always be *appropriate*, i. e., in keeping with the specific conditions of a region or the requirements of a specific urban situation. Admittedly, the term "concentration," if applied without qualification, is apt to be a mighty weapon in the hands of the land speculators whose power should not be rated any lower than that of the oil, chemical or steel combines. But the term "Concentration" should not be understood in a quantitative sense alone. Often, e.g. at the "Society through Concentration" Conference at Gelsenkirchen, 1963, the term is used in a qualitative sense, indicating a "spiritual" concentration process. Similarly, terms synonymous with "loosening-up" used to be applied, in the nineteen-twenties and thirties, not only to precise statements in terms of persons per acre but also qualitatively in order to indicate a state of mind. At that time, "loosening-up" was taken to imply proneness to contact-making; open-mindedness; absence of dogma, neurosis and bias–thus in Walter Serner's book "Letzte Lockerung" (Hanover, 1920).

The demand for concentration apparently reflects an urge for deliberate shaping, for greater emotional tension, for "densification," thus reversing the motto of the Gelsenkirchen Conference into "Concentration through Society." Spiritual concentration would thus also be in keeping with the demand for an "urban" type of housing, where the term "urban" is used in the sense of the following definition.

Definition of Urban Low-Rise Group Housing

"Urban" is a notion translated and handed down by the Romans from the Greek "asteiotes" which, apart from serving as the adjective to the noun "town," implies a refined mode of living, a deliberate intellectualism, related not only to individual persons or a ruling class but, to an even greater extent, to the democratic-social conscience of the public at large. The definition has been amplified by E. Salin to signify "fruitful cooperation of Man as a political being." Even apart from Athens and the Age of Pericles, Ancient Greece offers many highlights and examples of the active co-operation of citizens in creating a "polis," resulting in a symbiosis of intellectual and architectural achievement to which the term "urban" can rightfully be applied. To this period corresponds a heyday of urbanism in Medieval Europe where a wise and even ingenious social order and comprehension was accompanied by supreme achievements in the sphere of arts. This development can be ascribed to a "social intelligence" in the sense in which this term was used by Thomas Aquinas ("That which is good is wise") who regarded "Providentia" as the essential ingredient of perfect wisdom.

From these examples of the past, we gain the conviction that "social quality" is the only soil in which refined culture was and is able to prosper, and where supreme achievements are attained and emulated. The anonymous background of social quality is therefore just as necessary and important as a paramount achievement visible to the eye. This background must be regarded as an indispensable ingredient of all that is "urban," becoming even more manifest in simple houses, streets and squares than in monumental buildings such as places of worship, manor houses and town halls. We are therefore entitled to apply the term "urban" to a mode of urban development if it is derived from the collective intellectual effort of all citizens to obtain the right kind of housing, and an urban settlement deserves to be called "urban" in this more refined sense if care is taken to cater for all the different "activities," age groups, family combinations and their changes in the course of time. The term "urban" is thus meant to signify, not the condition

Auflockerung oder Verdichtung?

Die Menschheit vermehrt sich jährlich um 2%, das heißt, sie verdoppelt sich in etwa 40 Jahren. Diese alarmierende Tatsache einerseits und die heutige städtebauliche Praxis andererseits, nach der Siedlungen ebenso planlos wie hemmungslos das Land »überschwemmen«, haben zur Forderung nach Verdichtung geführt. Angesichts der »Zersiedlung« ganzer Provinzen und der sich daraus ergebenden negativen ästhetischen, gesellschaftlichen und ökonomischen Erscheinungen ist diese Forderung zweifellos zu begrüßen. Auch in »Die gegliederte und aufgelockerte Stadt« (J. Göderitz und R. Rainer gemeinsam mit dem Verfasser, 2. Aufl. 1964) wird ein verdichteter Flachbau gefordert. Darüber hinaus werden die Grenzen von Dichte und Auflockerung gezeigt und die notwendigen Folgerungen für eine gemäße Bauweise gezogen. Etwa in gleicher Art streben die englischen Städteplaner einen Ausgleich an, d. h., sie bemühen sich, den Flachbau stärker zu verdichten und die zu dicht bebauten, überbelegten Viertel von Industriestädten aufzulockern. In der Theorie werden unter dem Einfluß entgegengesetzter Leitbilder, extreme Konzentration einerseits – etwa durch William H. White in »The Exploding Metropolis« (New York, 1958) – und extreme Dezentralisation andererseits – durch Lloyd Rodwin in »The Future Metropolis« (London, 1962), Kevin Lynch in »The Image of the City« (Cambridge, 1960) und ebenso durch Lowdon Wingo in »Cities and Space. The Future Use of Urban Land« (Baltimore, 1963) – gefordert bzw. nachgewiesen. Wir meinen, daß »Dichte« immer *gemäß* sein sollte: den Bedingungen einer Region oder den Aufgaben einer Situation im städtischen Raum entsprechend. Das Wort »Verdichtung« ist, kommentarlos angewendet, allerdings eine prächtige Waffe für die Bodenspekulation, deren Macht nicht geringer eingeschätzt werden darf als die der Öl-, Chemie- oder Stahlkonzerne. Der Begriff »Verdichtung« wird jedoch nicht nur quantitativ verstanden. Er wird, wie auf der Tagung »Gesellschaft durch Dichte« (Gelsenkirchen 1963), häufig qualitativ, im Sinne einer »geistigen« Verdichtung angewandt. Auch mit dem Wort »Auflockerung« war in den zwanziger und dreißiger Jahren ebenso eine Qualität psychischer Art wie eine exakte Angabe über die Anzahl von Personen pro Hektar gemeint. »Auflockerung« hatte damals die Bedeutung: kontaktfähig, aufgeschlossen, undogmatisch, ausgeruht, ohne Vorurteil, z. B. Walter Serner »Letzte Lockerung« (Hannover, 1920).
Der Wunsch nach Dichte entspricht offenbar einem Streben nach Gestaltung, stärkerer Spannung, nach »Dichtung«, das heißt – in Umkehrung des Themas von Gelsenkirchen – nach einer Verdichtung durch Gesellschaft. Geistige Verdichtung würde somit auch der Forderung nach einer urbanen Form des Wohnens – im Sinn der folgenden Definition – entsprechen.

Definition »urban« und »Flachbau«

»Urban« ist ein von den Römern aus dem griechischen »asteiotes« übersetzter und vermittelter Begriff, der sich mit »städtisch« übersetzen läßt, mit der zusätzlichen Bedeutung einer feineren Lebensart, einer bewußten Geistigkeit, bezogen nicht nur auf einzelne Persönlichkeiten, eine führende Schicht, sondern in viel stärkerem Maße auf das demokratisch gesellschaftliche Bewußtsein der Allgemeinheit. E. Salin ergänzt die Definition durch die Umschreibung »fruchtbare Mitwirkung des Menschen als politisches Wesen«. Es gibt im antiken Griechenland außer Athen und dem Zeitalter des Perikles zahlreiche Höhepunkte und Beispiele aktiven Mitwirkens der Bürger an der Gestaltung einer Polis und daraus hervorgehender Übereinstimmung von geistiger Leistung mit der gebauten Stadtstruktur, die man als »urban« bezeichnen muß. Dieser Periode entspricht die Blütezeit des Städtewesens im Mittelalter Europas, in der sich eine kluge, ja geniale gesellschaftliche Ordnung und Einsicht, bei gleichzeitigen Höhepunkten auf dem Gebiet der Künste, erkennen läßt. Sie hat ihre Ursache in einer »Gemeinschaftsintelligenz«, im Sinne Thomas von Aquins (»Das Gute ist das Kluge«), der »Providentia« (Vorsorge) für den wesentlichen Bestandteil vollendeter Klugheit hielt.
Nur eine gesellschaftliche Qualität ist demnach der Boden, auf dem verfeinerte Kultur wachsen konnte und kann, auf dem Höchstleistungen als »Vorbilder« gedeihen. Die anonyme Basis einer gesellschaftlichen Qualität ist daher ebenso notwendig und wichtig wie die sichtbare Spitzenleistung. Sie muß als ein unentbehrlicher Bestandteil des Urbanen angesehen werden, das sich in einfachen Wohnbauten, Straßen und Plätzen noch stärker dokumentiert als in den Monumentalbauten Tempel, Schloß und Rathaus. Wir können also mit Recht eine Bebauungsweise »urban« nennen, wenn sie aus dem Mitdenken aller Bürger um die richtige Art von Wohnung und Haus entstanden ist, das heißt, wenn sie sich in das Ganze einordnet und einbindet. Wir vermögen ein Stadtgebilde als »urban« zu bezeichnen, wenn für die verschiedenen »Tätigkeiten«, Altersgruppen und Kombinationen der Familie und deren Wandlung Vorsorge getroffen ist. Urban bedeutet also nicht nur den Zustand, der durch eine relative Dichte entsteht, vielmehr eine »Verdichtung« im geistigen Sinne, die aus politischer Qualität erwächst.
Im allgemeinen Sprachgebrauch werden ein- und zweigeschossige Bauten als »Flachbau« be-

3. Gladsaxe, Denmark. Blocks of four, nine and sixteen storeys on a site which would have been spacious enough to provide a high percentage of dwellings in the form of low-rise housing. But the demonstration of building site rationalisation and prefabrication methods was regarded as more important than human and social requirements.

3. Gladsaxe, Dänemark. Vier-, neun- und sechzehngeschossige Wohnblocks auf einem Gelände, das weiträumig genug gewesen wäre, um einen hohen Anteil der Wohnungen im Flachbau zu errichten. Der Demonstration von Baustellen-Rationalisierung und Fertigbauweise wurde jedoch das Primat eingeräumt, vor menschlichen und gesellschaftlichen Bedürfnissen.

4. Multi-layer house in Sweden; Architect: E. Friberger. Efforts at augmenting the scarce building land through artificial stratification give rise to a new type of housing with additional structure. The low-rise dwelling erected on the artificially created platform has sufficient open space without, however, enjoying the quality of the grown soil.

4. Schichtenhaus in Schweden, Architekt E. Friberger. Bemühungen, den knappen Baugrund durch künstliche Schichten zu vermehren, führen zu einer neuen Bebauungsweise mit zusätzlicher Konstruktion. Flachbau auf künstlichen Schichten hat ausreichenden Freiraum, allerdings ohne die Qualität des gewachsenen Bodens.

Page/Seite 11:

5. The division of a traditional London house may exemplify the notion of "Urban Low-Rise Housing." The lower dwelling is associated with a private enclosure at ground level whilst the upper dwelling is merely connected to a public space at ground level. (Architects: R. Stout & P. Litchfield.)

5. Teilung eines traditionellen Londoner Hauses als Beispiel zur Definition des Begriffes »Flachbau«. Die untere Wohnung führt in einen ebenerdigen, privaten Bereich; die obere Wohnung dagegen lediglich in einen ebenerdigen, öffentlichen Raum. (Arch.: R. Stout & P. Litchfield.)

brought about by a relatively high population density, but a concentration in the intellectual sense, arising from a high level of political maturity.

In common parlance, the term "Low-Rise Housing" is generally reserved for buildings with one or two storeys, whilst buildings from two to six storeys are said to be of "medium-rise" and even higher ones are described as "multi-storey" buildings. But such a classification does not do full justice to the typical features of "low-rise housing." One might talk of "horizontally" and "vertically" grouped housing; but as there is an increasing tendency to adopt imbricated arrangements of dwellings, the terms "horizontal" and "vertical" have ceased to be the decisive criteria. This definition also tends to become ambiguous in the case of hillside housing.

Here, the term "Low-Rise Housing" is meant to denote dwellings which are directly associated with the ground, in contrast to the indirect association with the ground in the form of a jointly used staircase to which the occupiers of multi-storey houses are confined.

In low-rise housing, the direct link consists of the internal stairs or a door leading to a private garden, or possibly to a semi-private open space reserved for the occupiers of surrounding houses. In contrast, a "multi-storey dweller" must use a "public" staircase as a lock through which a public sphere—road or open space—can be reached.

A clear definition of the notion of "Low-Rise housing" therefore calls for an indication of the private or public character of the open space to which the dwelling is directly or indirectly linked. Urban Low-Rise Group Housing may therefore be defined as "high-density housing where each dwelling is directly linked with a private open space." It is the intimate association between dwelling and open space which is the vital criterion of low-rise housing.

In recent years, there have been frequent suggestions to the effect that the area available for buildings should be enlarged by an artificial scaffolding, a kind of "community carrier," rather like Le Corbusier's "Ville Radieuse." Among these suggestions are, inter alia, Winkler's "Stratified Town"; the ideas of the Japanese "Metabolists"; the plans for Toulouse designed by Candilis-Josic-Woods; the "space lattices" conceived by Frei Otto, Schulze-Fielitz and Friedmann, and the present author's elevated walkway systems envisaged for Berlin, Gelsenkirchen, and other places. Such designs may be classified as low-rise housing if the dwellings are associated with a terrace serving as a substitute for the natural ground; but they would have to be classified as multi-storey housing if the bye-laws require the provision of lifts.

In fact, such designs calling for an additional structural framework would seem to defy classification under either category. As the example of the "housing hill" at Stuttgart clearly shows, the objective is the combination, in a single unit, of different functions, ancillary services, car parks, and different types of dwellings. We are obviously confronted with an entirely new category of housing representing an urban concentration greater than that of the "Unité d'habitation." Whilst conventional multi-storey, medium and low-rise houses are erected on natural ground where roads, walkway, public and private open spaces are located, the natural ground is here merely used for the erection of a bearing structure, a "lattice work." Roads, walkways and piazzas, sometimes even building sites and open spaces, are mainly removed to artificially created platforms. The three-dimensional inter-relation of the urban elements is no longer, primarily dependent on natural conditions.

The range of housing types thus comprises "ground-based" housing with individual bearing structures for multi-storey, medium or low-rise housing, and will in future also comprise "platform-based" units where multi-storey, medium or low-rise buildings can be erected on artificially created ground. The "urban" character of platform-based units follows spontaneously from the logical and economic utilisation of the "platform." Correspondingly, the "urban" character of ground-based housing follows from a close group association where the individual building becomes an integral part of a planning unit.

History and Geographical Spread of Urban Low-Rise Group Housing

For a long time, most cities in our latitudes preserved the character of marked towns which lived, to some extent, on the surplus agricultural produce of their hinterland. They were dominated by the "farming townsman," and differed but little from villages. Later, although the houses became higher and narrower, the barn door remained, even if there was no longer any harvest to be sheltered. The age of manufacture and the conversion of the farming townsman to craftsman and merchant brought little change. Basically, his house was still modelled on the rural single-roof house.

Even the modern urban detached house which, to most of our contemporaries in Europe, represents the ideal mode of housing, is a copy of a rural house. But it is a miserable, crippled house with wrong proportions, which cannot deny its origin from the farmhouse with its necessarily large storage space under the roof.

It is no accident, either, that the Central European multi-storey house can be traced back to the

zeichnet, zwei- bis sechsgeschossige als »Mittelbau« und mehr als sechsgeschossige als »Hochbau«. Diese Beschreibung umreißt jedoch das Typische des »Flachbaus« nicht mit hinreichender Deutlichkeit. Man könnte auch von »nebeneinandergereihten« und »übereinandergestapelten« Wohnungen sprechen, aber es mehren sich Bemühungen, Wohnungen ineinanderzuschachteln, so daß Neben- und Übereinander nicht mehr entscheidende Kennzeichen sind. Auch bei Hangbebauung verliert diese Definition ihre Eindeutigkeit.

Flachbau ist eine Bebauungsweise, bei der die Wohnungen eine unmittelbare Verbindung mit dem Boden haben, im Unterschied zu der mittelbaren Verbindung mit dem Grund bei Mehrfamilienhäusern über das allgemein benutzte Treppenhaus. Die direkte Verbindung beim Flachbau erfolgt über das Medium der internen Treppe oder durch eine Tür in den privaten Bereich des Hausgartens – oder in eine private, nur einer Wohngruppe zugängliche Freifläche. Die indirekte Verbindung der Wohnung im Mehrfamilienhaus bedeutet, daß man ein »öffentliches« Treppenhaus als Schleuse benutzen muß, um in eine öffentliche Sphäre, Straße oder Freifläche, zu gelangen.

Zur eindeutigen Definition des Begriffes »Flachbau« bedarf es also einer Aussage über den privaten oder öffentlichen Charakter jener Freifläche, mit der die Wohnung direkt oder indirekt verbunden ist.

Urbaner Flachbau ist zu definieren als »eine geschlossene Bebauungsweise, bei der eine unmittelbare Verbindung der Wohnung mit einem Freiflächenbereich besteht, welcher der privaten Sphäre zugehört«. Der ineinandergreifende intime Bereich Wohnung–Freiraum ist das eigentliche Kriterium des Flachbaus.

In den letzten Jahren haben sich die Vorschläge gehäuft, die Bodenflächen – ähnlich wie schon Le Corbusiers »Ville Radieuse« – durch ein künstliches Gerüst, eine Art »Gemeinschaftsträger« zu vermehren. Dazu gehören etwa die »Schichtenstadt« von Winkler, die Vorschläge der japanischen Metabolisten, die Pläne für Toulouse von Candilis-Josic-Woods, die Raumgitter von Frei Otto, Schulze-Fielitz, Friedmann und Ruhnau, die Stegsysteme des Verfassers für Berlin und Gelsenkirchen u.a. Handelt es sich hier um Flachbau, wenn die Wohnungen eine den natürlichen Boden ersetzende Terrasse haben, oder um Wohnhochhäuser, wenn nach den Hochhausverordnungen Fahrstühle erforderlich werden?

Solche Gebilde auf einem zusätzlichen konstruktiven Gerüst lassen sich weder unter »Hochbau« noch »Flachbau« einordnen. Das Ziel ist, das zeigt der Stuttgarter Wohnhügel deutlich, in einer Einheit verschiedene Funktionen, Folgeeinrichtungen, Abstellplätze und unterschiedliche Wohnformen miteinander zu mischen. Es entsteht also offenbar eine ganz neue Kategorie von Bebauungsweisen, eine über die Unité d'habitation hinausgehende städtebauliche Konzentration.

Während Hoch-, Mittel- und Flachbau auf natürlichem Gelände aufbauen und für Straßen, Wege, öffentliche und private Freiflächen den gegebenen Boden voraussetzen, wird hier der natürliche Grund nur benutzt, um eine tragende Konstruktion, ein »Gitter«, aufzustellen. Straßen, Wege und Plätze, manchmal auch Bau- und Freiflächen, sind zum überwiegenden Teil auf künstliche Ebenen verlegt. Die räumlichen Beziehungen der urbanen Elemente untereinander sind nicht mehr primär abhängig von der Natur.

Es gibt somit bodengebundene Bebauungsweisen mit individueller Tragkonstruktion in Hoch-, Mittel- und Flachbau, und es gibt künftig schichtengebundene städtebauliche Einheiten, bei denen Hoch-, Mittel- oder Flachbau auf einem künstlich geschaffenen Grund errichtet werden können. Der urbane Charakter schichtengebundener Einheiten ergibt sich zwangsläufig durch die sinnvolle und ökonomische Ausnutzung des »Trägers«. Der urbane Charakter bodengebundener Bebauungsweisen entsteht dementsprechend durch eine enge gruppenhafte Verflechtung, in der sich der individuelle Bau der städtebaulichen Einheit unterordnet.

Zeitliche und räumliche Verbreitung des Flachbaus

Lange Zeit hindurch hatte die Mehrzahl der Städte in unseren Breiten noch den Charakter von Marktgemeinden, die zum Teil vom landwirtschaftlichen Überschuß der Umgebung lebten. Der »Ackerbürger« prägte das Gesicht dieser Städte, die sich noch kaum von Dörfern unterschieden. Später wurden zwar die Häuser höher und schmäler, aber das Scheunentor blieb, auch bei solchen, in denen keine Ernte unterzubringen war. Die Manufakturperiode und die Wandlung des Ackerbürgers zum Handwerker und Kaufmann änderte an diesem Zustand wenig. Die Form des Hauses blieb im Prinzip eine Nachahmung des landwirtschaftlichen Eindachhauses.

Auch das heutige städtische Siedlungshaus, das heißt jenes freistehende Einfamilienhaus, das für die Mehrzahl unserer Zeitgenossen in Europa ein Ideal darstellt, ist die Nachahmung eines Bauernhauses. Ein jämmerliches, verkrüppeltes, unproportioniertes Haus allerdings, das seine Herkunft vom Bauernhaus mit notwendigem großem Bergeraum unter dem Dach nicht verleugnen kann.

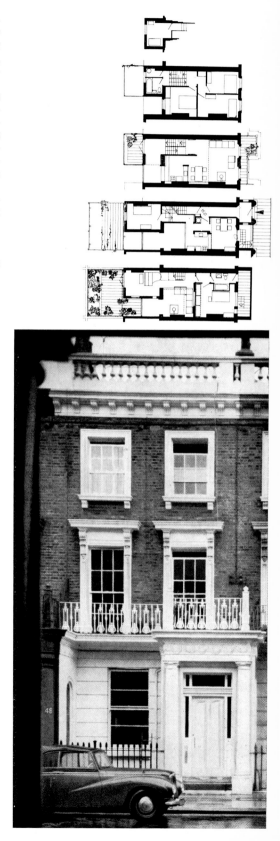

6. El Omrane near Tunis: An estate of low-rise houses grouped around a mosque. Patio houses with reinforced concrete vaults. A traditional method of building construction, continued with modern means.

6. El Omrane bei Tunis: Flachbausiedlung um eine Moschee gruppiert. Hofhäuser mit Tonnengewölbe in Stahlbetonkonstruktion. Fortführung traditioneller Bebauungsweise mit neuen Mitteln.

7. Pompei: House blocks of equal depth contain a tissue of patio and terrace houses of different sizes.

7. Pompeji: Wohnquartiere gleicher Blocktiefen enthalten ein Gewebe von Hof- und Reihenhäusern verschiedener Größe.

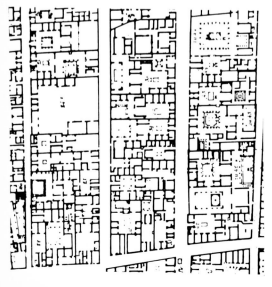

military barrack; in fact, the German term "Mietskaserne," signifying a "barrack for tenants," was by no means meant to be derogatory. In the absence of other examples, this type was initially influenced by Mediterranean designs. A different picture is encountered in North-West Europe. In Britain, in the Netherlands, and in the adjacent regions of Germany and France, the transition from primary agricultural production to secondary commercial activities took place earlier. In these countries, the rural heritage of the single-family house is therefore much more repressed than in the rest of Central Europe and in Eastern Europe. Not only were the wealthy "low" countries able to develop a particularly high dwelling culture, which spread along the entire North Sea and Baltic and, in the South, all the way to Spain; they also developed a type of urban single-family house which, by virtue of its plan and external appearance, may already be regarded as "urban low-rise housing" in the sense here defined.

According to an opinion widely held in Central Europe, it is the industrial revolution, and the hasty growth of our cities caused by it, which has given rise to urban concentration and to the advent of three-to-five-storey tenement houses in our medium-sized and large cities. But this opinion is based on an erroneous assumption of a casual relationship between two simultaneous phenomena. In the Anglo-Saxon and Low Countries, low-rise housing continued to prevail in the residential areas of the largest conurbations even after the industrial revolution. Even to-day, there is no city in England, including London, with a higher average population density than 9 persons per building. It is partly due to the high standard of dwelling culture in the Anglo-Saxon and Low Countries and in the adjacent regions, and to the "dwelling consciousness" developed in these regions, that the single-family house has been preserved as the predominant mode of housing.

That low-rise housing has been ousted by multi-storey housing in the cities of Central Europe is mainly due to the prevailing real estate and mortgage conditions which provide a greater incentive to uninhibited ground speculation than in the Anglo-Saxon countries. In England, remnants of the feudal system still remain. The feudal landlord who became property owner —the "landed gentry"—leases his land for a 99 years leasehold to developers who are responsible for the building of entire estates. Because of this legal differentiation between building and ground, mortgages can be obtained on the building alone, and slum clearance becomes easier. The unfortunate combination of mortgages on the building as well as on the ground, which in Germany dates back to the mortgage legislation introduced by Frederic the Great, is ruled out.

Apart from areas under European influence, multi-storey housing is the exception in other continents, too. The patio house can be traced back to the oldest cities in the east, and even to-day, cities like Esphahan with a population of some 300,000, exclusively consists of closely spaced low-rise houses. Wolf Schneider has this to say: "The dwelling comfort enjoyed by the inhabitants of Ur or Echet-Aton and the sanitary installations of Mohenjo Daro can put most of the tenement houses of the nineteenth century to shame, and our modern dwellings have, in any case, much less space than those of the cities of 4000 years ago" ("Überall ist Babylon," p. 59). In the seismic belt stretching from Macedonia through Persia and South-East Asia to Japan, the lightly built low-rise house is a vital safety requirement. Rather than imitating European multi-storey housing, it would here be more appropriate to revive the traditional low-rise timber house, suitably adapted to modern conditions, in order to create earthquake proof residential areas. The new towns built by Doxiadis in Pakistan and in Iraq represent a promising beginning in their renewed reliance on regional conditions. In 1963, the present author was able to see for himself that virtually no lives were lost in the low-rise "Turkish quarter" of Skopje, whilst the districts with solid multi-storey buildings showed a high death-roll.

Technical and Economic Comparison of Low-Rise and Multi-Storey Housing

In a discussion on the efficiency and economics of sliding windows compared with hinged windows, Mart Stam once said: "With us in Holland, sliding windows are more efficient and more economic because we like sliding windows." This dictum would be just as appropriate if one would substitute, for sliding windows, low-rise housing. This means first of all that technical, economic and other objections are overcome or are regarded as being of secondary importance, if a mode of housing stems from an inner compulsion; it also means, that it is difficult to argue for low-rise housing in countries where this mode of housing has been ousted for a long time. If we compare multi-storey housing with low-rise housing, the concentration of all plumbing installations and the savings in basement space and roof area must, prima facie, be regarded as technical-economic advantages of the former. In this respect, low-rise housing would indeed seem to be costlier, because of the relatively higher costs of foundations, basements and roofing, and because of the need for a private staircase in two-storey houses.

On closer investigation, however, it is found that, for technical reasons, the heavier load calls for more solid construction—and as a result of the bye-laws, public staircases are so much costlier

Es ist auch kein Zufall, daß sich das Mehrfamilienhaus in Mitteleuropa aus der Kaserne entwickelt hat, weshalb die Bezeichnung »Mietskaserne« durchaus nicht abwertend gemeint war. Infolge der fehlenden Vorbilder bediente sich dieser Typ zunächst mediterraner Formen. Ein gegensätzliches Bild zeigen die Verhältnisse in Nordwesteuropa. In England, den Niederlanden und angrenzenden Teilen Deutschlands und Frankreichs erfolgte der Übergang von der primären, landwirtschaftlichen Produktion zur sekundären, gewerblichen schon früher. In diesen Ländern ist daher der bäuerliche »Einschlag« des Einfamilienhauses weit stärker zurückgedrängt als im übrigen Mittel- und Osteuropa. In den wohlhabenden »niederen« Landen hat sich nicht nur eine besonders hohe Wohnkultur herausgebildet, die an der ganzen Nord- und Ostsee und bis nach Spanien Verbreitung fand, es hat sich auch eine Form des städtischen Einfamilienhauses entwickelt, die bereits nach Grundriß und in der äußeren Form als »urbaner« Flachbau bezeichnet werden kann.

Nach einer in Mitteleuropa weitverbreiteten Ansicht ist die Industrialisierung und das mit ihr verbundene rasche Anwachsen der Städte die Ursache einer Konzentration und Einführung des drei- bis fünfgeschossigen Mehrfamilienhauses in den Mittel- und Großstädten. Diese Betrachtungsweise bringt jedoch zwei parallele Erscheinungen fälschlich in einen ursächlichen Zusammenhang. In den angelsächsischen und niederländischen Gebieten blieb auch nach der Industrialisierung der Flachbau in den Wohnvierteln der größten Agglomerationen vorherrschend. Noch heute gibt es in England keine Stadt, einschließlich Londons, mit einer höheren Bebauungsziffer als neun Personen pro Haus. – »Wohnbewußtsein« und Wohnkultur der Angelsachsen, Niederländer und der angrenzenden Bereiche haben dazu beigetragen, das Einfamilienhaus als vorherrschende Wohnform zu erhalten.

Die Verdrängung des Flachbaues in den Städten des mittleren Kontinents durch das Mehrgeschoßhaus hat seine Ursachen vor allem in den hier gültigen Eigentums- und Beleihungsverhältnissen, die einer hemmungslosen Bodenspekulation mehr Anreiz gaben als in den angelsächsischen Ländern. Immer noch bestehen in England Reste des Lehnssystems: Der zum Eigentümer gewordene »Lehnsherr«, der Großgrundbesitzende Adel, verpachtet seine Ländereien auf 99 Jahre in Erbpacht an Unternehmer, die ganze Viertel bebauen. Durch diese Trennung von Bau und Boden können nur auf das Haus Hypotheken aufgenommen werden, und Sanierungen sind einfacher durchzuführen. Die unglückliche Verquickung einer Belastung von Bau und Grundstück wie in Deutschland, als Folge des von Friedrich dem Großen veranlaßten Hypothekengesetzes, ist nicht möglich.

Auch in anderen Kontinenten sind, ausgenommen Gebiete mit europäischem Einfluß, mehrgeschossige Häuser die Ausnahme! Das Hofhaus wurde schon in den ältesten Städten des Orients nachgewiesen, und auch heute noch sind Städte wie Esphahan mit rund 300 000 Einwohnern durchweg flach und dicht bebaut. Wolf Schneider sagt: »Vor dem Wohnkomfort von Ur oder Echet-Aton und den sanitären Anlagen von Mohendscho Daro müssen sich die meisten Mietskasernen des 19. Jahrhunderts schämen, und Platz haben wir in unseren Wohnungen sowieso viel weniger als die Bewohner jener Städte vor vier Jahrtausenden« (»Überall ist Babylon«, S. 59). Im Erdbebengürtel, der über Mazedonien, Iran, Insulinde bis nach Japan reicht, ist der leichtgebaute Flachbau eine Forderung der Lebenssicherheit. Hier sollte der traditionelle hölzerne Flachbau, entsprechend den heutigen Verhältnissen erneuert, wieder aufgenommen werden, um erdbebensichere Wohnviertel zu schaffen, anstatt europäische Mehrgeschoßhäuser nachzuahmen. Die Siedlungen von Doxiades in Pakistan und im Irak geben ein vielversprechender Anfang, wieder von den regionalen Bedingungen auszugehen. In Skopje 1963 konnte der Verfasser feststellen, daß in dem flach gebauten »Türkenviertel« fast niemand umgekommen ist, während in den Stadtgebieten mit mehrgeschossigen Massivbauten eine hohe Zahl von Todesopfern zu beklagen war.

Technisch-wirtschaftlicher Vergleich von Flach- und Hochbau

In einer Diskussion über die Zweckmäßigkeit und Wirtschaftlichkeit von Schiebefenstern oder Drehfenstern äußerte Mart Stam: »Bei uns in Holland sind Schiebefenster zweckmäßiger und wirtschaftlicher, weil wir Schiebefenster lieben!« Dieser Ausspruch wäre ebenso richtig, wenn man statt Schiebefenster »Flachbau« sagen würde. Das heißt erstens, daß technische, wirtschaftliche und sonstige Widerstände überwunden werden oder zweitrangig sind, wenn sich eine Bebauungsweise aus innerem Zwang ergibt, und zweitens, daß es schwierig ist, für neue Formen des urbanen Flachbaues in Ländern zu argumentieren, in denen diese Bebauungsweise seit geraumer Zeit verdrängt ist.

Die erneute Erörterung aller Vor- und Nachteile und ein Vergleich mit anderen Bebauungsweisen scheint unter den veränderten Bedingungen der Gegenwart notwendig, nicht um nachzuweisen, welche Wohnform die absolut günstigste ist. *Die* günstigste Wohnform gibt es nicht. Jede Wohnform hat Vorzüge und Nachteile, die von verschiedensten Faktoren abhängen.

8. Thera-Santorin: The modern patio houses erected after the earthquake are adapted to the pre-existing buildings in an exemplary manner.

8. Thera-Santorin: Die nach dem Erdbeben neu errichteten Hofhäuser moderner Konstruktion sind in hervorragender Weise der bestehenden Bebauung angepaßt.

9. Reconstruction of a house at Priene: A fusion, in Greece, of the patio house of southern and eastern origin with the Megaron house of northern origin.

9. Rekonstruktion eines Hauses in Priene: Verschmelzung des von Süden und Osten kommenden Hofhauses mit dem von Norden kommenden Megaronhaus in Griechenland.

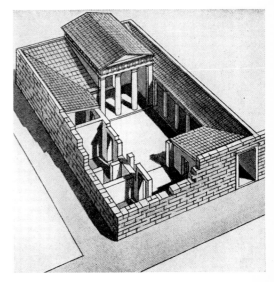

10. Chinese house. With its pavilions for different groups of one large family, this patio house is particularly flexible.

10. Chinesisches Haus. Pavillons für verschiedene Gruppen einer Großfamilie machen dieses Hofhaus besonders flexibel.

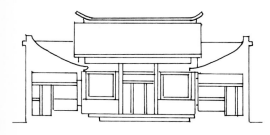

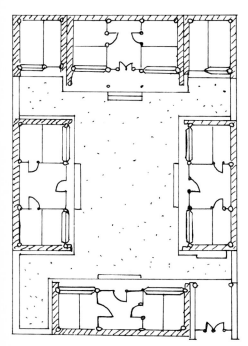

that, according to comparative surveys, it is only in a four-storey block with three flats per floor that the cost incidence of the staircase is reduced to that in a two-storey house. From the fifth or sixth storey onwards, the costs are considerably increased by the lift which then becomes indispensable as an internal means of transport. Moreover, modern bye-laws insist, in the case of multi-storey blocks of flats, on a second emergency staircase and a second lift. Because of the higher costs thus incurred for stairs and lifts and for the structure itself, a flat in a multi-storey block is, on an average, 30 per cent dearer than a low-rise dwelling. On the other hand, the two-storey–single-family house has the advantage that the space above or below the stairs can also be utilised, e. g. for a built-in cupboard, a shelf, or simply as storage space.

The economic aspects of providing a basement depend on the individual storage requirements. However, according to a survey carried out by the Austrian Building Research Institute, an average household will require a storage space of 20 sq. metres (215 sq. ft.). There is therefore no need for a basement covering the entire area of a low-rise house. Moreover, with modern building materials, rooms without basement can be insulated just as well, in fact even better, than rooms with basements. In any case, the low-rise house provides an easier and cheaper solution to the problem of ancillary and storage accomodation. In multi-storey buildings, the ratio of basement floor area and apartment floor area becomes more unfavourable with increasing height.

There thus remains, as the only genuine economic disadvantage of low-rise housing, the cost of the roof. But this must be balanced against other, and more weighty, expenses associated with multi-storey housing, especially with tower blocks. Being more exposed to atmospheric agents, the facades of multi-storey blocks call for a higher quality of finish, especially also in view of the high cost of subsequent repairs. On the building site, too, there arise differences in cost which increase with the height of the building: cranes rising with the structure, shuttering, and safety regulations. By comparison, the plant and equipment required for low-rise housing is less weighty.

Yet low-rise housing is particularly well suited for all types of light-weight construction methods. Savings in weight not only signify cheaper transport, representing a social benefit; they also greatly facilitate the erection of the buildings, especially as far as single-storey houses are concerned. Low-rise housing is virtually predestined for the application of prefabrication methods. According to detailed comparative calculations carried out by the Building Research Institute at Hanover, the costs per dwelling unit in two-storey houses are approximately 8 per cent higher than those of flats of the same size in a four-storey block. This survey was based on conventional types and construction methods.

Yet Herr Kräntzer, one of the civil engineers associated with the same Institute, has this to say about low-rise housing: "The costs of the building, especially with relatively flat roofs, are not higher than for flats of equal size and equipment in three-storey blocks with two flats per floor; in fact, they may even be lower."

The results become more favourable to low-rise housing if the comparsion is extended to houses without basements, with light storage sheds or ancillary rooms at ground level and with flat or nearly flat roofs without attics.

In recent years, the Austrian Building Research Institute has carried out very exact comparisons between the costs of a three-storey block of flats and those of different types of low-rise housing estates without basement. For most of the types of low-rise housing, the overall cost per cubic metre is lower (by up to 13 per cent!) than that of the three-storey block of flats.

It is not possible to state that this or that type of housing is absolutely cheaper than the other since conditions differ in each case. But it can be stated on the strength of the different cost comparisons that it is possible, under certain conditions, to produce dwellings in low-rise houses at the same or at a lower cost than dwellings in multi-storey blocks. If, drawing on a large pool of experience, one tries to probe the boundary line, one arrives at the following result: the costs per dwelling in a two-storey terrace house may range from 125 to 87 per cent and those in a single-storey house from 132 per cent to 90 per cent of the cost of equally large flats in a three-storey block. In England, in the Netherlands and the United States, low-rise housing is cheaper, in principle, than multi-storey housing as the costs are greatly influenced by living habits. In the United States, this even applies to the detached house!

Sociological and Psychological Considerations

What are the sociological or psychological arguments in favour of the multi-storey block?
There is, first of all, the fact that one does not want to become a slave of one's garden which, especially to the housewife, means an additional burden. Moreover, one may be afraid of the financial burden of ownership, the difficulties associated with the erection of a house, the costs for its maintenance, the stronger ties to a given place of residence, traffic difficulties, etc.

Vergleichen wir Hochhaus und Flachbau, so spricht in technisch-wirtschaftlicher Hinsicht die Konzentration aller Naßräume und Installationen sowie die Einsparung von Kellerräumen und Dachflächen zunächst für den Mehrgeschoßbau. Demgegenüber scheint der Flachbau in der Tat durch im Verhältnis vermehrten Aufwand für Fundament, Keller- und Dachflächen eine Verteuerung zu bringen, ebenso die besondere Treppe im zweigeschossigen Flachbau.

Bei genauerer Betrachtung ergibt sich jedoch, daß öffentliche Treppenhäuser aus technischen Gründen – die stärkere Belastung fordert eine solidere Ausführung – und infolge baupolizeilicher Auflagen soviel aufwendiger und teurer sind, daß nach vergleichenden Untersuchungen erst bei einem viergeschossigen Haus mit Dreispännern der Treppenhausanteil dem einer zweigeschossigen Wohnung im Flachbau gleichkommt. Vom fünften oder sechsten Geschoß an erhöht der, im Interesse einer reibungslosen Kommunikation im vielgeschossigen Haus, unerläßliche Fahrstuhl die Kosten ganz erheblich. Auch werden nach neueren Bestimmungen bei Wohnhochhäusern ein zweites Not-Treppenhaus und ein zweiter Fahrstuhl verlangt. Die höheren Aufwendungen für Kommunikation und Statik verteuern eine Wohnung im Hochhaus gegenüber einer solchen im Flachbau um durchschnittlich dreißig Prozent. Das zweigeschossige Einfamilienhaus hat dagegen den Vorteil, daß zum Beispiel auch der Raum über oder unter der Treppe genutzt werden kann, durch einen eingebauten Schrank, ein Regal oder als Abstellplatz.

Die Wirtschaftlichkeit des Kellers ist abhängig vom Grad der individuellen Vorratswirtschaft. Nach Erhebungen des Instituts für Bauforschung sind nur 20 qm für einen mittleren Haushalt erforderlich. Eine Vollunterkellerung ist also bei Flachbau nicht erforderlich. Neuzeitliche Baustoffe machen es zudem möglich, nichtunterkellerte Räume ebensogut, ja sogar besser zu isolieren als über Kellerräumen gelegene. Das Problem der Neben- und Abstellräume ist auf jeden Fall im Flachbau leichter und billiger zu lösen. Im mehrgeschossigen Haus wird das Verhältnis von Kellerfläche zu Wohnfläche bei wachsender Höhe ungünstiger.

Es blieben also nur die Kosten für das Dach als echte wirtschaftliche Mehraufwendung des Flachbaus. Dem stehen aber andere Aufwendungen beim Mehrgeschoßbau, vor allem beim Hochhaus, gegenüber, die schwerer ins Gewicht fallen. Fassaden von Hochhäusern erfordern, da sie der Witterung stärker ausgesetzt sind, eine qualitativ bessere Ausführung, vor allem auch im Hinblick auf teure Renovierungsarbeiten. Auch auf der Baustelle ergeben sich Kostenunterschiede, die mit der Höhe der Bauten wachsen: Kräne, die mit dem Bauwerk aufsteigen, Schalung und Sicherheitsvorschriften. Der Flachbau kommt demgegenüber mit leichteren Maschinen und einem geringeren Aufwand aus.

Flachbau ist aber ganz besonders für jede Art von Leichtbauweise geeignet. Gewichtsersparnisse bedeuten nicht nur einen Transport- und damit volkswirtschaftlichen Gewinn; sie erleichtern auch die Montage der Bauten erheblich, vor allem beim eingeschossigen Bau. Flachbau ist für das Bauen mit vorfabrizierten Elementen geradezu prädestiniert.

Das Institut für Bauforschung in Hannover hat sorgfältige Vergleichsberechnungen zwischen Mittelbau und Flachbau angestellt, wobei die Kosten für die Wohnungen im zweigeschossigen Haus rund 8% höher lagen als die für die gleich großen Wohnungen eines viergeschossigen Mehrfamilienhauses. Diesen Untersuchungen sind herkömmliche Typen und Konstruktionen zugrunde gelegt.

Diplomingenieur Kräntzer vom gleichen Institut sagt in bezug auf Flachbauten: »Ihre Gebäudekosten sind, insbesondere bei sparsamer Dachneigung, nicht höher als für gleich große und gleichartig ausgestattete Wohnungen in dreigeschossigen Zweispännern; sie können sogar niedriger sein.«

Die Ergebnisse werden günstiger für den Flachbau, wenn nichtunterkellerte Wohnungen mit leichten Abstellschuppen oder ebenerdigen Nebenräumen und flachen oder flachgeneigten Abdeckungen ohne Dachstuhl zum Vergleich herangezogen werden.

Das österreichische Institut für Bauforschung hat in den letzten Jahren verschiedentlich die Kosten dreigeschossiger Mehrfamilienhäuser mit denen mehrerer Flachbausiedlungen verglichen, die ohne Keller errichtet wurden. Der Kubikmeter-Endpreis ist bei der Mehrzahl der Flachbautypen niedriger als der des dreigeschossigen Stockwerkhauses (bis zu 13%!).

Man kann nicht sagen, diese oder jene Bebauungsweise ist absolut billiger als die andere, da die Bedingungen jeweils anders sind. Man kann aber auf Grund der verschiedenen Kostenvergleiche feststellen, daß es möglich ist, Wohnungen im Flachbau unter bestimmten Voraussetzungen mit gleichen oder geringeren Kosten herzustellen als im mehrgeschossigen Bau. Wenn man die Grenzwerte unter Zugrundelegung vieler Erfahrungen abtastet, kommt man zu folgendem Ergebnis: Die Kosten für die Wohnung des zweigeschossigen Reihenhauses können gegenüber denen für die gleich großen Wohnungen des dreigeschossigen Mehrfamilienhauses zwischen 25% höher und 13% niedriger, beim eingeschossigen Haus zwischen 32% höher und 10% niedriger liegen. In England, den Niederlanden und den USA ist der Flachbau grundsätzlich billiger als der Wohnungsbau im hohen Haus, da die Gewohnheit bei den Kosten eine erhebliche Rolle spielt. In den USA gilt das sogar für das freistehende Haus!

15

11. Turkish houses in Macedonia. Throughout the entire region formerly under Turkish suzerainty, there are many examples of a highly civilised terrace type timber house with one, two, or three storeys.

11. Türkische Häuser in Mazedonien. Im gesamten ehemaligen Bereich türkischer Herrschaft gibt es Beispiele eines sehr kultivierten ein- bis dreigeschossigen Reihen-Holzhauses.

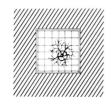

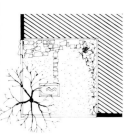

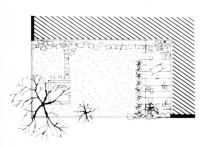

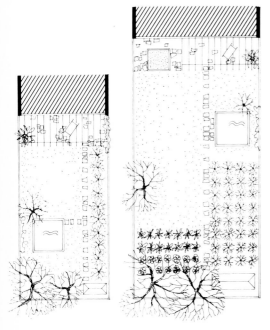

As regards the justifiable disinclination against the excessive burden of the garden, this argument is only valid in respect of low-rise housing of conventional type, with gardens which were originally meant to provide the fresh vegetables for the family. But the argument does not apply to "urban low-rise housing" where the open spaces are exclusively designed to serve for recreational purposes, as "outdoor living rooms." With gardens of a size ranging from say, 400 to 2,000 sq. ft., gardening as a spare-time hobby is not ruled out; but the garden can also be so designed that it requires hardly any work, either as a simple lawn or mainly laid out with flags. There is also a good deal of justification for the second argument, concerning the financial burden of ownership, since, in the German-speaking countries, multi-storey housing is virtually identical with tenancy, and low-rise housing with house ownership. But such identification is almost unknown in other countries, and is certainly not inherent in the mode of housing. In Italy, for instance, there are flats in multi-storey blocks owned by individual occupiers whilst in England, even low-rise dwellings are mainly rented. Tendencies in this direction are also apparent in Central Europe. In comparison to England, however, they are slight.

But if neither the size of the garden nor the association with house ownership constitute valid reasons against the one-family house, what are the remaining advantages in favour of multi-storey housing?

No doubt the "fine view." In this connection, however, every advocate of tower blocks merely has the flats on the top floors in mind, not those lower down.

Fred Forbat reports: "In the course of a Swedish survey based on interviews with mothers, no more than 55 per cent of those living in multi-storey blocks of flats expressed a preference for this type of housing whilst 31 per cent expressly preferred low-rise housing, and 81 per cent of those already living in low-rise houses expressed a preference for this type." This result points to a particular disadvantage of the multi-storey block: it does not satisfy the requirements of a family with children.

Tower blocks may be well suited for childless couples or single people who spend most of the day at their office or workplace; this applies, in particular, if the block of flats is associated with social amenities and with facilities for full or partial catering as in a boarding house.

In the countries where low-rise housing prevails, a decisive part is played by the entrance. Insistence on an individual entrance is not just a question of status symbol or exaggerated individualism. It symbolises the preservation of a frontier between two social spheres. In low-rise housing, the house entrance provides the best possible solution for the "lock" between private and public spheres. The occupier of a block of flats must overcome three obstacles: the door of the flat, the staircase or lift, and the main entrance door. Each time, there is a chance of meeting pleasant or unpleasant fellow residents. Both can be disturbing.

In contrast, the direct link of the dwelling with the town at large (subconsciously felt as an "escape route") conveys a feeling of security. This feeling is strengthened if the occupiers, and especially the children, have a second exit through the garden and can reach the open country through public open space.

That high blocks of flats are only tolerable if they are fitted with expensive sound insulation—which is not normally provided—has been proved by experience. But even if all reasonable precautions have been taken to avoid noise nuisance, the effects of a conglomeration of many people, living side-by-side or one above the other, remain. There can be no doubt that every person is more or less receptive to radiations from outside which can penetrate even the strongest concrete walls and which may, in particular, affect him subconsciously. Major aggregations of people affect the nervous system of particularly sensitive residents and keep it under tension. It is not only the effects of traffic and of excessive distractions which are the cause of the ever more widespread large-town neurosis. Such mass diseases are also due to excessive housing densities which give rise to tangible acoustic disturbances and intangible friction between many individuals confined to a narrow space who "get on each other's nerves." The open space around the house, supplementing the "interior" by a matching "exterior," meets a primary and vital need. This applies, in particular, if the open space is directly linked to the living room so that it visually forms the outward extension; or if there is easy access from the kitchen to an outdoor dining area; or if even the bedrooms have direct access to the garden. The reasons are not only psychological—the expansion of one's own zone of living—but also practical in that the open space provides opportunities for sunbathing, physical training and all kinds of spare-time occupations. Such an expansion of the dwelling is a particular requirement of modern city life when work is more and more concentrated in enclosed and air-conditioned premises. In the case of families with children, even a balcony, a terrace or roof garden are no substitute for the family garden—quite apart from the fact that roof garden flower tubs with sufficient garden earth, which must be at least 2 ft. deep, are costly to buy and maintain and are therefore, for the time being, reserved for the dwellings of the few well-to-do. The outdoor space represents the most important venue for the upbringing of the children. It constitutes a link between nature and enclosed space, providing visual contact with vegetation and sky. To the

16

Soziologisch-psychologische Gesichtspunkte

Welche soziologischen oder psychologischen Gründe sprechen für das Mehrfamilienhaus? Zunächst die Tatsache, daß man nicht zum Sklaven seines Gartens werden will, der vor allem für die Hausfrau eine zusätzliche Arbeit bedeutet. Ferner, daß man die Belastung durch Eigentum scheut, die Schwierigkeiten der Errichtung eines Hauses, die Kosten für seine Unterhaltung, die Bindung an einen Standort, Verkehrsschwierigkeiten usw.
Zu der berechtigten Abneigung gegen eine übermäßige Beanspruchung durch den Garten wäre zu sagen, daß dieses Argument nur auf den Flachbau bislang üblicher Art zutrifft, mit Gärten, die quasi für eine »Selbsternährung« vorgesehen waren. Es trifft nicht zu auf »urbanen Flachbau«, dessen Freiflächen so bemessen sind, daß sie der reinen Erholung, dem »Wohnen im Freien« dienen. Bei einer Größe zwischen 40 und 200 qm ist Gartenarbeit als Freizeitbeschäftigung nicht ausgeschlossen, aber der Garten kann auch so angelegt sein, daß er kaum Arbeit verursacht, etwa als Rasenfläche oder vorwiegend als Plattenhof.
Auch das zweite Argument, »Belastung durch Eigentum«, ist berechtigt, da in den deutschsprachigen Ländern auf der einen Seite Mehrfamilienhaus und die Rechtsform des Mieters und auf der anderen Seite Einfamilienhaus und »Eigentum« nahezu identisch sind, das heißt, der Bewohner juristisch auch Eigentümer ist. Diese Gleichsetzung ist jedoch in anderen Ländern fast unbekannt und hat nichts mit der Bebauungsart zu tun. So gibt es in Italien Eigentumswohnungen im Mehrgeschoßbau und in England vorwiegend Mietwohnungen im Flachbau. Ansätze in dieser Richtung gibt es auch in Mitteleuropa. Im Verhältnis zu England sind sie allerdings verschwindend gering.
Wenn das Einfamilienhaus aber weder durch die Größe des Gartens noch durch die Bindung an Eigentum eine Belastung darstellen muß, welche Vorteile sprechen dann noch für die mehrgeschossige Bauweise?
Sicherlich »die schöne Aussicht«. Jeder Befürworter von Wohnhochhäusern denkt dabei nur an die Wohnungen in den obersten Stockwerken, nicht an die in den mittleren und unteren.
Fred Forbat berichtet: »Bei Befragung im Hochhaus wohnender Mütter in Schweden zogen nur 55 % das Hochhaus vor, 31 % erklärten sich ausdrücklich für den Flachbau, während die im niederen Haus wohnenden zu 81 % an ihrem Haustyp festhielten.« Dieses Ergebnis weist auf den besonderen Mangel im höheren Haus hin: Es genügt nicht den Bedürfnissen einer Familie mit Kindern.
Für kinderlose Ehepaare oder Ledige, die den überwiegenden Teil des Tages in der Arbeitsstätte verbringen, ist diese Bebauungsweise geeignet, vor allem wenn Gemeinschaftsräume und Teil- oder Vollverpflegung wie beim Typ des Boarding-Hauses gegeben sind.
Eine entscheidende Rolle spielt bei den »Flachbaunationen« der individuelle Wohnungseingang. Das Festhalten an dieser Form des Zugangs ist nicht nur eine Frage der Repräsentation oder eines übersteigerten Individualismus. Es versinnbildlicht das Bewahren der Grenze zweier gesellschaftlicher Bereiche. Der Wohnungseingang im Flachbau ist die bestmögliche Lösung der »Schleuse zwischen Privatbereich und Öffentlichkeit«. Im hohen Haus muß der Bewohner eine dreifache Hemmung überwinden: die Wohnungstür, das Treppenhaus oder den Fahrstuhl und die Haustür. Jedesmal besteht die Möglichkeit, daß er mit ihm angenehmen oder unangenehmen Hausbewohnern zusammentrifft. Beides kann störend sein.
Dagegen gibt die unmittelbare Verbindung der Wohnung mit den übrigen Punkten der Stadt ein Gefühl der Sicherheit (der unbewußte »Fluchtweg«). Diese Empfindung wird noch verstärkt, wenn die Bewohner, vor allem die Kinder, über den Garten einen zweiten Ausgang haben und über öffentliche Grünflächen in die freie Natur des Stadtrandes gelangen können.
Daß hohe Wohnhäuser nur bei kostspieligen Schallisolierungen erträglich sind, die in der Regel nicht vorgenommen werden, zeigt die Erfahrung. Aber auch wenn alle Vorkehrungen getroffen sind, um akustische Störungen zu vermeiden, bleiben die Auswirkungen einer Zusammenballung vieler Menschen, die neben- und übereinander wohnen, bestehen. Zweifellos hat jeder Mensch eine persönliche Ausstrahlung, die auch stärkste Betonwände zu durchdringen vermag und die vor allem auf das Unterbewußtsein einwirkt. Größere Menschenanhäufungen beeinflussen das Nervensystem besonders sensibler Bewohner und halten es in Erregung. Nicht nur die Auswirkungen des Verkehrs und eine übermäßige Erlebnisdichte sind Ursache der immer stärker anwachsenden Großstadt-Neurosen. Auch übermäßige Wohndichten haben ihren Anteil an diesen Massenerkrankungen, durch materiell faßbare akustische Störungen und immaterielle Auswirkungen vieler Individualitäten auf engem Raum, die sich gegenseitig »irritieren«. Mit dem offenen Raum am Haus, der Ergänzung des »Innen« durch ein dazugehöriges »Außen« wird einer primären Lebensnotwendigkeit Rechnung getragen. Vor allem dann, wenn der Freiraum in unmittelbarer Verbindung mit dem Wohnraum steht, ihn optisch nach draußen fortsetzt, wenn von der Küche aus ein Eßplatz im Freien leicht erreichbar ist, oder wenn auch die Schlafräume direkten Zugang dazu haben, sowohl aus psychologischen Gründen der Weite des eigenen Bereichs als auch für Sonnenbad und Gymnastik und jede Art von Freizeitbe-

17

Page/Seite 16:

12. The sketches show typical solutions for patios and small gardens, indicating some possibilities of planting. Under different climatic conditions, this gave rise to those minute courtyards which the Japanese call "small Vase." Under Central European conditions, a garden court of say 400 square feet must be regarded as a minimum. The maximum still compatible with urban low-rise housing lies around 2000 sq. ft.

12. Die Skizzen zeigen typische Lösungen von Höfen und kleinen Gärten und deuten Möglichkeiten der Bepflanzung an. Unter anderen klimatischen Bedingungen sind jene winzigen Höfe entstanden, die der Japaner als »kleine Vase« bezeichnet. Für mitteleuropäische Verhältnisse ist ein Gartenhof von 36 qm das Minimum. Die Grenze, bis zu der man von urban sprechen kann, liegt etwa bei 200 qm.

13. The garden is a most essential "outlet" for children's activities.

13. Für Kinder ist der Garten notwendigster »Auslauf« und »Spielraum«.

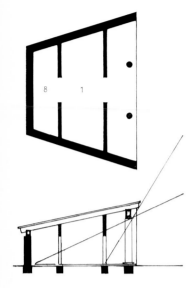

14. House of Socrates. Socrates developed, from the "Megaron Type," a functional house which makes the most of the winter sun yet excludes the summer sun. On the north side, the house is insulated by store rooms.

15. Diagram illustrating the relationship between the degree of latitude, the number of storeys, and the floor space index. Because of the steeper angle of the sun, higher densities can be permitted in southern latitudes. A floor space index of 3.0 might indicate the upper limit.

14. Haus des Sokrates. Sokrates entwickelte aus dem »Megaron-Typ« ein funktionelles Haus, das die Wintersonne maximal ausnutzt und die Sommersonne ausschließt. Vorratsräume isolieren gegen Norden.

15. Graphische Darstellung der Beziehung Breitengrad – Geschosse – Geschoßflächenzahl. Infolge des steileren Einfallswinkels der Sonne nimmt die mögliche Dichte nach Süden zu. Die Grenze dürfte bei GFZ 3,0 liegen.

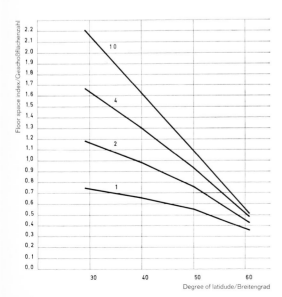

child, the garden is an aid in apprehending the phenomena of life and natural surroundings. It is a space where the child can move, dig and romp about, or do some handiwork in fresh air, alone or with friends, under the direct supervision of the mother. But even to the adults, the possibility of occasionally having a quiet moment by sending the children of "active" age directly from the house to a play ground is an advantage which should not be underrated.

Influence of Different Sunlight Intensities

Before dealing with the area requirements of concentrated low-rise housing, some general considerations concerning the relationship between density and sunlight access are called for. Housing density is, first of all, dependent on the geographical position. As has already been pointed out by Hilberseimer, buildings in Leningrad would have to be spaced at about twice the distance as equally high buildings in Paris, if they are to receive the same amount of sunlight.

The patio of an atrium type house in Munich must have a minimum depth of about 20 ft. A similar patio in Stockholm would require a depth of approximately 36 ft., corresponding to an area approximately 3½ times as large.

That these conditions are more or less taken into account is apparent from the maximum net floor space indices laid down for inner urban areas in different countries: Sweden up to 1.6; Germany up to 2.0; Austria up to 2.5.

The relationship between geographical position (sunlight access) and housing density is also reflected in the maximum net densities for residential areas in different cities:

London	approx. 250 persons per acre;	target: 140 to 200 persons per acre
Berlin	approx. 400 persons per acre;	target: 160 to 200 persons per acre
Vienna	approx. 500 persons per acre;	target: 200 to 240 persons per acre
Naples	approx. 800 persons per acre;	target: 320 to 400 persons per acre
Barcelona	approx. 1000 persons per acre;	target: 400 persons per acre

Because of the considerably heavier cloud cover of the northern sky, the differences in sunlight intensity are increased still further. In northern latitudes, the psychological effect of sunlight is at least as important as the germicidal effect. Hamburg has 1200 hours of sunshine per annum (27 per cent), Magdeburg 1500 (34 per cent), Graz 1800 (41 per cent), Lienz 2000 (45 per cent).

If urban housing were concentrated in proportion to the rising angle of the sun, one would arrive at high floor space indices in the South (e. g. Athens, 3.0). New York, situated on the 41st Parallel, the same as that of Naples, even permits a maximum floor space index of 10.0; this figure, however, is not so much governed by hygienic or traffic considerations, but adapted to the existing building density in the central business district.

The poor traffic conditions in New York are notorious. The city's 3½ million daily commuters must travel in great discomfort. The supply of goods to the central area is beset with considerable difficulties. The parking space available is minute; but also the space available for moving traffic is far from adequate. For the improvement of such precarious situations, recourse to different traffic levels is not just a necessity; it is in fact the only possibility of preserving the viability of areas with high population density. But, because of the necessary vertical links, the number of levels available is limited. Broad calculations based on such considerations point to a maximum floor space index of 3.0 for large cities in southern as well as northern latitudes.

Even as far as residential areas are concerned, there are good reasons why the floor space index in the South should not be increased in accordance with the angle of the sun. In the North, e. g. in Scandinavia, it is a vital necessity to take in a certain amount of the sunlight during the summer in order to see the winter through. In the South, where the "stone culture" is at home, it is necessary, in contrast, to seek protection in the summer against the high midday sun and the shafts of stagnant air which are dangerous to health. Here, air movement is a hygienic requirement almost as important as the sun in the North. Housing estates are, if possible, placed on undulating ground in order to intercept the wind. If possible, the hillside streets are so orientated that they are open to the prevailing summer winds. Here, too, a certain density in the utilisation of private and public space must not be exceeded.

It is difficult to arrive, by these means, at an exact calculation of the width required for adequate ventilation. There is, however, another criterion: the so-called "open space index" which indicates the ratio of gross floor area and private open space.

An average requirement would be about 25 sq. metres (say, 270 sq. ft.) of open space per person which, with a present-day dwelling standard of approximately 100 sq. metres (say 1080 sq. ft.) per dwelling and, say, four persons per household, would correspond to a ratio of 1 in 1, viz. 100 sq. metres of gross floor area compared with 100 sq. metres of private open space. In our latitudes, the minimum requirement would be around 10 sq. metres (say, 100 sq. ft.) of open space per person, the maximum around 50 sq. metres (540 sq. ft.) per person, corresponding

schäftigung. Eine derartige Ergänzung der Wohnung ist ein besonderes Erfordernis des heutigen Großstadtlebens, das überwiegend Arbeit in geschlossenen, mehr und mehr vollklimatisierten Räumen bedeutet. Der Hausgarten ist bei Familien mit Kindern kaum durch einen Balkon, eine Terrasse oder einen Dachgarten zu ersetzen, abgesehen davon, daß Tröge mit genügend Erde, das heißt mindestens 60 cm Tiefe, teuer in der Herstellung und Unterhaltung sind, also vorläufig nur für die Wohnungen der wenigen Begüterten in Frage kommen. Der freie Raum bildet das wichtigste »Habitat« für die Heranbildung der Kinder. Er stellt ein Bindeglied zwischen Natur und künstlichem Raum dar, in dem man Pflanzen und den Himmel sieht. Dem Kind ist er eine Hilfe zum Begreifen der Lebensvorgänge und der natürlichen Umwelt. Ein Freiraum, in dem das Kind sich in frischer Luft bewegen, buddeln und toben, basteln kann – allein oder mit Freunden unter direkter Beaufsichtigung der Mutter. Aber auch die Möglichkeit, Kinder im »Bewegungsalter« aus der Wohnung unmittelbar auf Spielflächen zu schicken, um gelegentlich Ruhe vor ihnen zu haben, ist für die Erwachsenen von nicht zu unterschätzender Bedeutung!

In der Rangordnung der Freiflächen: Sport-, Spielplätze, Kleingärten usw. steht die unmittelbar an der Wohnung gelegene Freifläche an der Spitze. Der Flachbau ist wegen dieses unentbehrlichen »Auslaufs« die prädestinierte Wohnform für die Familie mit Kindern.

Einfluß der unterschiedlichen Besonnung

Wenn im folgenden der Flächenbedarf eines verdichteten Flachbaues untersucht werden soll, so sind zuvor einige Überlegungen über das Verhältnis von Dichte und Besonnung anzustellen. Die Wohndichte ist zunächst abhängig vom Standort. Schon Hilberseimer wies darauf hin, daß Gebäude gleicher Höhe in Leningrad etwa den doppelten Abstand voneinander haben müssen wie in Paris, um gleiche Besonnungsverhältnisse zu erreichen.

Der Hof des Atriumhauses in München muß mindestens 6 m tief sein. Der Hof des gleichen Typs in Stockholm erfordert dagegen eine Tiefe von rund 11 m, das heißt auf die Fläche bezogen etwa die dreieinhalbfache Weiträumigkeit.

Daß diesen Verhältnissen in etwa Rechnung getragen wird, zeigen die eine Höchstausnutzung festlegenden Geschoßflächenzahlen (GFZ) verschiedener Länder: Schweden bis zu 1,6 GFZ netto in Innenstädten, Deutschland bis zu 2,0 GFZ netto in Innenstädten, Österreich bis zu 2,5 GFZ netto in Innenstädten.

Auch die vorhandenen und angestrebten maximalen Dichten der Wohngebiete verschiedener Städte weisen auf die Wechselbeziehung zwischen Standort (Besonnungsverhältnisse) und Wohndichte hin:

London	rund 600 Einwohner je ha netto, geplant	340– 500 Einwohner je ha netto
Berlin	rund 1000 Einwohner je ha netto, geplant	400– 500 Einwohner je ha netto
Wien	rund 1200 Einwohner je ha netto, geplant	500– 600 Einwohner je ha netto
Neapel	rund 2000 Einwohner je ha netto, geplant	800–1000 Einwohner je ha netto
Barcelona	rund 2500 Einwohner je ha netto, geplant	1000–1200 Einwohner je ha netto

Durch die erheblich stärkere Bedeckung des Himmels im Norden werden die Unterschiede in der Intensität der Besonnung noch gesteigert. Ihre psychologische Wirkung ist in diesen Breiten mindestens so wichtig wie die keimtötende. Die Zahl der Sonnenstunden pro Jahr beträgt in Hamburg 1200 = 27%, in Magdeburg 1500 = 34%, in Graz 1800 = 41%, in Lienz 2000 = 45%. Verdichtet man nun in den Städten proportional dem steigenden Einfallswinkel der Sonne, so kommt man für den Süden zu hohen Geschoßflächenzahlen – Athen GFZ 3,0. Für das auf dem 41. Breitengrad, das heißt auf der Höhe Neapels gelegene New York ist sogar eine, der gegenwärtigen Dichte der City angepaßte GFZ von 10,0 als Höchstgrenze zugelassen.

Bekannt sind die ausgesprochen schlechten Verkehrsverhältnisse dieser Stadt. Von den dreieinhalb Millionen Menschen, die New York täglich »aus- und einatmet«, werden größte Strapazen in Kauf genommen, um den Weg zur Arbeitsstätte zu bewältigen. Die Belieferung der inneren Stadt ist nur unter erheblichen Schwierigkeiten durchzuführen. Der verfügbare Parkraum ist minimal, aber auch der Raum für den fließenden Verkehr reicht nicht im entferntesten aus. Um solche prekären City-Situationen zu verbessern, ist die Anlage von mehreren Verkehrsschichten nicht nur eine Notwendigkeit: es ist die einzige Möglichkeit, Gebiete mit hohem Verdichtungsgrad lebensfähig zu erhalten. Die Zahl der Ebenen ist jedoch infolge der notwendigen vertikalen Verflechtung begrenzt. Aus diesen Erwägungen ergibt sich nach überschlägigen Berechnungen eine maximale GFZ von 3,0 für Großstädte sowohl in südlichen als auch in nördlichen Breiten.

Auch für Wohngebiete bestehen Gründe, die GFZ im Süden nicht dem Stand des Sonnenwinkels entsprechend zu erhöhen. Im Norden, etwa in Skandinavien, ist es eine Lebensnotwendigkeit, im Sommer ein gewisses Maß an Sonne zu »tanken«, um den Winter durchhalten zu können. Im Süden, im Bereich der »Steinkultur«, muß man sich dagegen vor den steil einfallenden Strahlen der Mittagssonne und den gesundheitsgefährdenden stehenden Luftsäulen im Sommer schüt-

16. Hugo Häring's centre corridor house with "loosened" plan. To obtain maximum sunlight for the dwelling facing east and west, the frontage is also opened towards south.
17. Distance between houses, and shade effect at different latitudes and in different seasons. For the same sunlight hours, the distance between houses on the 50th parallel must be about three times as great as on the 30th parallel.

16. Hugo Härings »Mittelganghaus mit ›aufgerauhtem‹ Grundriß«. Um für die ost- und westorientierten Wohnungen eine möglichst lange Besonnung zu erhalten, ist die Front auch nach Süden geöffnet.
17. Hausabstand und Schattenbildung bei verschiedenen Breitengraden und Jahreszeiten. Am 50. Breitengrad muß der Hausabstand rund dreimal so groß sein wie am 30. Breitengrad, um die gleiche Besonnung zu erreichen.

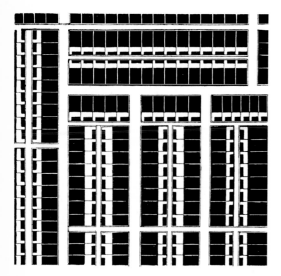

18. Exaggerated individualism leads to its opposite, i. e. mass concentration. In this English working class district of the 19th century, the density is at the rate of 40 houses per acre.

19. Curve indicating the housing density or floor space density for single-storey and two-storey low-rise housing: On the assumption of a density of 25 sq. metres (270 sq. ft.) of gross floor area per person, and four persons per dwelling, it is possible to read, from the abscissa, both the housing densities and the floor space indices. The scale of the ordinate indicates the net building land available for housing. From the curve of roofed areas required for single-storey and two-storey housing, it is possible to determine, for a given density, the remaining private open space per person. In this diagram, the front garden has been ignored since a garden flanking a residential road may be reduced to a minute protective strip which may have little effect on the results. The graph also shows the area requirements for a private car (on the assumption of one car per dwelling) and their effect on housing density if the car is garaged on public land or on net building ground. In this diagram, the critical limits are specially marked.

18. Überspitzter Individualismus führt zur Vermassung. In diesem englischen Arbeiterquartier des 19. Jahrhunderts wurden 100 Einfamilienhäuser auf einen Hektar gezwängt.
19. Kurve der Wohndichte oder Geschoßflächendichte für ein- und zweigeschossigen Flachbau: Bei Annahme einer Belegungsdichte von 25 qm Bruttogeschoßfläche je Person und vier Personen je Wohnung lassen sich auf der Abszisse sowohl die Wohnungsdichten wie auch die Geschoßflächenzahlen ablesen. Auf der Ordinate ist die Skala des Netto-Wohnbaulandes aufgetragen. An der Kurve der überbauten Flächen bei ein- und zweigeschossigem Flachbau läßt sich ablesen, welcher private Freiflächenanteil bei der jeweiligen Dichte verbleibt. Der Vorgarten ist bei dieser Darstellung vernachlässigt, da er als Schutzstreifen neben Wohnwegen geringe Ausmaße annehmen kann und daher die Ergebnisse kaum beeinflußt. Es ist auch zu erkennen, welcher Flächenbedarf für das Auto (bei Annahme von einem Auto je Wohnung) einzusetzen ist. Besonderer Wert wurde darauf gelegt, Grenzwerte kenntlich zu machen.

to a net building plot of approximately 330 sq. metres (say, 3500 sq. ft.) per dwelling unit, or 30 dwellings per hectare (12 dwellings per acre). This ratio of open space and floor area has already served as a basis for the examination of housing densities in the book "Die gegliederte und aufgelockerte Stadt," already referred to.
The application of such an "open space index" would thus have certain advantages compared with the "floor space index" embodied in present German legislation.

Area Requirements for Urban Low-Rise Housing

The main argument advanced against low-rise housing in urban areas is the allegedly much greater area requirement.
This prejudice has persisted although the examination in "Die gegliederte und aufgelockerte Stadt" provided convincing proofs that the built-up area required for concentrated low-rise housing was not much greater than that required for multi-storey housing. The prejudice is no doubt due to the fact that the notion of low-rise housing is spontaneously associated with that large suburban sprawl which surrounds our cities.
This prejudice is not confined to Central Europe. In nearly all countries, the advantages of the ancient type of concentrated low-rise housing have been forgotten, and low-rise housing is associated in peoples' minds with the wide expanse of suburbia. The German building regulations, for instance, specify the maximum floor space index of 1.0 for housing construction outside the central areas of the towns. Within this limit, as is apparent from the curve of housing densities, it is possible to provide two-storey housing with up to 100 dwelling units per hectare (40 units per acre). In fact, if the calculation were exclusively based on the distance rule of 1 in 2, it would even be possible to raise the density to 118 dwelling units per hectare (48 units per acre), i.e. the floor space index of 1.0 may even be exceeded by nearly 20 per cent, always assuming a mean density of 25 sq. metres (270 sq. ft.) of floor area per person. In England, the density of about 100 sq. ft.(or, say, 10 sq. metres) per person encountered in the back-to-back houses in the working-class districts of the industrial cities of the nineteenth century even

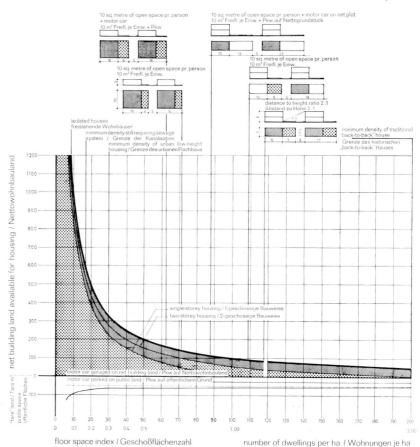

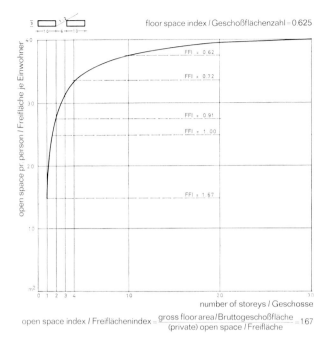

floor space index / Geschoßflächenzahl = 0.625

open space pr person / Freifläche je Einwohner

FFI = 0.62
FFI = 0.72
FFI = 0.91
FFI = 1.00
FFI = 1.67

number of storeys / Geschosse

$$\text{open space index / Freiflächenindex} = \frac{\text{gross floor area / Bruttogeschoßfläche}}{\text{(private) open space / Freifläche}} = 1.67$$

20. Increase in open space with increasing number oт storeys, on the assumption of a gross floor area of 25 sq. metres (270 sq. ft.) per resident and a constant floor space index of 0.625, applicable to single-storey housing and an angle of the sun of 1:2. The abscissa indicates the number of storeys, the ordinate the open space per resident. Single-storey housing leaves 15 sq. metres (160 sq. ft.) of open space per resident, corresponding to an open space index of 1.67. Two-storey housing leaves an open space of 27.5 sq. metres (290 sq. ft.) per resident, corresponding to an open space index of 0.91. From the tenth storey onwards, there is hardly any further increase in open space.

21. Nineteenth century houses in Hamburg. The interval between the houses is a mere 8 ft. or so, and daylight must be caught by mirrors. In the intervening 100 years, hygienic minimum requirements were worked out, such as minimum floor space per person, minimum distances, minimum daylight access and the like, which govern the housing densities.

20. Zunahme der Freifläche bei steigender Geschoßzahl: Voraussetzung ist eine Bruttogeschoßfläche von 25 qm je Einwohner und eine gleichbleibende GFZ von 0,625, die bei eingeschossiger Bebauung und bei einem Sonneneinfallswinkel von 1:2 ermittelt wurde. Auf der Abszisse ist die Geschoßzahl und auf der Ordinate die Freifläche je Einwohner abzulesen. Eingeschossige Bebauung ergibt eine Freifläche von 15 qm je Einwohner, entsprechend einem FFI von 1,67. Zweigeschossige Bebauung ergibt eine Freifläche von 27,5 qm je Einwohner; das entspricht einem Freiflächenindex von 0,91. Vom zehnten Geschoß an nimmt die Freifläche kaum noch zu.

21. »Hamburger Schlitzbauweise«. Der Hausabstand beträgt ganze 2,50 m, das Licht wird durch Spiegel in die Wohnräume geholt. In den inzwischen vergangenen 100 Jahren wurden »hygienische Mindestforderungen« erarbeitet, wie Wohnfläche pro Person, Mindestabstände, Belichtung und ähnliches, die die Bebauungsdichten bestimmen.

zen. Luftbewegung wird hier zu einem nahezu ebenso wichtigen Element der Hygiene wie Besonnung im Norden. Man ist bestrebt, Siedlungen auf bewegtem Gelände anzulegen, um Wind einzufangen. Die Straßen werden nach Möglichkeit in einer Richtung so zum Hang angelegt, daß sie der Sommerwind durchstreichen kann. Auch hier darf im privaten und im öffentlichen Raum eine gewisse Dichte nicht überschritten werden.

Die für eine genügende Durchlüftung notwendige Weite läßt sich mit den genannten Mitteln exakt schwer erfassen. Es gibt jedoch ein anderes Maß: das Verhältnis von umbautem Kubus zur privaten und öffentlichen Freifläche oder, genauer ausgedrückt, das Verhältnis von Geschoßflächen zur privaten Freifläche, den »Freiflächenindex«.

Eine mittlere Dichte wären 25 qm Freifläche je Person, wodurch nach dem heutigen Wohnungsstandard etwa ein Verhältnis 1:1 entstehen würde, das heißt 100 qm Bruttogeschoßfläche auf 100 qm privaten Freiraum, vier Personen je Familie im Schnitt gerechnet. Das Minimum läge in unseren Breiten etwa bei 10 qm Freifläche je Person, das Maximum etwa bei 50 qm je Person, das sind rund 330 qm Nettobauland je Wohnung und 30 Wohnungen je Hektar. – Bereits in »Die gegliederte und aufgelockerte Stadt« wurde der Untersuchung über Wohndichte das Verhältnis von Freiraum zu Geschoßfläche zugrunde gelegt.

Die Anwendung eines Freiflächenindex hätte also manche Vorzüge gegenüber dem in der deutschen Gesetzgebung festgelegten Geschoßflächenindex.

Flächenbedarf des urbanen Flachbaus

Das Hauptargument gegen die Anwendung von Flachbau im städtischen Raum ist der angeblich weit größere Flächenbedarf.

Obgleich in der bereits genannten Untersuchung »Die gegliederte und aufgelockerte Stadt« überzeugende Beweise dafür erbracht wurden, daß verdichteter Flachbau nur eine geringe Vergrößerung der bebauten Fläche gegenüber dem Hochbau erfordert, ist jenes Vorurteil geblieben. Es rührt offenbar daher, daß »Flachbau« automatisch mit jenen weiträumigen vorstädtischen Streusiedlungen gleichgesetzt wird, die unsere Städte umgeben, und daß es noch nicht genügend und lebendig gestaltete Beispiele eines verdichteten Flachbaus gibt, um der Allgemeinheit den Unterschied deutlich zu machen.

Diese Erscheinung finden wir nicht nur in Mitteleuropa. Bei fast allen Nationen der Welt sind die Vorzüge des verdichteten historischen Flachbaus in Vergessenheit geraten, und man versteht unter »Flachbau« die ausgedehnten Gebiete von »suburbs« oder Gartenstädten. Die deutsche Baunutzungsverordnung zum Beispiel legt für den Wohnungsbau außerhalb des Kerngebiets der Städte eine Geschoßflächenzahl – im folgenden kurz GFZ genannt – von 1,0 als obere Begrenzung der Ausnutzung fest. Innerhalb dieses Rahmens ist, wie die Kurve der Wohnungsdichten zeigt, ein zweigeschossiger Flachbau bis zu 100 Wohnungen je Hektar netto realisier-

22. Urban area and height of buildings. If the built-up areas of the residential districts are related to the gross areas of the town, the gain obtainable by multi-storey housing is minute. Savings in tare areas result in greater advantages than excessive concentration by multi-storey housing. A Courtyard and garden, B Parking space, C Streets and Squares, D Parkland, E Sports and play grounds, F Cemeteries, G Allotment gardens, H Public buildings, I Urban woodlands, K Lakes, rivers, etc., L Railway land, M Industry, storage, etc.

22. Stadtfläche und Bauhöhe. Bezieht man die bebauten Flächen der Wohngebiete auf die Bruttoflächen der Stadt, so sind die Gewinne durch höhere Bebauung minimal. Einsparungen der Taraflächen ergeben größere Vorteile als übermäßige Verdichtung durch Wohnhochhäuser. A Hof und Garten, B Parkplätze, C Straßen und Plätze, D Park, E Sport- und Spielflächen, F Friedhof, G Kleingärten, H Öffentliche Gebäude, I Stadtwald, K Wasserflächen, L Eisenbahn, M Industrie, Lagerflächen.

permitted a population density of 1000 to 1500 persons per hectare (400 to 600 persons per acre). With the advent of coloured immigrants, these slum quarters have even, occasionally, experienced population densities of up to 3000 persons per hectare (1200 persons per acre).

A healthy average density for urban low-rise housing lies around 200 to 300 persons or 50 to 75 dwellings per hectare (80 to 120 persons in 20 to 30 dwelling units per acre). But densities up to 500 persons per hectare (200 persons per acre) are quite feasible with two-storey housing and, on undulating ground, even with single-storey housing. With three-storey "low-rise" houses of 5 metres (16½ ft.) frontage, it would even be possible to provide 133 dwellings per hectare (54 per acre) with a floor area of 100 sq. metres (say 1080 sq. ft.) each and with 10 sq. metres (say, 100 sq. ft.) of open space per person.

The limit of maximum spaciousness in urban low-rise housing lies around 30 dwellings per hectare (12 per acre), i.e. 330 sq. metres (say, 3500 sq. ft.) of net building plot area per family and 50 sq. metres (540 sq. ft.) of private open space per person. Larger private open spaces can no longer be maintained without major effort, and the provision of roads and mains becomes too expensive. Another limit lies at 15 dwellings or 60 persons per hectare (6 dwellings with 24 persons per acre), corresponding to a net area of 600 sq. metres (say, 640 sq. ft.) sufficient for the sewage disposal of a household of 4 persons. With this density, there is therefore no strict need for canalisation. Haphazard developments are nearly always initiated on this assumption of a "cheap" town planning solution with the result that, when canalisation becomes necessary after all, the local authorities are burdened with heavy expenses. Compared with a mean density of urban low-rise housing of 60 dwellings per net hectare, i.e. 166.7 sq. metres per dwelling, (24 dwellings per acre, approx. 1800 sq. ft. per dwelling), a detached house on a site of 1000 sq. metres requires 6 times as much area; if the site is 1200 sq. metres (13,000 sq. ft.), the area per dwelling becomes nearly 7½ times as large. But the costs of providing access and mains increase in proportion to almost one third of the area of the site, i.e. the costs are doubled if the area is six times larger.

Higher floor space indices than 1.0 are, in Germany, permitted in business districts only where they may rise to 2.0 for office and commercial buildings. If this density is compared with the maximum possible utilisation in two-storey low-rise housing, viz. 80 to 100 dwellings per hectare (32 to 40 dwellings per acre), broadly corresponding to a floor space index of 1.0, the saving in area amounts, with very high floor space indices, to approximately one third. But no savings can be claimed in the costs of providing access and mains since, in the central area, the road space requirements for moving traffic are greater than in purely residential districts.

If the savings in area obtainable from multi-storey housing are related to the total area per person required in a town—assessed by the author at 200, and by Göderitz even at 250 sq. metres per person (2150 to 2700 sq. ft.) as shown in page 22 the area used for two-storey housing accounts for approximately 3 per cent of the total of the town area. On the assumption that 50 per cent of all buildings are of the low-rise housing type, the difference between two-storey housing and ultra-high multi-storey housing (approx. 25 storeys) is no greater than 2.5 per cent!

The index of "200 sq. metres per person" signifies a very economically planned city. The average figure for 40 major German cities works out at 455 sq. metres (4900 sq. ft.) per person! If the agricultural areas, amounting to approximately 30 per cent, are deducted, there remain some 300 sq. metres (3200 sq. ft.) per person. In practice, the percentage gain obtainable by multi-storey housing is therefore in fact still lower! Much greater possibilities of savings in area are afforded by active town planning policies. Even greater savings could be obtained if industry or traffic installations were placed underground, or if the "open" type of housing were abandoned. Such measures would yield area gains of up to 50 per cent!

From the one extreme of sprawling and shapeless suburbs, some theoreticians now tend to turn to another, advocating housing densities which exceed those of the worst slum districts, created by land speculation. In refugee settlements near Hongkong, for example, population densities of some 6000 persons per hectare (2400 per acre) were found. The "American Institute of Planners" is now asking rather naively whether "in the absence of any detrimental effects, the present standards and conceptions of spaciousness in town planning can be maintained."

It is apparently intended to wait until all these poor Chinese have perished.

Extremely high densities are advocated even by Jane Jacobs who, in her book "Death and Life of large American Cities" propounds many a clever idea. In her opinion, the mixed development with 2500 persons per hectare (1000 persons per acre) in the case of Boston-North-End, chosen by her as an example, contains all grades of differentiation.

That such excessive densities are advocated not for the sake of the residents but rather for the sake of the developers is apparent from the admission, quoted on p. 130 of her book, by the economist Philipp M. Hauser: "...because such population concentrations represent the best production and consumption units which our society has produced so far. The very size, density and concentration of our conurbations, objected to by some of our town planners, are among our most precious economic assets"(!).

bar. Ja, wenn man lediglich von der Abstandsregel 1:2 ausgeht, lassen sich sogar 118 Wohnungen unterbringen, das heißt, GFZ 1,0 kann sogar um fast 20% überschritten werden – immer eine mittlere Belegungsdichte von 25 qm Geschoßfläche je Person vorausgesetzt. Die Belegungsdichte von 10 qm je Person in den Back-to-back-Häusern englischer Industriestädte des vorigen Jahrhunderts ermöglichte es sogar, in den Arbeitervierteln 1000 bis 1500 Einwohner je Hektar netto unterzubringen. Das Nachrücken einer farbigen Bevölkerung in diese Elendsviertel läßt hier stellenweise Dichten bis zu 3000 Einwohner je Hektar netto entstehen!

Die gesunde mittlere Dichte für den urbanen Flachbau liegt bei 200 bis 300 Einwohnern oder 50 bis 75 Wohnungen je Hektar netto. 500 Einwohner je Hektar netto sind bei zweigeschossigen Flachbauten durchaus möglich, auf Hanggelände sogar bei eingeschossigem Flachbau. Bei dreigeschossigen Flachbauten mit 5 m Frontbreite sind sogar 133 Wohnungen bei einer Geschoßfläche von 100 qm und bei 10 qm Freifläche je Einwohner möglich!

Die Grenze der größten Weiträumigkeit für den urbanen Flachbau liegt etwa bei 30 Wohnungen je Hektar, das sind 330 qm Nettogrund je Familie und rund 50 qm je Person. Größere private Freiflächen können nicht mehr ohne Anstrengung unterhalten werden, die Aufschließung wird außerdem zu kostspielig. Ein weiterer Grenzwert liegt bei 15 Wohnungen oder 60 Einwohnern je Hektar netto. Dieser Wert entspricht einem Nettogrund von 600 qm, der ausreicht, die geklärten Abwässer eines Haushalts von vier Personen zu verrieseln. Unter dieser Dichte ist eine Kanalisation nicht unbedingt erforderlich. Unsere »wilden« Siedlungsbezirke werden fast immer unter dieser Voraussetzung einer »billigen« städtebaulichen Lösung begonnen, um dann später die Gemeinde, wenn trotzdem Folgeeinrichtungen nötig werden, als Ergebnis der Planlosigkeit mit ungeheuren Summen zu belasten. Gegenüber einer mittleren Dichte des urbanen Flachbaus von 60 Wohnungen je Hektar netto (pro Wohnung 166,6 qm) beansprucht das freistehende Eigenheim auf 1000 qm Grund die sechsfache Fläche; bei 1200 qm Grund steigt der Flächenanteil auf fast das Siebeneinhalbfache! Dabei wachsen aber die Kosten für Aufschließung fast proportional zu einem Drittel der Grundstücksgröße, das heißt, bei sechsfacher Fläche etwa auf das Doppelte!

Höhere Ausnutzungszahlen als GFZ 1,0 werden in Deutschland nur in reinen Geschäftsgebieten (Kerngebieten) zugelassen, das heißt bis zu GFZ 2,0 bei reinen Büro- und Geschäftshäusern. Vergleichen wir diese Dichte mit der höchstmöglichen Ausnutzung im zweigeschossigen Flachbau, 80–100 Wohnungen je Hektar netto (etwa GFZ 1,0), dann beträgt der Gewinn an Grund bei sehr hohen Geschoßzahlen annähernd ein Drittel. Eine Einsparung der Kosten für die Aufschließung kann jedoch nicht in Rechnung gestellt werden, da im Stadtkern mehr Straßenraum für Ziel- und Quellverkehr benötigt wird als in reinen Wohngebieten.

Setzt man den Flächengewinn bei Mehrgeschoßbauten in ein Verhältnis zu der für eine Stadt erforderlichen Gesamtfläche je Person – nach Ermittlungen des Verfassers 200, nach Göderitz sogar 250 qm je Person – wie in der Tabelle auf Seite 22 dargestellt, dann hat die zweigeschossige Überbauung einen Anteil von rund 3% an der Stadtfläche. Die Differenz zwischen zweigeschossiger und sehr hoher Bebauung (etwa 25 Geschosse) beträgt nur rund 2,5% (!) unter der Annahme, daß 50% aller Bauten im Flachbau errichtet werden.

»200 qm je Einwohner« bedeutet eine sehr ökonomisch geplante Stadt. Bei 40 deutschen Großstädten sind es im Durchschnitt 455 qm je Einwohner! Zieht man die landwirtschaftlichen Flächen, etwa 30%, ab, verbleiben rund 300 qm je Einwohner. Der prozentuale Gewinn durch Häufung der Geschosse ist also in der Praxis noch geringer! Weit größere Einsparungen lassen sich erreichen, wenn Industrien und Verkehrsanlagen unter die Erde verlegt werden oder durch Aufhebung der »offenen Bauweise«. Diese Maßnahmen würden Flächengewinne bis zu 50% erbringen!

Von dem *einen* Extrem weiträumiger und formloser Vororte verfallen einige Theoretiker heute in ein anderes: die Forderung nach Wohndichten, die jene der übelsten Spekulationsviertel übertreffen. In Flüchtlingssiedlungen bei Hongkong wurden zum Beispiel Einwohnerdichten von rund 6000 Einwohnern je Hektar festgestellt. Das »American Institute of Planners« fragt nun in aller Naivität, »ob beim Ausbleiben nachteiliger Folgen die bisherigen Normen und Vorstellungen städtebaulicher Weiträumigkeit aufrechterhalten bleiben können«.

Offenbar will man abwarten, bis jene bedauernswerten Chinesen ausgestorben sind.

Auch Jane Jacobs, die in »Tod und Leben großer amerikanischer Städte« manchen gescheiten Gedanken vorträgt, verfällt auf die Forderung extremer Dichten. Ihr Musterbeispiel Boston-North-End enthält angeblich mit 2500 Einwohnern je Hektar bei gemischter Bebauung alle Stufen der Differenzierung.

Daß solche übermäßigen Verdichtungen nicht den Einwohnern, sondern der Wirtschaft zuliebe propagiert werden, geht aus dem von ihr (S. 130) zitierten Bekenntnis des Wirtschaftsexperten Dr. Philipp M. Hauser hervor: »...weil derartige Bevölkerungsballungen die besten Produktions- und Konsumeinheiten darstellen, die unsere Gesellschaft bisher ausgebildet hat. Gerade die Größe, Dichte und Konzentration unserer Stadtregionen, gegen die manche Stadtplaner Einwendungen erheben, gehören zu unseren kostbarsten wirtschaftlichen Vorzügen(!).«

23. Pedestrian precincts at Hook. A system of walkways is provided which is independent of the carriageways for vehicular traffic. The project provides for moderate densities, approx. 100 persons per net acre. There is a higher concentration around the centres which contain some multistorey buildings with central functions.

23. Fußgänger-Bereiche in Hook. Neben dem Fahrstraßen-System ist ein Fußgänger-Wegnetz ausgebildet. Die Stadt zeigt maßvolle Verdichtung: etwa 250 Einwohner je Hektar netto. Die Zentren sind stärker verdichtet und enthalten Geschoßbauten mit zentralen Funktionen.

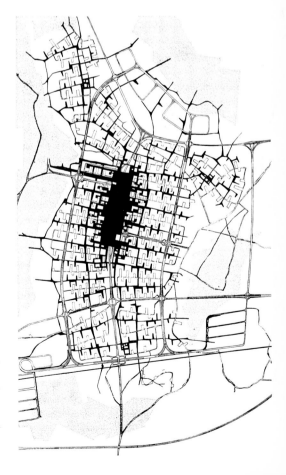

24. Levittown, an American suburb, with 16,000 detached, single-storey houses. Mechanised romanticism and lack of central features create monotony whilst the lack of economic spacing entails long journeys to work.

24. Levittown, eine amerikanische Suburb, mit 16 000 freistehenden, eingeschossigen Einfamilienhäusern. Mechanisierte Romantik und fehlende Zentren schaffen Langeweile; unökonomische Aufschließung hat lange Berufswege zur Folge.

Table of specified housing densities for different housing ranges and climatic regions

Floor Space Index	Population Density (Persons pr. ha.)	Housing Density (Dwellings pr. hectare)	Cubic Content Index	Housing Range				Climatic Region
0.1	40	10		No canalisation				
0.15	60	15						
0.2	80	20	0.8					
0.3	120	30	1.2					
0.4	160	40	1.6					
0.5	200	50	2.0	Range of urban low-height group housing	Range of low-height housing	Range of residential housing		
0.6	240	60	2.4					
0.7	280	70						
0.8	320	80	3.2					
0.9	360	90						
1.0	400	100	4.0					
1.2	480	120	4.8					
1.5	600	150	6.0				Range of central area housing	Scandinavian countries
2.0	800	200	8.0					Germany
2.5	1000	250	10.0					Austria
3.0	1200	300	12.0					Tropical countries
10.0	4000	1000	40.0					New York City

In this table, the following mean values have been assumed:
25 sq. metres of gross floor area per person; 4 persons per household; 3.0 metres storey height.

Area requirements of cities

		Part areas in sq. metres (Figures in brackets denote floor areas)			
		per person			per household of 4 persons
		Minimum	Average	Economic maximum	Average
Net areas	Area covered by residential buildings	10 (20)	15 (25)	25 (30)	60 (100)
	Courtyard, garden and front garden	10	25	50	100
	Private car park	(underground)	3 (partly underground)	5	12 (partly underground)
	Totals	20	43	80	172
Tare areas	Streets, roads, piazzas	10	15	15	60
	Sports and play grounds	5	13	20	52
	Cemeteries	2	3	3	12
	Parks	4	12	15	48
	Allotment gardens	4	6	7	24
	Public buildings and minor industry	5	8	10	32
	Totals	30	57	70	228
Gross areas	Totals, excluding industry, woods, etc.	50	100	150	400
	Railways	10	20	25	80
	Water, woods	5	50	60	200
	Industrial and storage areas	10	30	45	120
	Subtotals	25	100	125	400
	Whole town	75	200	275	800

This table is based on the following floor space index assumptions:
for minimum values, 1.2; for average values, 0.6; for maximum values, 0.3.

Tabelle der festgesetzten Dichten nach Bebauungs- und Klimabereichen

Geschoß-flächen-zahl, GFZ	Einwoh-nerdichte E/Ha netto	Wohn-dichte Wo/Ha netto	Bau-massen-zahl, BMZ	Bebauungsbereich			Klimabereich
0,1	40	10		Keine Ka-			
0,15	60	15		nalisation			
0,2	80	20	0,8				
0,3	120	30	1,2				
0,4	160	40	1,6		Flach-	Wohn-	
0,5	200	50	2,0	Bereich	bau-	bau-	
0,6	240	60	2,4	des	bereich	bereich	
0 7	280	70		urbanen			
0,8	320	80	3,2	Flach-			
0,9	360	90		baues			
1,0	400	100	4,0				
1,2	480	120	4,8				Maximale Dichten für:
1.5	600	150	6,0			City-bereich	Skandinavische Länder
2,0	800	200	8,0				Deutschland
2,5	1000	250	10,0				Österreich
3,0	1200	300	12,0				Tropische Länder
10,0	4000	1000	40,0				New York City

Voraussetzung sind mittlere Werte:
25 qm Bruttogeschoßfläche je Person; 4 Personen je Familie; 3,0 m Geschoßhöhe.

Flächenbedarf von Städten

		Flächenanteile in qm (in den Klammern Wohnfläche)			
		Je Person			Je Familie (4 Personen)
		Minimum	Mittlerer Wert	Ökonomisches Maximum	Mittlerer Wert
Entspricht Nettoflächen	Überbaute Wohnbauflächen	10 (20)	15 (25)	25 (30)	60 (100)
	Hof, Garten und Vorgarten	10	25	50	100
	Privater Parkplatz	(unter-irdisch)	3 (zum Teil unterirdisch)	5	12 (zum Teil unterirdisch)
	Insgesamt	20	43	80	172
Entspricht Taraflächen	Straßen, Wege, Plätze	10	15	15	60
	Sport- und Spielplätze	5	13	20	52
	Friedhof	2	3	3	12
	Park	4	12	15	48
	Kleingärten	4	6	7	24
	Öffentliche Gebäude und Kleingewerbe	5	8	10	32
	Insgesamt	30	57	70	228
Entspricht Brutto-flächen	Bruttoflächen ohne Industrie, Wald etc. insgesamt	50	100	150	400
	Eisenbahn	10	20	25	80
	Wasser, Wald	5	50	60	200
	Industrie, Lager	10	30	45	120
	Insgesamt	25	100	125	400
	Bruttoflächen d. Gesamtstadt	75	200	275	800

Der Tabelle sind folgende Dichten zugrunde gelegt:
bei den Minimum-Werten GFZ 1,2; bei den mittleren Werten GFZ 0,6; bei den Maximum-Werten GFZ 0 3.

25. Increase of the floor space index with the height of the buildings. The diagram shows the variation of the floor space index with the height of the buildings, assuming the same sunlight conditions and the same floor space requirement per person. The ordinate shows, for each curve, the floor space index for the given storey height. The curve has been plotted for the same angle of the sun and, thus, for a constant space requirement (or open space index) per person. The diagram shows four curves which are in use for different situations within the usual density range based on hygienic minimum requirements. The bottom curve applies to the height-distance ratio of 1 in 3; in the case of schools and hospitals, a ratio of 1 in 2.5 is regarded as sufficient. From the first to the seventh storey, the floor space index increases from 0.5 to 0.9. Beyond this value, the increase in utilisation efficiency becomes insignificant. The constant open space index of 1.11, with 22.5 sq. metres (244 sq. ft.) per person, corresponds to a garden of approx. 90 sq. metres (say, 1000 sq. ft.) for a household with four persons.
OSI Open space index, OS/P Open space pr. person.

25. Wachsen der GFZ bei höherer Bebauung: Die Kurve zeigt die Änderung der Geschoßflächenzahl mit höherer Bebauung, bei gleichen Besonnungsbedingungen und gleichem Flächenanteil je Person. An der Ordinate ist die GFZ bei der jeweiligen Geschoßhöhe an der entsprechenden Kurve abzulesen. In dem Diagramm sind vier Kurven dargestellt, die, im Bereich der im Städtebau angewandten Dichten, auf hygienischen Mindestforderungen für verschiedene Situationen basieren. Die unterste Kurve zeigt das Verhältnis Höhe:Abstand = 1:3, für Schulen und Krankenhäuser bis 1:2,5 ausreichend. Die Geschoßflächenzahl (GFZ) steigt vom ersten bis zum siebenten Geschoß von 0,5 auf 0,9. Darüber hinaus ist die Steigerung der Ausnutzung minimal. Der konstante Freiflächenindex (FFI) 1,11 mit 22,5 qm FF/E ergibt bei vier Personen einen Hausgarten von rund 90 qm.

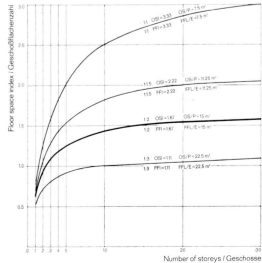

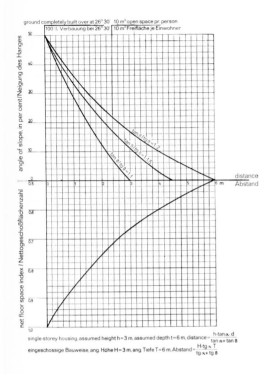

ground completely built over at 26°30'   10 m² open space pr. person
100 % Verbauung bei 26°30'   10 m² Freifläche je Einwohner

angle of slope, in per cent / Neigung des Hanges

tan α/tg α = 1:2
tan α/tg α = 1:1.5
tan α/tg α = 1:1

net floor space index / Nettogeschoßflächenzahl

distance
Abstand

single-storey housing, assumed height h = 3 m, assumed depth t = 6 m, distance = $\frac{h \cdot \tan \alpha \cdot d}{\tan \alpha + \tan \beta}$

eingeschossige Bauweise, ang. Höhe H = 3 m, ang. Tiefe T = 6 m, Abstand = $\frac{H \cdot tg \alpha \cdot T}{tg \alpha + tg \beta}$

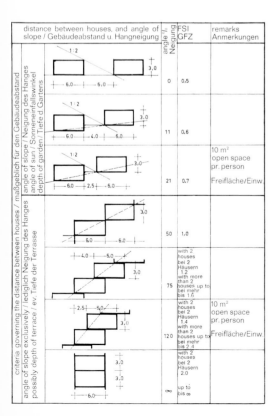

distance between houses, and angle of slope / Gebäudeabstand u. Hangneigung	angle / Neigung	FSI GFZ	remarks Anmerkungen
1:2 6,0 6,0 3,0	0	0,5	
1:2 6,0 4,0 6,0 3,0	11	0,6	
1:2 6,0 2,5 6,0 3,0	21	0,7	10 m² open space pr. person Freifläche/Einw.
6,0 6,0 3,0	50	1,0	
4,0 6,0 3,0	75	with 2 houses bei 2 Häusern 1.2 with more than 2 houses up to bei mehr bis 1.6	
2,5 6,0 3,0	120	with 2 houses bei 2 Häusern 1.4 with more than 2 houses up to bei mehr bis 2.4	10 m² open space pr. person Freifläche/Einw.
6,0 3,0 3,0	∞	with 2 houses bei 2 Häusern 2.0 up to bis ∞	

criteria governing the distance between houses / maßgeblich für den Gebäudeabstand
angle of slope exclusively / lediglich Neigung des Hanges
possibly depth of terrace / ev. Tiefe der Terrasse
angle of sun / Sonneneinfallswinkel
depth of garden / Tiefe d Gartens

"Diagonal" Housing

The advantages of horizontal and vertical arrangements of dwelling units can be combined by adopting a "diagonal" arrangement.

The diagonal may be a natural slope so that housing construction is governed by topographical conditions; but the diagonal can also be artificially created in the form of superimposed platforms resulting in a "stratified" design. If the slope is gentle, free space remains between the houses. If the slope is steeper, the houses must imbricate; the free space is on the roof of the house below. The first alternative might be called hill-side housing, the second terraced housing. The latter has the advantage that the walking distances to the ground are short. On a very steep slope, however, the arrangement becomes more akin to multi-storey housing.

The possibilities of diagonal arrangements on natural or artificially created ground have been in the foreground of discussion for some time. Up to now, practical examples have mostly been confined to natural slopes. Early examples of terraced houses are found in Finland (Aalto), Sweden (Backström and Reinius), Japan (Kenzo Tange), and Germany (Frey, Schröder).

Apart from ideological and creative possibilities, the sloping ground has the advantage of better utilisation, and therefore of higher housing density, compared with level ground. The steeper the slope, the shorter the necessary distance between buildings. Where the angle of the slope reaches 90°, the house is suspended on the rock as is sometimes the case in Italian hill towns.

An increase in density is advantageous, particularly in single-storey housing. The limits of the utilisation of net building land are given by the distance/height ratio of 2 in 1. The angle of 22.5° more or less corresponds, in Central Europe (48th Parallel), to the angle of the sun still touching the window sill at noon 21st December (19.5°). With a slope of 25 per cent, for example, it is possible to obtain a floor space index of approximately 0.75, compared with one of 0.5 on level ground. With a slope of 50 per cent, the utilisation can be doubled, i.e. the area can be completely built over (corresponding to a floor space index of 1.0).

With the aid of a curve, or families of curves, obtained by plotting the slope in per cent. (ordinate) against the distance between houses in metres (abscissa), the house spacing corresponding to the angle of the sun can be ascertained for any slope up to 50 per cent.

On the assumption of a house of H = 3.0 metres height and T = 6.0 metres depth, the curves indicating the house spacing for an angle of the sun β = 1:2 (purely residential areas), 1:1.5 (residential districts in central areas) and 1:1 (purely commercial areas) have been determined for our latitudes (Fig. 26).

For this calculation, the following general formula has been developed:

$$a = \frac{H - \tan \alpha \cdot T}{\tan \alpha + \tan \beta}$$

where a signifies the distance between the two buildings, α the slope of the ground, and β the angle of the sun.

With the aid of this formula, it is possible to determine the distance between buildings, for houses of any given height or depth, even beyond the range of the diagram.

The diagram also permits the determination, in terms of floor space indices, of the densities corresponding to the relevant house spacing (ordinates ,downwards). If the slope of the ground exceeds 50 per cent (26°30'), the houses overlap. In this case, the housing density is exclusively governed by the angle of slope, or by the minimum terrace area regarded as open space.

26. The diagram enables the distance between houses to be read off for a given angle of the sun within an angle of slope up to 50 per cent. The lower curve indicates the corresponding floor space indices.

27. Graphic presentation of the basic data on which the calculation of the slope and housing density is based. The graph covers the entire range of slope from 0 to ∞.

26. Die graphische Darstellung ermöglicht ein Ablesen des Hausabstandes bei einem bestimmten Sonneneinfallswinkel, im Bereich einer Hangneigung bis zu 50%. An der unteren Kurve lassen sich die entsprechenden Geschoßflächenzahlen ablesen.

27. Graphische Darstellung der Grundlagen, nach denen die Berechnung von Hangneigung und Bebauungsdichte erfolgt. Erfaßt ist der ganze Bereich der Hangneigung zwischen 0 und ∞.

Diagonalbebauung

Die Vorzüge des »Nebeneinanderstellens« und des »Aufeinandersetzens« von Wohnungen lassen sich durch Anordnen in der Schräge miteinander verbinden.

Die Diagonale kann ein natürlicher Hang sein, wodurch eine »bodengebundene« Bauweise entsteht, sie kann aber auch durch ein künstliches Gerüst gegeben sein, auf dem oder in dem eine Wohnsiedlung erstellt wird, also eine »schichtengebundene« Bauweise. Bei geringer Neigung des natürlichen Geländes entsteht der Freiraum zwischen den Gebäuden. Bei stärkerer Neigung müssen die Bauten übereinander geschoben werden; das Dach des darunterliegenden Gebäudes wird zum Freiraum. Die erste Möglichkeit kann man als Hangbebauung, die zweite als Terrassenbebauung bezeichnen. Die Terrassenbebauung hat den Vorteil einer kurzen Verbindung zum Boden. Bei sehr steilem Gelände nähert sie sich aber den Eigenschaften des Hochbaues.

Die Möglichkeiten diagonaler Bebauung auf natürlichem oder künstlichem Träger werden seit einiger Zeit stark diskutiert. Die Realisierung beschränkt sich zunächst vorwiegend auf natürliche Hänge. Erste Beispiele von Terrassenhäusern gibt es in Finnland (Aalto), Schweden (Backström und Reinius), Japan (Kenzo Tange) und Deutschland (Frey, Schröder, Schmidt).

Neben den ideellen und gestalterischen Möglichkeiten bietet das Hanggelände gegenüber dem ebenen Baugrund den Vorteil einer besseren Ausnutzung und damit größeren Dichte. Die Abstände von Baukörper zu Baukörper können um so geringer gehalten werden, je steiler der Hang ist. Wenn der Neigungswinkel 90° erreicht hat, entspricht die Anlage einem am Felsen hängenden Haus, wie es in italienischen Bergstädten vorkommt.

Eine Steigerung der Dichte ist vor allem bei eingeschossiger Bebauung vorteilhaft. Die Grenzen der Ausnutzung von Nettobauland sind durch das Verhältnis von Abstand zu Höhe wie 2:1 gegeben. 22,5° entsprechen in Mitteleuropa (48. Breitengrad) etwa dem Neigungswinkel der Sonne von 19,5°, die am 21. Dezember um 12 Uhr die Unterkante des Fensters noch berühren soll. Bei einer Neigung von 25% kann zum Beispiel eine GFZ von etwa 0,75 erreicht werden, gegenüber einer GFZ von 0,5 im ebenen Gelände. Bei einem Hang mit 50% Neigung ist die doppelte Ausnutzung, das heißt eine volle Überbauung möglich (= GFZ 1,0).

Bei der Annahme eines Hauses mit der Höhe H = 3,0 m und der Tiefe T = 6,0 m wurden die Kurven für die Hausabstände unter Annahme eines Sonneneinfallswinkels β = 1:2 (reine Wohngebiete), 1:1,5 (Wohngebiete in der City) und 1:1 (reine Geschäftsgebiete) in unseren Breiten ermittelt (Abb. 26).

Für vorstehende Berechnung wurde die allgemeine Formel

$$a = \frac{H - tg\,\alpha \cdot T}{tg\,\alpha + tg\,\beta}$$

aufgestellt. Dabei ist: a = Abstand der beiden Gebäude, α = Neigungswinkel des Geländes, β = Sonneneinfallswinkel.

Mit Hilfe dieser Formel kann der Städteplaner, über die Werte der graphischen Ermittlung hinaus, den Abstand der Gebäude bei jeder Haushöhe oder Haustiefe erfassen.

Das Diagramm ermöglicht auch, die durch den jeweiligen Hausabstand entstehenden Dichten in Geschoßflächenzahlen abzulesen (Ordinate nach unten). Übersteigt die Neigung des Hanggeländes 50% = 26° 30', so schieben sich die Häuser übereinander. Für die Dichte der Bebauung ist dann nur die Hangneigung bzw. der erforderliche Terrassenanteil, der als Freifläche gerechnet wird, maßgebend. (Darstellung der mathematischen Beziehungen unter Mitarbeit von Frau Dipl. Ing. Spielhofer.)

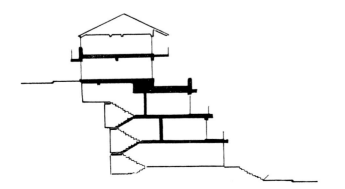

28. The "Habitat" project designed for the Montreal World Exhibition, 1967, has succeeded in creating a housing group which, though of economically high density, conveys a lively impression; this has been achieved by making use of the diagonal. The quality corresponds to that of ground level low-rise buildings.

29. Gröndahl near Stockholm, architects: Backström and Reinius, providing an early example of diagonal housing. Favourable utilisation of a steep slope with access at bottom and top level.

28. Bei dem Projekt »Habitat« für die Weltausstellung 1967 in Montreal ist es gelungen, durch Anwendung der Diagonale ein ebenso ökonomisch dichtes wie lebendiges Gebilde zu schaffen. Die Qualität entspricht der des ebenerdigen Flachbaues.

29. Gröndahl bei Stockholm, Architekten Backstroem und Reinius, ein frühes Beispiel einer Diagonalbebauung. Günstige Ausnutzung eines Steilhanges mit unterem und oberem Zugang.

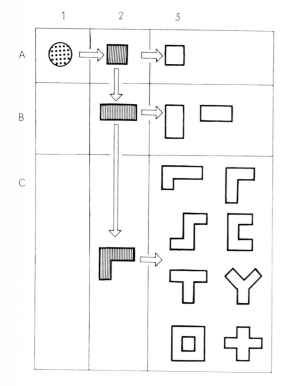

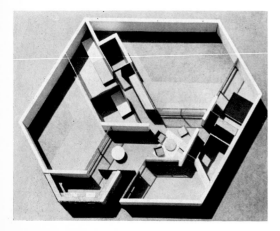

30. Theoretical derivation of low-rise housing types according to Meyer-Bohe.
1 Origin, 2 Basic type, 3 Variants, A Point house, B Oblong house, C Angle house.
31. Model of a hexagonal patio house, designed by Kapfhammer and Wegan (Seminar Professor Hoffmann).

30. Ableitung der Flachbau-Typen nach Meyer-Bohe.
1 Ursprung, 2 Grundform, 3 Varianten, A Punkthaus, B Langhaus, C Winkelhaus.
31. Modell eines hexagonalen Hofhauses. Entwurf Kapfhammer und Wegan (Seminar Professor Hoffmann).

Typology of Low-Rise Housing

Since the advent of the urban house, a few types of terrace houses with one, two or three storeys have been developed and are still with us to-day. This group (1), formerly confined to simple rectangular plans with one, two or three bays, has been enriched by some new variants with projecting or recessed frontages, staggered storeys, etc.

In contrast to it is group (2), "Patio Houses," which spread horizontally in all directions and provide a greater mutual penetration of enclosed and open space. Even now, the manifold potentialities of ground-level housing have not yet been fully recognized. In this group, new designs and transitional solutions, e.g. in conjunction with two-storey components or staggered storeys or with utilisation of a hillside position, emerge all the time so that a recognition of typical features has become difficult. The present typology is therefore no more than an attempt to register the present state of development.

1 Terrace houses (Key to plans see page 174)
Three-bay houses. These date back to the farmhouse with the hall in the centre. Because of the greater floor span technically possible to-day, houses of this type are nowadays rare. They are confined to larger houses where the frontage exceeds the depth.
1a Two-storey houses with three bays are mainly encountered in south orientation. Kitchen, dining area and transversely placed living rooms and studies are on the ground floor, the bedrooms on the upper floor, the corridors and ancillary rooms on the north side. Less frequent is an east-west type where the ground floor rooms face west and the upper floor bedrooms east.
1b With single-storey houses of the three-bay kind, the frontages are even longer (in excess of 40 ft. or so) so that the living rooms and bedrooms, mainly facing south, can be placed side-by-side. As with two-storey houses, the loads are transmitted by the party walls and intermediate parallel walls so that the front windows and doors can be made as wide as desired.
Two-bay houses:
1c The two-storey, two-bay house is the one most frequently encountered to-day, in particular the variant with a flight of stairs parallel to the party walls. The frontage length ranges from, say, 20 to 30 ft. This simple and appropriate design, where the stair landing is supported by the centre wall, is already encountered in the Fugger houses, in the Potsdam types, and in nearly all the Dutch and English terrace houses. On the upper floor are two, three or four bedrooms and bathroom, on the ground floor the living rooms. In Scandinavia, where heavy snowfalls must be reckoned with, the living rooms are often on the upper floors. The kitchen is best placed on the garden side although, at present, the variant with the kitchen facing the road is still equally frequent. With increasing use of reinforced concrete, the spiral staircase is becoming more and more popular. It avoids the loss in space caused by the landing and has the advantage of permitting a particularly economic plan. Moreover, an uninterrupted flight of spiral stairs is less dangerous to elderly people than an interrupted flight.
1d In contrast to those houses where the bearing walls are at right angles to the road, there are also types where the bays are placed parallel to the road, although this solution is structurally less favourable. The layout of such houses is mainly governed by orientation towards the sun, i.e., living and bedrooms are on the garden side, whilst entrance, stairs and bathroom/W.C. occupy the smaller bay along the road.
1e With single-storey houses, the rooms may either be lined up on the south side (garden side), or may be orientated in two directions. The frontages exceed 40 ft. in length. All the plan variants encountered with multi-storey houses can also be used, with suitable modifications, for single-storey houses.
Single-bay houses:
1f With single-storey and two-storey terrace houses, there is a tendency to loosen the frontages. In particular, a parallel stagger of the two bays offers the advantage not only of better sunlight but also of better accessibility of the centre of the house. Moreover, a plan of this type facilitates future extension as well as the segregation of a small self-contained dwelling for lodgers. "T-Types" already represent a transition to the "L-Type" of the patio house. They are particularly suitable where terrace houses with rectangular plan would result in an unfavourable orientation.
1g The higher the terrace house, the shorter is, in general, the frontage and the greater the depth. Terrace houses with three or four storeys are thus nearly always designed in accordance with the single-bay principle. A minimum frontage of about 12 ft. is sufficient. Staircase, bathroom, kitchen, W. C. and ancillary rooms are placed in the interior of the house. In narrow houses, the stairs may be of the spiral or landing type. To achieve better connections with the other rooms, the main rooms are often, with this house type, placed on the intermediate floor. The ground floor often contains, apart from ancillary and spare rooms, a study which may also serve as an extra bedroom.

Flachbau-Typologie

Seit der Entstehung des städtischen Hauses haben sich einige wenige, auch heute noch gültige Typen des ein- bis dreigeschossigen Reihenhauses herausgebildet. Diese Gruppe (1), früher auf einfache, rechteckige Grundrisse beschränkt, mit ein bis drei Schiffen, wurde durch vor- und zurückspringende Fronten, versetzte Geschosse und Kombinationen mit anderen Bebauungsweisen um neue Abarten bereichert.

Ihr steht die Gruppe (2) der »Hofhäuser« gegenüber, die sich in die Fläche ausbreiten, und bei denen sich umbauter Raum und Freiraum stärker durchdringen. Die Vielfalt der Möglichkeiten ebenerdiger Bebauungsweise ist noch gar nicht erkannt. Immer neue Varianten und Übergangslösungen, etwa in Verbindung mit zweigeschossigen Bauteilen oder Geschoßversetzung und Ausnutzung von Hanglagen, entstehen bei dieser Gruppe, so daß eine Erfassung des Typischen schwierig geworden ist. Diese Typologie ist daher nur ein Versuch, den gegenwärtigen Stand der Entwicklung zu fassen.

1 Reihenhäuser (Legende zu den Grundrissen siehe Seite 174)

Dreischiffige Anlagen: Sie sind aus dem Bauernhaus mit in der Mitte angeordneter Diele entstanden. Infolge der heute technisch möglichen Deckenspannweiten werden sie nur noch selten angewendet. Sie beschränken sich auf größere Wohnungen, deren Front breiter ist als die Tiefe.

1a Zweigeschossige Anlagen mit drei Schiffen gibt es vor allem als südgerichtete Typen. Küche, Eßplatz und breitgelegte Wohn- und Arbeitsräume befinden sich im Erdgeschoß, Schlafräume im Obergeschoß und Flure und Nebenräume auf der Nordseite. Weniger häufig ist ein Ostwest-Typ, bei dem die Räume des Erdgeschosses nach Westen und die Schlafräume im Obergeschoß nach Osten orientiert sind.

1b Bei eingeschossigen, dreischiffigen Anlagen sind die Fronten noch breiter, über 12 m, um die vorwiegend nach Süden gerichteten Wohn- und Schlafräume nebeneinander aufreihen zu können. Brandmauern und parallele Zwischenmauern nehmen, wie bei zweigeschossigen Anlagen, die Decken- und Dachlasten auf, so daß die Fronten beliebig weit für Fenster und Türen geöffnet werden können.

Zweischiffige Anlagen:

1c Das zweigeschossige, zweischiffige Haus ist bis heute am häufigsten angewendet worden, und zwar die Variante mit einer Treppe parallel zur Brandmauer. Die Frontbreite liegt zwischen 6 und 9 Metern. Die Fugger-Siedlung, die Potsdamer Typen und nahezu alle holländischen und englischen Reihenhäuser folgen diesem einfachen und zweckmäßigen Prinzip, bei dem der Treppenwechsel durch die Mittelmauer aufgefangen wird. Im Obergeschoß liegen zwei bis vier Schlafräume mit Bad, im Erdgeschoß die Wohnräume. In Skandinavien befinden sich die Wohnräume, da mit großen Schneehöhen zu rechnen ist, oft im Obergeschoß. Die Küche liegt am günstigsten auf der Gartenseite, obgleich die Variante mit der Küche an der Straßenseite auch heute noch ebenso häufig ist. Mit zunehmender Verwendung von Stahlbeton setzt sich die Wendeltreppe mehr und mehr durch. Sie vermeidet den durch ein Podest gegebenen Raumverlust und bietet den Vorteil, daß eine besonders ökonomische Grundrißbildung möglich ist. Außerdem ist für alte Leute die gleichmäßig gewendelte Treppe nicht so gefährlich wie die halbgewendelte.

1d Im Gegensatz zu jenen Anlagen, bei denen die tragenden Mauern senkrecht zur Straße angeordnet sind, gibt es auch Typen, deren Schiffe parallel zur Straßenfront verlaufen, obgleich diese Lösung konstruktiv ungünstiger ist. Solche Anlagen sind vorwiegend einseitig sonnengerichtet, das heißt, Wohn- und Schlafräume befinden sich an der Gartenseite, Eingang, Treppe und Naßgruppe im schmaleren Schiff an der Straßenseite.

1e Bei eingeschossigen Anlagen ist sowohl die Aufreihung mit Südorientierung an der Gartenseite als auch die Ausrichtung nach zwei Himmelsrichtungen möglich. Die Frontbreiten überschreiten 12 Meter. Alle Grundrißsysteme, die bei mehrgeschossigen Bauten üblich sind, können entsprechend abgewandelt auch ebenerdig Anwendung finden.

Einschiffige Anlagen:

1f Bei ein- und zweigeschossigen Reihenhäusern ist eine Tendenz zur Auflockerung der Fronten zu beobachten. Vor allem die Parallelverschiebung der beiden Schiffe gegeneinander hat nicht nur den Vorteil einer besseren Besonnung, sondern auch der besseren Zugänglichkeit des Hauskerns. Darüber hinaus fördert der bewegte Grundriß die Möglichkeit der Erweiterung und der Abtrennung einer selbständigen Wohneinheit für Einlieger. »T-Typen« bilden bereits einen Übergang zum »L-Typ« des Atriumhauses. Sie sind besonders dann anzuwenden, wenn die Orientierung in der Reihe bei rechteckigem Grundriß ungünstig wäre.

1g Je höher das Reihenhaus wird, um so schmaler ist im allgemeinen die Frontbreite und um so tiefer der Hauskörper. So folgen drei- bis viergeschossige Reihenhäuser fast immer dem einschiffigen Prinzip. Für die Frontbreite reichen 3,70 m als Minimum aus. Treppenhaus, Naßgruppe und Nebenräume sind im Hausinnern vorgesehen. Die Treppe ist bei schmalen Häusern

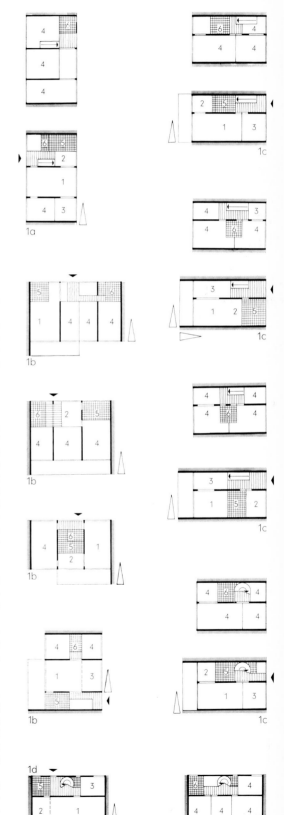

1a

1b

1b

1b

1d

1c

1c

1c

1c

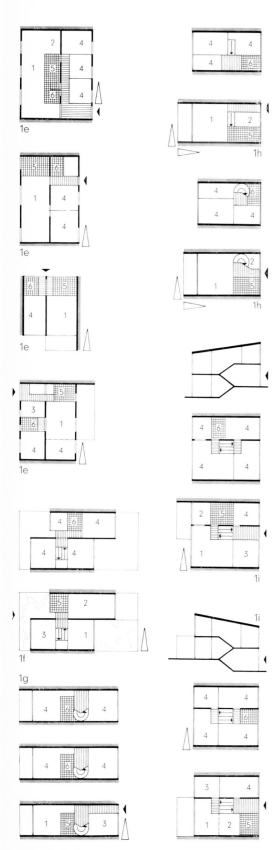

1e

1e

1e

1e

1f

1g

1h

1h

1h

1i

1i

1h With single-bay, two-storey houses, the stairs may again either be of the spiral type or placed at right angles to the party walls (Dammerstock Estate, designed by Gropius). Because of the short frontage, the kitchen must face the road. The upper floor contains two or two and a half bedrooms only.

1i Two-storey or three-storey terrace houses with staggered floors permit diversified rooms, yet are economic in plan. Because of the central position of the stairs, the plans are quadratic rather than deep. The kitchen may be placed on the entrance side or on the garden side. Among the possible variants is an entrance with a half-flight of stairs upwards or downwards, depending on the hillside position.

1k Single-storey types of great depth require top lighting or patios and thus become "Patio Houses." Even Hugo Häring's prototype house demonstrated the advantages of the single-storey house. The possibility of providing toplighting for parts of the dwelling so that, e.g., the kitchen and possibly even bedrooms can be placed in the interior of the house, gives rise to new plan combinations. Concentrated low-rise housing brings further advantages.

The choice between these plan types of terrace houses depends not only on the size but also on the orientation of the house. Rows of terrace houses are preferably given an east-west orientation, or are turned at an angle not exceeding about 22° towards east. Living rooms and the minority of bedrooms should face west, the majority of bedrooms east or east-north-east. This arrangement is particularly easy with the two-bay type where living room, kitchen, one of the bedrooms and the entrance are on the ground floor whilst bathroom and the other bedrooms are on the upper floor. A variant with nearly square plan is obtained where the floor area is strictly limited. The three-bay type requires so much open space that it can no longer be regarded as "Urban Low-Rise Housing" in the sense here defined. Three-storey or four-storey terrace houses are extremely economic, but have the disadvantage of requiring much use of the stairs. Single-storey terrace houses are relatively uneconomic but have the special advantage of combining all functions on a single level.

2 Patio Houses

Any terrace house where the living room is connected with an open space not surrounded by walls, may also be regarded as a type of Patio House. A transitional type is represented by the single-storey terrace houses where the patio is placed parallel or at right angles to the road. These may also be called I-Types. With patio houses, the structural feature of the "bays" cannot be regarded as a definition criterion as the types are either of the single-bay variety, or the bays are so staggered or turned in relation to each other that clear definitions are no longer possible.

2a In the I-Type of patio house, the rooms are concatenated so that the house may have a length of up to 66 ft. or so. The patio is placed parallel to the building. One advantage is that the garden can be reached from the road yet, because of its depth, preserves the seclusion of a patio.

2b L-Type layouts (whose development owes much to Hilberseimer) can be used in many varieties. One wing contains the main bedrooms, the other the living rooms. With but two variants, it is possible to build in any position and to attain proper orientation. In that case, however, the second variant will be a "semi-patio house," i.e., not all the doors and windows face the patio.

2c With U-Type layouts, the patio is enclosed on three sides. The size of such houses exceeds the normal space requirements of a family which can already, in all cases, be satisfied by the L-Type. Frequently encountered is the arrangement with the living rooms in the centre, flanked by two bedroom wings.

2d D-Type layouts represent genuine patio houses in the classical sense, where the patio is enclosed at all sides by rooms in daily use. This type should preferably be confined to cases where space requirements are particularly great, e.g., combination with a surgery, or where, as may be the case in Mediterranean countries, connecting corridors can be omitted.

2e B-Type layouts. This type, too, is of ancient origin. Plots of great depth are nearly wholly built over. The rooms receive daylight through two or more patios some of which are also used as utility courtyards. Luxury types of great flexibility, with one, two or even three bays (Chermayeff, page 147; Coderch, page 144) offer interesting, dispersed layouts. The combination of a two-storey terrace house with a single-storey patio group (Lyons, page 38; van den Broek and Bakema, page 44) offers further possibilities of variation.

gewendelt oder eine Podesttreppe. Bei diesem Typ liegen die Haupträume oft, aus Gründen der günstigen Verbindung zu den übrigen Räumen, im mittleren Geschoß. Das Erdgeschoß enthält außer Neben- und Gasträumen häufig ein Studio, das auch als Schlafraum dienen kann.

1h Bei einschiffigen, zweigeschossigen Anlagen wird die Treppe ebenfalls gewendelt oder senkrecht zur Brandmauer angelegt (Gropius, Siedlung Dammerstock). Infolge der geringen Frontbreite muß die Küche an der Straßenseite liegen. Das Obergeschoß enthält nur zwei bis zweieinhalb Schlafräume.

1i Zwei- bis dreistöckige Reihenhäuser mit versetzten Geschossen ermöglichen differenzierte Räume bei sparsamer Flurausbildung. Infolge der mittig angelegten Treppe sind die Grundrisse eher quadratisch als tief. Die Küche kann an der Eingangs- oder der Gartenseite liegen. Variationsmöglichkeiten: Eingang mit Halbtreppe nach unten oder oben, entsprechend der Hanglage.

1k Sehr tiefe eingeschossige Typen erfordern Oberlicht oder Höfe und verwandeln sich dann in Hofhäuser. Schon Hugo Häring hat mit seinem Versuchshaus auf die Vorteile des ebenerdigen Hauses hingewiesen. Die Möglichkeit, Teile der Wohnung mit Oberlicht zu versehen, das heißt Küche und eventuell auch Schlafräume ins Hausinnere zu legen, ergibt neue Grundrißkombinationen. Der eingeschossige Flachbau gewinnt den Vorzug weiterer Verdichtung.

Welcher der genannten Grundrißtypen des Reihenhauses gewählt wird, hängt, neben der Größe, von der Orientierung ab. Nach Möglichkeit versucht man den Reihenhauszeilen eine Ostwest-Orientierung zu geben, mit einer maximalen Drehung bis zu 22 Grad nach Osten. Die Wohnräume und der kleinere Teil der Schlafräume sollten nach Westen gerichtet sein, der größere Teil der Schlafräume nach Osten oder Ostnordosten. Dieser Anordnung kommt besonders der zweischiffige Typ entgegen, bei dem Wohnraum, Küche, ein Schlafraum und Eingang im Erdgeschoß, Bad und weitere Schlafräume im Obergeschoß liegen. Eine dem Quadrat angenäherte Lösung entsteht bei sehr knappen Wohnflächen. Der dreischiffige Typ erfordert so große Freiräume, daß er kaum noch als urbaner Flachbau anzusprechen ist. Drei- oder viergeschossige Reihenhäuser sind äußerst ökonomisch, haben jedoch den Nachteil des Treppensteigens. Eingeschossige Reihenhäuser sind etwas unwirtschaftlicher, haben aber den besonderen Vorteil, alle Funktionen auf einer Ebene zu vereinigen.

2 Hofhäuser

Alle Reihenhäuser lassen sich, wenn sie einen mit dem Wohnraum in Verbindung stehenden, nicht ummauerten Freiraum haben, auch als eine Form des Hofhauses auffassen. Einen Übergangstyp stellen besonders die eingeschossigen Reihenhäuser dar, deren Hof parallel oder senkrecht zur Straße angeordnet ist. Sie können auch als I-Typen bezeichnet werden. Das konstruktive Merkmal der »Schiffe« läßt sich zur Definition des Hofhauses nicht verwenden, da die Typen entweder einschiffig sind oder das Verschieben und winkelige Aneinandersetzen der Schiffe keine eindeutigen Abgrenzungen zuläßt.

2a Der senkrecht zur Straße angeordnete I-Typ des Hofhauses reiht die Räume hintereinander und erreicht dadurch eine Länge bis zu 20 Metern. Der Hof liegt parallel zum Baukörper. Vorteilhaft ist, daß man vom Wohnweg in den Garten gelangen kann, der dennoch durch seine Tiefe die Intimität eines Atriums besitzt. Die Raumfolge ist ähnlich wie bei Typ 1k, mit dem Unterschied, daß die Besonnung über den langgestreckten Hof durch Seitenlicht erfolgt. Bei der Ostwest-Variante dieses Typs ist der Flur auf der Westseite angeordnet, und es entstehen zwei Höfe.

2b L-Typen, um deren Entwicklung sich Hilberseimer besondere Verdienste erworben hat, sind vielfältig anwendbar. Ein Flügel enthält vorwiegend die Schlafräume, der andere die Wohnräume. Mit zwei Varianten kann man in jeder Lage bauen und die richtige Orientierung erreichen. Der zweite Typ ist dann allerdings ein »Semi-Atriumhaus«, das heißt, nicht alle Öffnungen liegen am inneren Hof.

2c Bei U-Typen wird das Atrium auf drei Seiten umschlossen. Ihre Größe übersteigt den normalen Raumbedarf einer Familienwohnung, der bereits im L-Typ immer befriedigt werden kann. Häufige Anordnung ist der in der Mitte gelegene Wohntrakt mit zwei Schlafflügeln.

2d D-Typen verkörpern echte Atriumhäuser im Sinne der klassischen Anordnung eines Wohnhofes, der auf allen Seiten von genutzten Räumen umschlossen ist. Dieser Typ ist zweckmäßig nur bei sehr großem Raumbedarf anzuwenden, etwa Kombination mit einer Praxis, oder bei Verzicht auf Flurverbindungen wie zum Beispiel in südlichen Ländern.

2e B-Typen. Auch diese Form kennen wir aus der Antike. Sehr tiefe Grundstücke sind nahezu ganz überbaut. Die Räume erhalten Licht durch zwei oder mehr Höfe, die zum Teil auch als Wohnhöfe genutzt werden. Ein-, zwei-, aber auch dreischiffige Luxustypen von großer Flexibilität (Chermayeff, S.147; Coderch, S.144) bieten interessante, aufgelockerte Grundrisse. Die Kombination von zweigeschossigem Reihenhaus mit eingeschossigem Atriumteil (Lyons, S. 38; van den Broek und Bakema, S. 44) ergibt weitere Variationsmöglichkeiten.

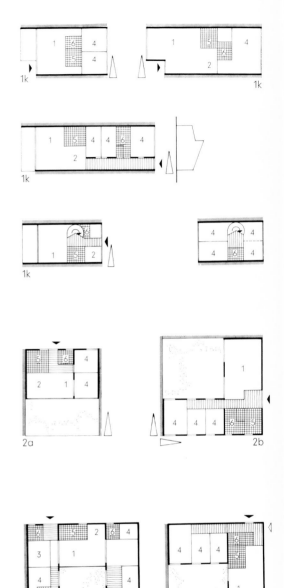

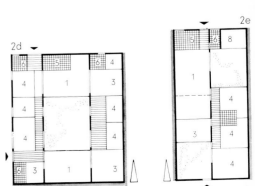

32. Isometric view of a "General Panel" house, architects: Gropius and Wachsmann. As early as 1925, Gropius predicted that "in future, a house would be bought from stock, like a shoe." He himself made a major contribution to this development by his many experiments.
33. "Packaged House System." Houses which are easy to erect and to dismantle promote the mobility of a town.

32. Isometrie eines »General-Panel«-Hauses, Architekten Gropius und Wachsmann. Schon 1925 prophezeite Gropius, »daß man in Zukunft ein Haus wie einen Schuh vom Lager beziehen« werde. Er hat diese Entwicklung durch viele Experimente gefördert.
33. »The Packaged-House-System«. Leicht auf- und abzubauende Häuser fördern die Mobilität der Stadt.

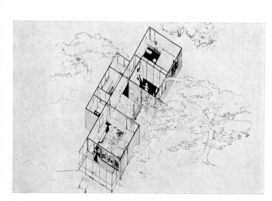

Industrial Prefabrication

The "Industrial Prefabrication" of building components has the effect that the individual components become larger. In this way, the laborious assembly of minute building elements by manual labour on the site can be replaced by rapid erection work.

The size of industrially produced components depends, first of all, on the weight of the material, on the purpose, and on the local circumstances. The scale ranges from the largest component which can still be handled by one man without mechanical aids, and from storey-high and storey-deep units to entire walls and floors, and finally to complete pre-assembled units such as bathroom, kitchen or bedroom.

Prefabricated houses, so-called, are low-rise houses which are erected form large-size components in the same way as industrially produced multi-storey buildings. All that is fixed beforehand is the prototype house and the price whilst, in either case, a rigid plan must be adopted, such as the stereotype four-and-a-half room dwelling so that the house functions are largely predetermined. It is only in this respect that the numerous prefabricated houses on the market differ from each other; they hardly offer any real margin for variation.

Gropius, well aware of this drawback, suggested that prefabrication should be confined to room-sized units which could be assembled and supplemented as desired. An even greater margin of freedom as between home functions and home structure would be obtained if the planner would be content to point out the logical potentialities inherent in the structural system whilst leaving the realisation of any specific solution to the occupier (cf. page 34 et. seq.). Among the great number of prefabricated houses on offer, there are, as yet, but few products which can be regarded as ultimately satisfactory both structurally and aesthetically. They are not cheaper than conventionally constructed houses; but they have the advantage that their price is fixed, that their features are known beforehand, and that a long building period with many unknown factors can be avoided.

Particularly unfavourable is their town planning effect. Prefabricated houses give further impetus to disorderly sprawl over large areas. The individualism of the "little man" is superseded by the even more strident form of contractors' self-sufficiency. There is hardly any attempt at subordination to a common plan; nor would such subordination even be possible with so many different products on the market. A fact not appreciated so far, and even now only beginning to become apparent (e. g. in England), is that prefabricated houses need not necessarily be arranged in open layouts, i. e. with plots of uneconomic size, but that they also lend themselves to erection in more concentrated clusters.

It is obviously important also to pay attention to developments in the United States. According to a survey carried out by the Bureau of the Census, the number of owner-occupiers had, by 1956, already reached 60 per cent of all households, compared with 47.8 per cent in 1930.

"During the economic crisis, such favourable methods of financing were developed that, even with a modest income, it has become quite feasible to own one's house. The average capital cost of a house ranges from two to three times the annual family income. The owners contribution is comparatively small. As a rule, a single mortgage is taken up which may amount to as much as 97 per cent of the estimated value of a house." ("Neue Heimat," January, 1959.)

Since the Second World War, house construction in the United States has reached the rate of about 1 million dwelling units per annum! There, too, interminable suburbs spread over the landscape, matching in their monotony the old tenement house districts in the central areas. A return to high-density urban districts is advocated, but with little success. Even after 1956, the percentage of owner-occupiers has continued to increase.

A strong impetus to this development is supplied by the building industry whose production of wholly or partially prefabricated low-rise houses has greatly increased in recent years (thus, in the case of wholly prefabricated houses, from 5 to 25 per cent, compared with an increase in Germany, in 1964, by 5 per cent). Moreover, prefabricated units—mainly of wood—are used for nearly all low-rise houses; pre-assembled plumbing units often consist of plastics.

"The government leaves housing construction to private initiative but facilitates financing through the 'Federal Housing Administration.' This government authority reinsures private institutes against the failure of mortgagors to repay long-term loans." Kurt Brändle, "Bauwelt," No. 17/64.

The American prefabrication methods as well as the financing system should be thoroughly studied by us. The monthly outgoings for a low-rise dwelling are generally lower than the rent for a flat in a multi-storey block.

If these methods are transferred to high-density low-rise housing, the costs (fire protection measures; roads and mains, etc.) are bound to decrease further.

Industrielle Vorfertigung

»Industrielle Vorfertigung« von Bauteilen bedeutet, daß einzelne Bauelemente größer werden. Auf diese Weise kann das langdauernde Zusammensetzen kleinster Bauelemente in Handarbeit auf der Baustelle durch kurzfristige Montage ersetzt werden.

Die Ausmaße der industriell gefertigten Teile sind in erster Linie abhängig vom Gewicht des Materials, vom Verwendungszweck und von der örtlichen Situation. Die Skala reicht vom großformatigen Bauteil, das ein Mann ohne maschinelle Hilfe versetzen kann, über geschoßhohe und -tiefe Elemente bis zur Größe ganzer Wände und Decken und schließlich bis zu fertigen Raumeinheiten wie Bad, Küche oder Schlafzimmer.

Die sogenannten Fertighäuser sind Flachbauten, die ebenso aus großformatigen Bauteilen montiert werden wie industriell hergestellte Mehrgeschoßbauten. »Fertig« sind nur das Musterhaus und der feste Preis, während hier wie dort ein starrer Grundriß vorgeplant ist, etwa die stereotype Viereinhalbzimmerwohnung, durch den Lebensvorgänge in bestimmter Weise fixiert werden. Die zahlreichen Firmenangebote differieren nur in der Vorbestimmung des Funktionsablaufes, lassen aber kaum wirkliche Variationsmöglichkeiten zu.

Gropius hat diesen Mangel bereits erkannt und den Vorschlag gemacht, lediglich Raumelemente auszubilden, die nach Bedarf aneinandergefügt und ergänzt werden können. Einen noch größeren Spielraum zwischen Lebensfunktion und baulicher Hülle erhielte man, wenn der Planer nur die, dem Konstruktionssystem entsprechenden, sinnvollen Möglichkeiten aufzeigen würde, die Realisierung der einen oder anderen Lösung aber dem Bewohner überlassen bliebe (siehe S. 35 ff.). Unter dem riesigen Angebot an Fertighäusern gibt es heute erst wenige Erzeugnisse, die im Endergebnis konstruktiv und formal befriedigen. Sie sind nicht billiger als traditionell hergestellte Bauten, haben aber den Vorteil eines festen Preises, voraufgehender Kenntnis des Typs und Vermeidung einer langen Bauzeit mit zahlreichen Unbekannten.

Denkbar ungünstig ist die städtebauliche Auswirkung: Die Flut der ungeordneten Besiedlung ganzer Landschaften wird durch vorfabrizierte Häuser verstärkt. Der Individualismus des Kleinbürgers tritt in der noch krasseren Form des Firmen-Egoismus auf. Eine städtebauliche Eingliederung wird kaum versucht, sie ist bei so unterschiedlichen Markterzeugnissen auch gar nicht möglich. Was bislang fast unbekannt war und sich erst in Ansätzen zeigt (zum Beispiel in England), ist die Tatsache, daß vorgefertigte Häuser ebenso gut in verdichteter, das heißt geschlossener Bauweise errichtet werden können wie in offener — mit unökonomischer Grundstücksgröße.

Wichtig erscheint es auch, die Entwicklung in den USA zu betrachten. Nach einer Untersuchung des Bureau of the Census (Amt für Statistik) wohnten 1956 bereits 60% aller Wohnungsinhaber in Wohnungen, deren Eigentümer sie sind, 1930 waren es 47,8%.

»Während der Wirtschaftskrise wurden so günstige Finanzierungsmethoden entwickelt, daß es auch bei einem bescheideneren Einkommen durchaus tragbar ist, ein Eigenheim zu besitzen. Ein Eigenheim kostet im Durchschnitt das zwei- bis dreifache Jahreseinkommen einer Familie. Die Eigenleistung ist verhältnismäßig gering. In der Regel wird nur eine Hypothek in Anspruch genommen, die unter Umständen bis zu 97% des geschätzten Wertes eines Hauses betragen kann.« (Neue Heimat, Januar 1959.)

Etwa seit Ende des Zweiten Weltkrieges werden in den USA ungefähr eine Million Wohnungseinheiten jährlich errichtet! Auch dort breiten sich unübersehbare Suburbs in die Landschaft, in ihrer Monotonie das Gegenstück zu den Mietskasernen der Innenstädte. Eine Rückkehr in die geschlossenen Stadtgebiete wird zwar propagiert, aber mit geringem Erfolg. Der Anteil an Eigenheim-Besitzern ist auch nach 1956 weiter angestiegen.

Ein starker Motor dieser Entwicklung ist die Bauindustrie, deren Produktion an teilvorgefertigten Flachbauten in den letzten Jahren stark zugenommen hat (bei reinen Prefab-Häusern von 5 auf 25%, in Deutschland 1964 um 5%). Im übrigen werden bei fast allen Flachbauten vorgefertigte Einzelteile — vorwiegend Holzkonstruktionen — verwendet; fertig eingebaute sanitäre Zellen bestehen häufig aus Kunststoff.

»Der Staat überläßt den Wohnungsbau privater Initiative, erleichtert allerdings die Finanzierung durch die ›Federal Housing Administration‹ (FHA). Diese staatliche Stelle versichert langfristige Hypothekendarlehen privater Institute gegen die Leistungsunfähigkeit des Hypothekenschuldners.« (Kurt Brändle, »Bauwelt« Nr. 17/64.)

Sowohl die amerikanischen Vorfertigungsmethoden als auch das Finanzierungssystem sollten bei uns gründlich studiert werden. Die monatliche Belastung der Flachbauwohnung ist im allgemeinen niedriger als die einer Mietwohnung im Mehrfamilienhaus!

Bei einer Übertragung dieser Verfahren auf einen verdichteten Flachbau können die Kosten (Feuerschutzmaßnahmen, Aufschließung usw.) nur geringer werden.

34. A prefabricated room-sized unit in the course of erection (Calder Homes, Basildon, Architects Harding & Horseman). As manual work is superseded by industrial methods, the elements become larger, and part of the assembly work is anticipated at the factory.

35. Erection of a Finnish prefabricated house, architects K. and H. Siren.

34. Eine vorgefertigte Raumeinheit wird eingehoben (Calder Homes, Basildon, Architekten Harding & Horseman). Mit der Ablösung der handwerklichen durch die industrielle Bauweise werden die Bauelemente größer, die Montage erfolgt zum Teil schon in der Fabrik.

35. Montage eines finnischen Fertighauses, Architekten K. und H. Siren.

a / b	c f	c %	d f	d %	g	h / i	2 c f	2 c %	3 d f	3 d %	e (2+3)
3	39	6,7	–	–	A	🏃	39	17,1	–	–	10
15	174	29,7	–	–	A	🏃🏃	87	38,1	–	–	24
	1 2	2 0	–	–	B	🏃 ⋯ 🏃	6	2,6	–	–	
28	81	13,8	162	24,0	A	🏃🏃🏃	27	11,9	54	33,4	30
	81	13,8	27	4,0	B	🏃🏃 ⋯ 🏃	27	11,9	9	5,6	
24	–	–	156	23,2	A	🏃🏃🏃🏃	–	–	39	24,1	19
	96	16,6	48	7,2	B	🏃🏃🏃 ⋯ 🏃	24	10,5	12	7,4	
14	–	–	60	8,8	A	🏃🏃🏃🏃🏃	–	–	12	7,4	9
	60	10,2	30	4,4	B	🏃🏃🏃🏃 ⋯ 🏃	12	5,3	6	3,7	
	–	–	30	4,4	C	🏃🏃🏃 ⋯ 🏃🏃	–	–	6	3,7	
7	–	–	36	5,3	B	🏃🏃🏃🏃🏃 ⋯ 🏃	–	–	6	3,7	4
	18	3,1	36	5,3	C	🏃🏃🏃🏃 ⋯ 🏃🏃	3	1,3	6	3,7	
3	–	–	21	3,1	B	🏃🏃🏃🏃🏃🏃 ⋯ 🏃	–	–	3	1,8	2
	–	–	21	3,1	C	🏃🏃🏃🏃🏃 ⋯ 🏃🏃	–	–	3	1,8	
6	24	4,1	48	7,2	C	🏃🏃🏃🏃🏃🏃 ⋯ 🏃🏃	3	1,3	6	3,7	2
100	585	100	675	100			228	100	162	100	100

36. H. P. Bahrdt and J. Lehmbrock have investigated the important question of the possible compositions and sizes of households within a housing unit of approx. 300 dwellings with 12,00 residents, determining the percentage distribution of these households over multi-storey and low-rise housing. The aim of this investigation was to determine the minimum number of types of households, with their variants, and to ascertain the number of dwellings to be built in low-rise and multi-storey housing, respectively. The result, indicating 15 possible different household compositions, differs but little from the conclusions of Scharoun who found 16 possibilities. The calculated percentage shares differ, also in respect of the occupations of the residents.

A 1 Household, B 1 Household and 1 independent person, C 1 Household and 2 independent persons, a Number of persons, b Per cent of all persons, c In multi-story housing, d In low-rise housing, e Per cent of all dwellings, f Number, g Type, h Households, i Persons.

36. H. P. Bahrdt und J. Lehmbrock untersuchten die wichtige Frage der möglichen Familienzusammensetzungen und -größen in einem Wohnbereich von etwa 300 Wohnungen mit 1200 Personen und stellten die prozentuale Verteilung dieser Familien auf Wohnungen im Hoch- und Flachbau fest. Das Ziel der Untersuchung war es, die Mindestzahl von Familientypen und dazugehörigen Varianten zu ermitteln und weiter, eine Aussage darüber zu ermöglichen, wieviel Wohnungen im Flachbau und wieviel im Hochbau zu errichten sind. Das Ergebnis, 15 mögliche unterschiedliche Familienzusammensetzungen, unterscheidet sich nur geringfügig von dem der Untersuchungen Scharouns, der 16 Gruppierungen feststellte. Die errechneten Anteile sind unterschiedlich und differieren auch hinsichtlich der Berufszugehörigkeit der Bewohner.

A 1 Haushalt, B 1 Haushalt und 1 selbständige Person, C 1 Haushalt und 2 selbständige Personen, a Anzahl der Personen, b Prozent aller Personen, c im Hochbau, d im Flachbau, e Prozent aller Wohnungen, f Anzahl, g Form, h Haushalte, i Personen.

Mobility of the Town

It is strange to find that there has been an increase in urban immobility just at a time when an adaptation to the rapid and continuous changes in industrial society would be required, so that the discrepancy between the 'petrified' city and technical progress becomes apparent on a catastrophic scale. There is a danger that our cities, already greatly impaired in their functional viability, will eventually cease to function altogether.

Apart from other causes such as the exaggerated ground ownership conceptions of Roman Law and the immense investments in traffic and supply installations, the immobility of a modern town is mainly attributable to the conventional type of solid four-to-five-storey tenement houses. Where the timber floors of such buildings dating back to the boom time of industrial revolution begin to fail, they are replaced by solid floors although the standard of the dwellings falls short of present-day hygienic as well as technical requirements. Such immobility is reinforced by multi-storey housing. Investments are greater so that the developer must reckon with a longer useful life, and therefore a longer depreciation period.

In general, residential buildings are reckoned to have a useful life of 100 years—a period which is, however, often exceeded in practice. This is in contrast to the rapid depreciation of industrial and office buildings. The latter are reckoned to last between 30 and 50 years, factories between 10 and 20 years. The mobile and flexible workplaces are therefore in contrast to a rather "static" approach to housing construction where the useful life is reckoned to be between two and five times as long. As a result, there are wastefully long distances between home and workplace—well illustrated by the examples of the Ruhr District or the Siemens Works in Berlin. Areas with central functions call for multi-level structures or platforms if they are to cope with the more concentrated activities. Such structures, however, tend to increase the immobility of these districts still further. "Mobile structures are not obtainable as long as we insist on wholly outdated conceptions of real estate law which impedes the adaptation of the urban structures to changing requirements in every conceivable way" (G. Rabeler).

But low-rise housing, making use of light-weight materials and associated with prefabrication, offers a possibility of achieving a better adaptation of housing construction to the internal and external development of the city. In particular, prefabricated houses of the bungalow type ensure great flexibility in urban development. If the basement can be omitted, investment costs are low; the house can be dismantled or moved without difficulties. One should get used to the idea of regarding the house as designed for just *one* generation, giving the next generation the chance of reshaping their environment in accordance with their own wishes and ideas and, in particular, in keeping with their latest technical standards. In the Middle Ages, whole districts fell victim to conflagrations whilst, in Japan, the light-weight house consisting of timber and paper was deliberately destroyed after the death of the owner.

So far, the production of prefabricated light-weight houses has been almost wholly confined to detached houses. Recent investigations have shown, however, that prefabrication can be equally well applied to the sphere of high-density low-rise housing, and that it is possible to obtain flexibility also in this way. Bearing walls or cross-walls, e. g. in single-storey or two-storey terrace houses, do not impede such a renewal, especially as these house types are increasingly built by semi-prefabrication methods inasmuch as certain components such as front walls, floors and roofs are prefabricated light-weight units. These can be replaced without difficulty since the geometrically simple space between the bearing walls leaves sufficient margin to permit, on renewal, compliance with the most variegated wishes in regard to layout.

Mobilität der Stadt

Vergleichen wir unsere gegenwärtigen Städte mit denen vergangener Zeiten, etwa des Mittelalters, so erweisen sich die Ergebnisse der heute üblichen Städteplanung als weit weniger wandlungsfähig.

Merkwürdig ist die Tatsache, daß der immobile Charakter der Stadt gerade in einer Zeit, in der eine Anpassung an die rasche und ständige Veränderung der industriellen Gesellschaft erforderlich wäre, eine Verstärkung erfahren hat, wodurch sich die Diskrepanz zwischen zurückgebliebener Stadt und den Veränderungen der Technik in katastrophaler Weise bemerkbar macht. Es besteht die Gefahr, daß unsere Städte ganz aufhören zu funktionieren, nachdem sie heute bereits eine äußerst mangelhafte Funktionsfähigkeit aufweisen.

Neben anderen Ursachen, wie dem überspitzten Eigentumsbegriff des römischen Rechts am Boden, den riesigen Investierungen in Verkehrs- und Versorgungsanlagen, ist die Immobilität der heutigen Stadt ganz besonders durch den üblichen vier- bis fünfgeschossigen massiven Wohnungsbau entstanden. Nachdem die Balkenlage von Bauten der Gründerjahre Mängel zeigt, wird sie durch Massivdecken ersetzt, obgleich ihre Wohnungen weder unseren hygienischen noch unseren technischen Anforderungen entsprechen. Wohnhochhäuser verstärken diese Immobilität: Die Investierungen sind höher, und damit wird vom Bauherrn eine längere Lebensdauer beziehungsweise Amortisation einkalkuliert.

Im allgemeinen rechnet man bei Wohnbauten heute noch mit einer Lebensdauer von hundert Jahren, eine Grenze, die allerdings oft überschritten wird. Im Gegensatz dazu steht die rasche Abwertung von Industrie- und Bürobauten: Bei Bürohäusern rechnet man mit dreißig bis fünfzig Jahren, bei Fabriken mit zehn bis zwanzig Jahren. Den beweglichen und anpassungsfähigen Arbeitsstätten steht also ein »statischer« Wohnungsbau mit einer zwei- bis fünffachen Lebensdauer gegenüber. Die Folge: unproduktive weite Wege zwischen Wohnung und Arbeitsplatz, wofür das Ruhrgebiet oder die Siemenswerke in Berlin deutliche Beispiele abgeben. Schichten oder Gemeinschaftsträger sind für Flächen mit zentralen Funktionen erforderlich, um das verdichtete Leben bewältigen zu können. Ihre Anwendung verstärkt jedoch die Immobilität dieser Gebiete. »Mobile Strukturen sind so lange nicht erreichbar, als wir auf einem völlig antiquierten Bodenrecht beharren, das die Anpassung des Stadtgefüges an wechselnde Erfordernisse in jeder nur denkbaren Weise erschwert« (G. Rabeler).

Flachbau in Leichtbauweise, kombiniert mit Vorfabrikation, ist jedoch eine Möglichkeit, den

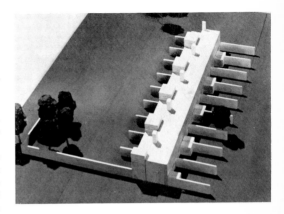

39, 40. The growing house of architects van den Broek and Bakema. The core is a two-storey terrace house which can be extended by single-storey out-buildings.

39, 40. Das wachsende Haus der Architekten van den Broek und Bakema. Der Kern ist ein zweigeschossiges Reihenhaus, das durch eingeschossige Anbauten erweitert werden kann.

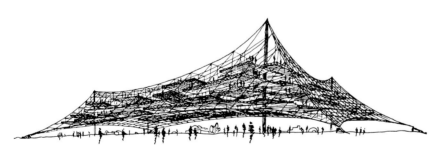

Wohnungsbau den inneren und äußeren Bewegungen der Stadt besser anzugleichen. Vor allem eingeschossige, vorfabrizierte Häuser erlauben eine städtebauliche Flexibilität. Verzichtet man auf den Keller, dann sind die Investitionen gering; das Haus kann ohne Schwierigkeiten abgebrochen oder verlagert werden. Man sollte sich auch daran gewöhnen, das Haus als Hülle für *eine* Generation zu betrachten und der nächsten die Chance geben, ihre Umwelt wieder nach eigenen Wünschen und Vorstellungen, vor allem aber auch nach dem neuesten technischen Standard zu gestalten. Im Mittelalter fielen in jeder Generation ganze Quartiere Bränden zum Opfer, während in Japan das leichte, aus Holz und Papier bestehende Haus nach dem Tode des Besitzers bewußt vernichtet wird.

Bislang hat sich die Produktion vorgefertigter Leichtbauten fast nur auf freistehende Wohnhäuser beschränkt. Neue Arbeiten zeigen jedoch, daß eine Vorfabrikation im Bereich des verdichteten Wohnungsbaus in gleicher Weise möglich ist und auch auf diese Weise Flexibilität erreicht werden kann. Brandmauern oder tragende Querwände, bei ein- oder zweigeschossigen Reihenhäusern etwa, bilden kein Hindernis für eine Erneuerung, zumal sich bei diesen Typen eine Tendenz zum Halbmontagebau abzeichnet. Das heißt, bestimmte Teile wie Frontwände, Decke und Dach sind leichte vorgefertigte Elemente. Sie können ohne Schwierigkeit ersetzt werden, da der einfache geometrische Raum zwischen den tragenden Mauern genügend Variationsmöglichkeiten zuläßt, um bei der Erneuerung verschiedensten Wünschen der Grundrißgestaltung gerecht zu werden.

37, 38. Basic framework system according to Frei Otto. Into a given framework structure, equipped with all the necessary installations, individual buildings of leightweight units are inserted. The dwellings are let by square metres of prepared urban area.

37, 38. Grundraster nach Frei Otto. In die vorgegebene Rahmenkonstruktion mit allen Installationen werden individuelle Bauten aus Leichtbauelementen eingefügt. Die Vermietung erfolgt nach Quadratmetern vorbereiteter urbaner Fläche.

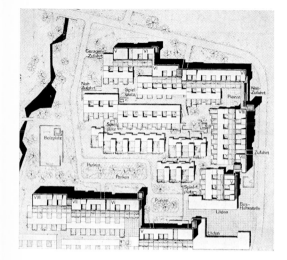

Combination With Other Types of Housing

High-density low-rise housing is no more expensive than multi-storey housing and is undoubtedly healthier for the family. But it would be equally wrong and misconceived if cities were made to consist exclusively of low-rise houses of one, two or three storeys. Objections against such a course include sociological as well as town planning and aesthetic considerations. English cities of the nineteenth century which are examples of highly concentrated low-rise housing are frightening in their monotony, and even the designers of the "New Towns" have not always succeeded in avoiding monotony by such measures as intimate precincts, preservation of old trees, variety of housing types, etc. If the Greater London Council decided to erect multi-storey blocks in their slum clearance areas, this is by no means meant to be a break, in principle, with English housing tradition, nor is it prompted by the desire to obtain more intensive land use. The reasons are of a sociological kind, associated with the desire for a three-dimensional, plastic revival of the earlier mono-cultures of Limehouse, the East End, and other districts with monotonous and featureless streets of two-storey terrace houses.

Utilitarian mentality is fond of tidy separation, alleged to provide simpler "clearer" solutions. In reality, concatenation and uniformity are by no means synonymous with tidiness. It is only by careful differentiation that better orientation can be achieved and each space unit can be distinguished by its own characteristic features.

The aim should be a mixture, as variegated as possible, of different occupations, income groups, education levels and family compositions so that even smaller units reflect, more or less, a sociological cross-section of the town as a whole. Town Planning units capable of comprising all occupational groups and all family compositions must have some 80 to 120 dwellings, just big enough to support such community facilities as, e.g., a playground for young children up to 10 years. There will however be some inevitable difference between residential areas in the town centre, where the intellectual professions account for a higher share and where the population composition is more liable to fluctuate, and in the outskirts where families with children still belonging to a common household account for a higher percentage. Similarly, a certain differentiation will also result from differences in the size and function of the city.

In this way, everybody should have the opportunity of finding a suitable dwelling within a given housing unit. Under present conditions, there are not many people who live exactly as they would like to live; much is left to chance, and to the developers' own notions of economic housing. Such opportunism is entirely out of keeping with the importance of a high dwelling standard which symbolizes our very standard of living; nor is it in keeping with the notion, postulated by CIAM, of the "Habitat" which is meant to signify an environmental atmosphere providing the most favourable conditions for the healthy development of individuals and families. The blending of multi-storey, medium-rise and low-rise housing in small, town planning units makes for much livelier groupings than the principle of segregation. If low-rise housing is diversified by single-storey and two-storey types; if three-storey low-rise buildings are adopted; if multi-storey and low-rise housing are combined; if even within the different categories, the frontage widths are varied; and if the different types are not uniformly concatenated but deliberately arranged to form small neighbourhood units, then the possibilities of variation are so great that it is not difficult to create units with "unmistakably" individual features. Bakema and van den Broek have carried out very thorough and excellent research on the prototype of such groups, but they tend to repeat them within the development plan in a somewhat ornamental and rectangular fashion with too few variations. Examples for good intermingling are the Mixsiepen-Remscheid housing development designed by Köngeter-Arns (page 160) and the Alton Estate, Roehampton, London, created by the Greater London Council (page 96).

In contrast to the dictatorship of uniform cornice height, housing units with a lively alternation of High and Low provide a *symbol of living democracy*.

41, 42. Residential area at Buxtehude, Germany; architect: F. Spengelin. One- and two-storey low-rise housing is surrounded in angular fashion by higher blocks of maisonettes. The possibilities of increasing the housing density by making use of natural slopes or artificial platforms are well utilized. With its blending of different housing types and the general arrangement of the housing unit, this project must be regarded as very successful.

41, 42. Wohngebiet in Buxtehude, Deutschland, Architekt F. Spengelin. Ein- und zweigeschossiger Flachbau wird von höheren Maisonetteblocks winkelförmig umschlossen. Die Möglichkeiten einer Verdichtung durch Bebauung von Hängen und künstlichen Erhöhungen sind gut genutzt. Dieser Vorschlag ist in der Mischung der Bebauungsweisen und auch in der Gliederung der Wohneinheit ein gutes Beispiel.

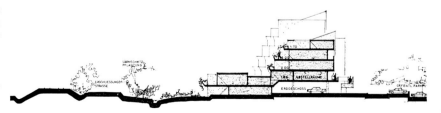

Mischung mit anderen Bebauungsarten

Der urbane Flachbau ist nicht teurer als Hochbau, und ohne Zweifel ist er gesünder für die Familie. Es wäre jedoch einseitig und ein erneutes Mißverständnis, wenn man Städte *nur* im ein- bis zwei- oder dreigeschossigen verdichteten Flachbau errichten würde. – Dagegen sprechen sowohl soziologische Erwägungen als auch räumlich-formale. Englische Städte des 19. Jahrhunderts, die Beispiele eines sehr dichten Flachbaus sind, erschrecken durch ihre Langeweile, und selbst bei den Newtowns ist es nicht immer gelungen, durch intime Raumbildungen, Schonung alter Bäume, Wechsel der Typen usw. eine gewisse Eintönigkeit zu vermeiden. Wenn das »Greater London Council« etwa sich entschlossen hat, in den Sanierungsgebieten Wohnhochhäuser zu errichten, so ist damit keineswegs ein grundsätzlicher Bruch mit der englischen Wohntradition beabsichtigt oder eine höhere Ausnutzung des Grundes. Es sind soziologische Gesichtspunkte und gleichzeitig die einer räumlich-plastischen Belebung der früheren Monokulturen von Lime-House, East End und anderer Viertel mit stumpfsinniger, ungestalter zweigeschossiger Reihenhausbebauung.

Utilitaristisches Denken liebt es zu sortieren, angeblich ist es einfacher, »klarer«. In Wirklichkeit ist die Reihung, die Gleichförmigkeit gar nicht übersichtlicher. Erst das sorgfältige Differenzieren führt zu einer besseren Übersicht und läßt jeden Raum in seiner Eigenart erkennbar werden. Eine möglichst vielfältige Mischung von Berufen, Einkommensklassen, Bildungsschichten und Familienzusammensetzungen sollte angestrebt werden und in kleineren Bereichen etwa dem soziologischen Querschnitt einer ganzen Stadt entsprechen. Städtebauliche Einheiten, in denen alle Berufsgruppen und Familienzusammensetzungen möglich sind, umfassen 80–120 Wohnungen, das heißt eine Größe, der etwa ein »Spielplatz« für die Kinder bis zu zehn Jahren zugeordnet werden sollte. Ein gewisser Unterschied wird sich allerdings ergeben zwischen Wohnbereichen im Stadtkern, mit einem höheren Anteil an intellektuellen Berufen und stärker fluktuierenden Bevölkerungsschichten, und den zum Stadtrand gelegenen Vierteln mit einem größeren Anteil an Familien mit Kindern, die noch zum gemeinsamen Haushalt gehören. Ebenso wird eine gewisse Differenzierung nach Größe und Aufgabe der Städte erfolgen.

Auf diese Weise ist innerhalb jeder Wohngruppe jedem die Chance gegeben, die geeignete Wohnung zu wählen. Heute wohnt kaum jemand so, wie er wohnen möchte, sondern »er wird irgendwie gewohnt«, nach Zufälligkeiten und den Vorstellungen, die Wohnungsbaugesellschaften von Wirtschaftlichkeit haben. Dieses »irgendwie« steht in einem diametralen Gegensatz zu der Bedeutung des Wohnens, das unsere Existenz schlechthin ist, oder zu dem von den CIAM postulierten »Habitat«, das soviel heißt wie »die Atmosphäre eines Raumes, der die günstigsten Bedingungen für das Wachsen und Gedeihen des einzelnen und der Familie enthält«.

Die Mischung von Hoch-, Mittel- und Flachbau in kleinen städtebaulichen Einheiten ermöglicht weit lebendigere Gruppierungen als das Prinzip der Sortierung. Wenn der Flachbau in ein- und zweigeschossigen Typen differenziert wird, dreigeschossige Flachbauten und kombinierte Hoch-Flachbauten gewählt werden, wenn die Typen selbst verschiedene Frontbreiten besitzen und nicht gleichmäßig aufgereiht sind, sondern mit dem Bestreben, kleine nachbarschaftliche Räume zu bilden, dann stehen so viele Elemente, um eine Gruppe zu variieren, zur Verfügung, daß es nicht allzu großer Bemühungen bedarf, um »unverwechselbare Einheiten« zu schaffen. Bakema und van den Broek haben sehr eingehende und ausgezeichnete Studien über den Prototyp von Gruppen geschaffen, aber sie wiederholen sie in einem Bebauungsplan ornamental und rechtwinklig mit zu geringen Variationen. Gute Durchmischung zeigen zum Beispiel die Siedlungen Mixsiepen-Remscheid von Köngeter-Arns (Seite 160) und Alton-Estate, Roehampton-London vom GLC (Seite 96).

Wohnbereiche mit gruppenhafter Gebundenheit im Nebeneinander von Hoch und Niedrig ergeben abweichend von Traufengleiche fordernder Diktatur ein *Sinnbild lebendiger Demokratie.*

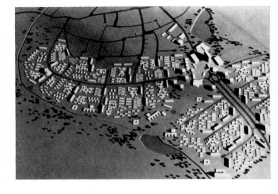

43. Norf expanded town, architects Hubert Hoffmann in association with Block and Schulze zur Wische, Timmel. Lively grouping of single-storey and two-storey low-rise houses. The otherwise two-storey centre is emphasized by a few multi-storey blocks.

43. Erweiterung Norf, Architekten Hubert Hoffmann mit Block und Schulze zur Wische, Timmel. Lebendige Gruppierung von ein- und zweigeschossigem Flachbau. Wenige Hochhäuser betonen das zweigeschossige Zentrum.

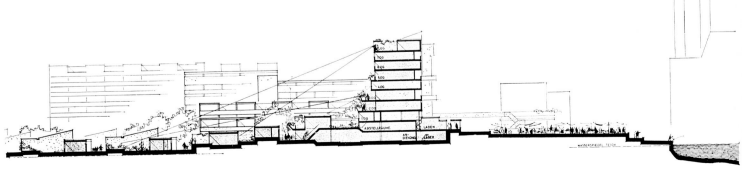

"Corner Green" terrace houses, Blackheath, London (1959)
Architect: Eric Lyons

Einfamilienreihenhäuser »Corner Green« in Blackheath bei London (1959)
Architekt: Eric Lyons

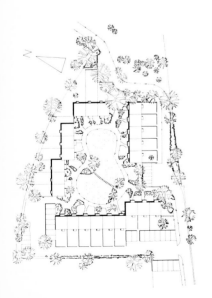

A number of excellent housing schemes designed by Eric Lyons and built by Townsend prove that a long and close association of architect and contractor is apt to raise the quality standard if both partners are imbued by the same ideals. From a town-planning point of view, the houses designed by this architect are exemplary for congenial dwellings, and for economic yet spacious environmental design, always supported by careful landscaping. "Corner Green" comprises 23 two-storey terrace houses with 21 garages. They are placed around a common which is reserved for pedestrians. To each house belongs a small, secluded garden. Construction: 1 ft. visible brickwork; upper floor cladding of horizontal timber boards painted white; timber beam roof with three layers of "Stramit" boards slightly inclined. The all-glass ground floor frontages consist of shop-assembled double-pane window units. Gross floor area 800 sq. ft. (74 sq. metres); floor space index 0.3.

Eine Anzahl ausgezeichneter Siedlungen, gemeinschaftlich errichtet von Lyons als Architekt und Townsend als Unternehmer, erweisen, daß die enge und langjährige Zusammenarbeit von Ausführendem und Planendem zu einer Steigerung der Qualität führen kann, wenn beide ein geistiges Ziel verfolgen. Städtebaulich sind die Wohnungen Musterbeispiele für intimes Wohnen, für ökonomische und doch weiträumige Gestaltung der engsten Nachbarschaft, die stets durch sorgfältige Gartengestaltung unterstützt wird. »Corner Green« umfaßt 23 zweigeschossige Einfamilienreihenhäuser mit 21 Garagen. Sie umschließen einen gemeinsamen Anger, der nur Fußgängerverkehr aufnimmt. Zu jeder Wohnung gehört ein kleiner abgeschlossener Hausgarten. Konstruktion: 30 cm sichtbares Ziegelmauerwerk, im Obergeschoß waagrechte, weißgestrichene Holzverschalung und ein Holzbalkendach mit drei Lagen »Stramit«-Platten in leichtem Gefälle. Die vollverglasten Erdgeschoßfenster bestehen aus vorfabrizierten, doppelt verglasten Einheiten. Bruttogeschoßfläche 74 qm, GFZ 0,3.

1. Eastern part of "Corner Green" housing scheme. The houses surround a carefully kept lawn.
2. Site plan, 1 in 2000. The space inside the estate is exclusively reserved for pedestrians.
3. Garden side of a row of houses.
4. Ground floor plan and first floor plan, 1 in 200.
The ground floor of the two-storey houses contains kitchen and living rooms, the upper floor three bedrooms, bathroom and W.C. The ground floor is designed for maximum flexibility. The additional room can be used as an extension of the sitting room, as a separate study, or as a fourth bedroom.
5. The house entrance is emphasized by the projecting porch.
6. Private garden outside the sitting room.

1. Blick in den östlichen Teil der Siedlung. Die Zeilen gruppieren sich um eine gepflegte, liebevoll gestaltete Grünfläche.
2. Lageplan 1:2000. Der innere Bereich der Siedlung ist ausschließlich den Fußgängern vorbehalten.
3. Die Gartenfront einer Zeile.
4. Grundrisse Erd- und Obergeschoß 1:200.
Im Erdgeschoß der zweigeschossigen Häuser befinden sich Küche und Wohnräume, im Obergeschoß drei Schlafräume mit Bad und WC. Das Erdgeschoß ist so geplant, daß ein Maximum an Flexibilität gegeben ist. Der zusätzliche Raum kann verwendet werden für die Erweiterung des Wohnraumes, als abgeschlossenes Studio oder als vierter Schlafraum.
5. Der vorgezogene Windfang betont den individuellen Eingang.
6. Blick in den kleinen Hausgarten vor dem Wohnraum.

Key to plans see page 174.
Legende zu den Grundrissen siehe Seite 174.

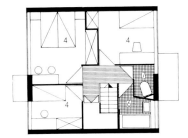

Housing scheme at West Ham, London (1964)
Architects: C Barr, O. Cox, M. Welbank, and others

Siedlung West Ham, London (1964)
Architekten: C. Barr, O. Cox, M. Welbank und andere

This housing scheme is a "demonstration project" of the Ministry of Housing and Local Government which was created in order to test the technical, planning and sociological effects of the "Parker Morris Standards." In the planning, the recommendations contained in "Homes for Today and Tomorrow" were taken into account. The planning was also preceded by an extensive social survey into local conditions. The design meets the expressed wishes for a private garden space, a communal landscaped area, and adequate parking facilities for motor vehicles. The 39 dwellings are composed of highly differentiated house types, ranging from single-storey to three-storey terrace houses, with dwelling units of different sizes and with the possibilities of sub-dividing the rooms. Structurally, the houses are of conventional type: brick walls, with timber cladding on the upper floor. Heating is by electric block storage heaters, using cheaper night-time current. Gross floor areas of the different types 1 000–1 200 sq.ft.; floor space index 0.6.

Die Wohnhausanlage Westham ist ein »Demonstrativbauvorhaben« des Ministry of Housing and Local Government, das errichtet wurde, um »Parker Morris Standards« in ihrer technischen städtebaulichen und soziologischen Auswirkung zu erproben. Bei der Planung wurden die Empfehlungen von »Homes for Today and Tomorrow« berücksichtigt. Voraus gingen außerdem eingehende Untersuchungen der örtlichen soziologischen Situation. Dem Wunsch nach einem kleineren individuellen Garten wurde ebenso entsprochen wie der Forderung nach einer gemeinsamen Freifläche und ausreichenden Abstellplätzen für Kraftfahrzeuge. Die neununddreißig Wohnungen verteilen sich auf sehr differenzierte Haustypen von ein- bis dreigeschossigen Reihenhäusern und unterschiedlicher Möglichkeit, die Räume zu unterteilen. Die Bauausführung erfolgte in traditioneller Konstruktion: Ziegelwände, die im Obergeschoß holzverschalt sind. Für die Beheizung wurden elektrische Nachtspeichergeräte gewählt. Bruttogeschoßfläche der einzelnen Typen: 91–112 qm, GFZ 0,6.

1. General view from the south. The houses have been kept well back from the main road which has been screened by a high brick wall.

1. Gesamtansicht der Siedlung von Süden. Interessant die konsequente Abkehr von der Hauptverkehrsstraße, gegen die die Siedlung durch eine Mauer abgeschlossen ist.

2, 3. The north and north-east sides are mainly enclosed. The contrast between the bright brick walls and the dark timber facing is effective.
4. Site plan, 1 in 1000.

2, 3. Nord- und Nordostseite sind weitgehend geschlossen. Wirkungsvoll ist der Kontrast der hellen Ziegelwände zur dunklen Holzverschalung.
4. Lageplan 1:1000.

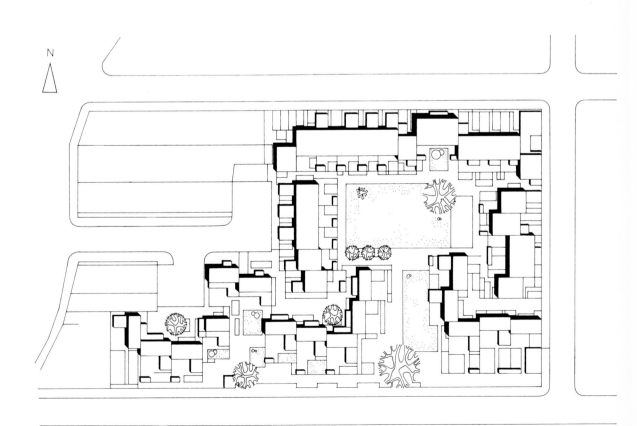

5. Plans of the different house types, 1 in 300. The plans are carefully considered and are economic inasmuch as the hall is used as dining space and the bedrooms have been kept small. The partition and cupboard units, made available by the housing manager, ensure a high degree of flexibility.

5. Grundrisse verschiedener Haustypen 1:300. Die Grundrisse sind sorgfältig durchdacht und ökonomisch durch die Ausnutzung der Diele als Eßraum und durch sparsame Bemessung der Schlafräume. Durch Wand- und Schrankelemente, die die Hausverwaltung zur Verfügung stellt, ist in hohem Maße Flexibilität gegeben.

6. To each house belongs a small garden where the children are able to play undisturbed, and safe from road traffic.

7, 8. The layout of the estate is such that any monotony has been avoided, and the attractively aligned foothpaths provide a variety of surprising vistas.

9. Dining space adjacent to the kitchen of a five or six-room flat.

6. Zu jedem Haus gehört ein kleiner Garten, in dem die Kinder ungestört und ungefährdet vom Straßenverkehr spielen können.

7, 8. Die Anordnung der Häuser vermeidet jede Eintönigkeit und läßt reizvoll gewundene Fußwege mit immer neuen überraschenden Ausblicken entstehen.

9. Eßplatz mit anschließender Küche in einer Fünf- bis Sechszimmerwohnung.

"Klein Driene" housing scheme, Hengelo, Netherlands (1957–1959)
Architects: J. H. van den Broek and J. B. Bakema, with Stokla

Siedlung »Klein Driene« in Hengelo, Niederlande (1957–1959)
Architekten: J. H. van den Broek und J. B. Bakema mit Stokla

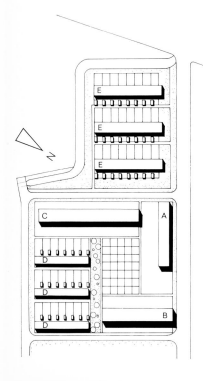

In this housing scheme, of 662 dwellings, the attempt was made to create an architectural and town-planning unit by using six "repeatable groups of houses" with a total of five house types for families of different size and occupations. Each group comprises one house of three and four storeys (B+C) for small families (4 to 5 beds), and three types of two-storey terrace houses (A, D, E) for larger families (5 to 9 beds). Each group includes a central playground for children, away from vehicular traffic. The terrace houses are approached by spur roads. In keeping with Dutch tradition, the plans are very economic without, however, impairing utility. The ratio of gross floor area and number of beds is good. Construction: Raw brick walls with solid floor slabs; timber clad entrance and eaves. Type A: gross floor area 110 sq. metres (1180 sq. ft.); floor space index 0.8 (with 160 sq. metres, i. e. 1720 sq. ft.). Type D: gross floor area 76 sq. metres (810 sq. ft.); floor space index 0.5 (with 160 sq. metres). Type E: gross floor area 100 sq. metres (1080 sq. ft.); floor space index 0.7 (with 160 sq. metres).

Bei dieser Siedlung mit 662 Wohnungen ist der Versuch unternommen, eine bauliche und städtebauliche Einheit zu erreichen durch sechs »wiederholbare Wohnhausgruppen« mit insgesamt fünf Typen für verschiedene Familiengrößen und Berufe. Jede Gruppe umfaßt je ein drei- und viergeschossiges Wohnhaus (B und C) für kleine Familien (4–5 Betten) und drei Typen zweigeschossige Einfamilienreihenhäuser (A, D, E) für größere Familien (5–9 Betten). Die Hausgruppe umschließt einen vom Fahrverkehr nicht berührten Kinderspielplatz. Die Einfamilienhäuser werden durch Wohnwege aufgeschlossen. Die Grundrisse sind in Fortführung einer holländischen Tradition sehr ökonomisch, ohne die Erfüllung der Funktion zu beeinträchtigen. Das Verhältnis zwischen Bruttogeschoßfläche und Anzahl der Betten ist günstig. Konstruktion: Unverputzter Klinkerbau mit Massivdecken. Eingang und Dachgesims holzverschalt. Typ A: Bruttogeschoßfläche 110 qm, GFZ 0,8; Typ D: Bruttogeschoßfläche 76 qm, GFZ 0,5; Typ E: Bruttogeschoßfläche 100 qm, GFZ 0,7 (bei jeweils 160 qm Netto-Bauland).

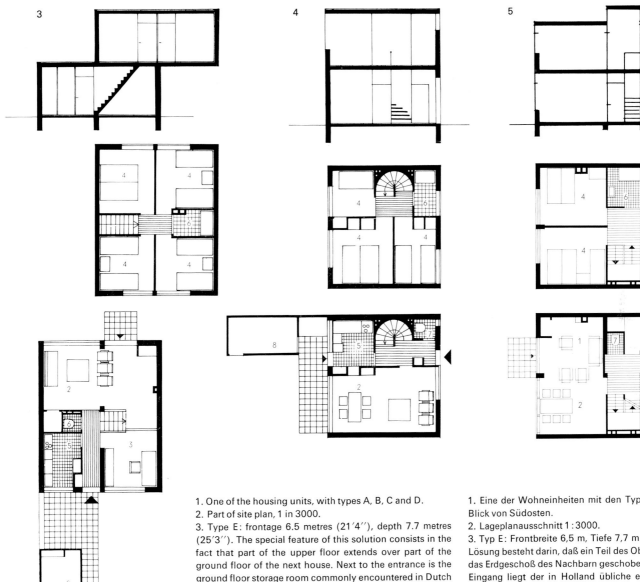

1. One of the housing units, with types A, B, C and D.

2. Part of site plan, 1 in 3000.

3. Type E: frontage 6.5 metres (21'4''), depth 7.7 metres (25'3''). The special feature of this solution consists in the fact that part of the upper floor extends over part of the ground floor of the next house. Next to the entrance is the ground floor storage room commonly encountered in Dutch housing. Kitchen, W. C. and sitting room are accessible from a hall. The rear part of the sitting room can be used as a separate study or as a spare bedroom (in which case the house has accommodation for ten beds). The upper floor contains four bedrooms and a bathroom. There is conspicuously little space for cupboards.

4. Type D: frontage 6.3 metres (20'8''), depth 6 metres (19'8''). The conventional two-bay type of house is skilfully modified by the use of a space-saving spiral stair. A small hall with stairs, W. C. and kitchen are placed in the narrower one of these two bays whilst the broader bay is taken up by an open-plan sitting room, with the dining area facing the garden.

5. Type A: frontage 6.5 metres (21'4''), depth 8.5 metres (27'11''). From the porch, one enters a central hall, giving access to all the rooms and the stairs. Opposite the kitchen is a spacious shed, directly accessible from the entrance. On the upper floor are four bedrooms and the bathroom. The shed outside the kitchen ensures privacy.

1. Eine der Wohneinheiten mit den Typen A, B, C und D. Blick von Südosten.

2. Lageplanausschnitt 1:3000.

3. Typ E: Frontbreite 6,5 m, Tiefe 7,7 m. Der »Trick« dieser Lösung besteht darin, daß ein Teil des Obergeschosses über das Erdgeschoß des Nachbarn geschoben wird. Neben dem Eingang liegt der in Holland übliche ebenerdige Abstellraum. Ein Flur erschließt Küche, WC und Wohnraum. Der rückwärtige Teil des Wohnraumes kann als Arbeits- oder Schlafraum verwendet werden; das Haus wird so zum Zehn-Betten-Typ. Das Obergeschoß enthält vier Schlafräume und ein Bad. Es fällt auf, daß für Schränke kaum Platz vorhanden ist.

4. Typ D: Frontbreite 6,3 m, Tiefe 6 m. Der traditionelle zweischiffige Haustyp ist durch die raumsparende Wendeltreppe geschickt abgewandelt. Ein kleiner Flur mit Treppe, WC und Küche liegen im schmaleren Schiff; der durchgehende Wohnraum mit dem Eßplatz bildet das breitere Schiff. Schlafräume und Bad befinden sich im Obergeschoß.

5. Typ A: Frontbreite 6,5 m, Tiefe 8,5 m. Vom Windfang gelangt man in die Diele, von der alle Räume und die Treppe zugänglich sind. Der Küche gegenüber ist ein geräumiger Abstell- und Vorratsraum vorgesehen, mit unmittelbarem Zutritt vom Eingang. Das Obergeschoß enthält vier Schlafräume und ein Bad. Der Abstellraum vor der Küche schützt gegen Einblick.

6. Street frontage of a row of type A houses.
7. Entrance side of two rows of type D houses.
8, 9. Entrance of type A (at the top) and type D house.

6. Eine Zeile des Typs A. Ansicht der Straßenfront.
7. Zwei Zeilen des Typs D, Eingangsseite.
8, 9. Eingang des Typs A (oben) und des Typs D.

Terrace houses at Hatertseveld, Nijmegen, Netherlands (1960)
Architect: E. F. Groosman, with P. C. Bos

Einfamilienreihenhäuser in Hatertseveld-Nimwegen, Niederlande (1960)
Architekt: E. F. Groosman, Mitarbeiter: P. C. Bos

The architects were asked to plan a housing unit with 700 dwellings. The development plan was designed in close collaboration with the planning authorities. The different housing requirements were catered for by resorting to different types of housing. It proved difficult to include, in the plan, the desired percentage of multi-storey blocks as the Dutch have a traditional preference for the one-family house. The attempt was made to separate vehicular traffic as far as possible from pedestrian traffic and to create, between the small private gardens, broad passages serving as playgrounds for older children. The alternation of single-storey, two-storey and four-storey houses has resulted in differentiated and lively groupings. But the rigidly rectangular pattern of the development plan has little regard to orientation. Construction: visible walls of common brick; structural floors of reinforced concrete with "Isoliet" floor coverings; facades mainly consisting of pre-assembled units, partly with timber cladding. Type A: Gross floor area 82 sq. metres (880 sq. ft.); floor space index 0.6. Type B: Gross floor area 98 sq. metres (106 sq. ft.); floor space index 0.7.

Die Architekten wurden mit der Planung einer Stadteinheit von 700 Wohnungen beauftragt. Der Bebauungsplan entstand in enger Zusammenarbeit mit dem Stadtplanungsamt. Den verschiedenen Wohnbedürfnissen wird durch unterschiedliche Bebauungsweisen entsprochen. Dabei war es schwierig, einen gewissen Prozentsatz mehrgeschossiger Häuser mit einzuplanen, da in Holland das Einfamilienhaus traditionell bevorzugt wird. Es wurde versucht, den Fahrverkehr vom Fußgängerverkehr zu trennen und zwischen den kleinen Hausgärten breite Spielwege für die größeren Kinder zu schaffen. Durch den Wechsel von ein-, zwei- und viergeschossigen Bauten entstehen unterschiedliche und lebendige Gruppierungen. Trotz des strengen rechtwinkligen Bebauungsplanes wird die Orientierung wenig berücksichtigt. Konstruktion: Das sichtbare Mauerwerk wurde in der üblichen Ziegelbauweise ausgeführt, die Decken in Stahlbeton mit »Isoliet«-Fußböden, während die Fronten überwiegend in Montage-Bauweise, zum Teil mit Holzverkleidung ausgeführt sind. Typ A: Bruttogeschoßfläche 82 qm, GFZ 0,6. Typ B: Bruttogeschoßfläche 98 qm, GFZ 0,7.

1. On the spacious lawns between the rows of houses, the children are able to play undisturbed and without danger from motor traffic.

1. Auf breiten Grünstreifen zwischen den Zeilen können die Kinder ungestört und ungefährdet durch Autoverkehr spielen.

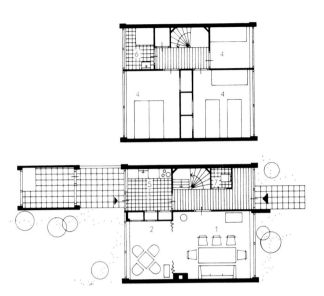

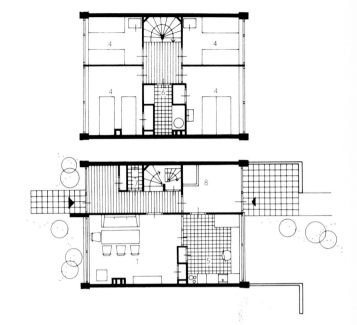

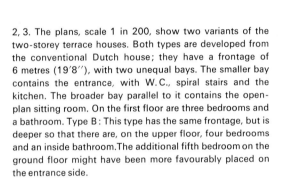

2, 3. The plans, scale 1 in 200, show two variants of the two-storey terrace houses. Both types are developed from the conventional Dutch house; they have a frontage of 6 metres (19′8″), with two unequal bays. The smaller bay contains the entrance, with W.C., spiral stairs and the kitchen. The broader bay parallel to it contains the open-plan sitting room. On the first floor are three bedrooms and a bathroom. Type B: This type has the same frontage, but is deeper so that there are, on the upper floor, four bedrooms and an inside bathroom. The additional fifth bedroom on the ground floor might have been more favourably placed on the entrance side.

2, 3. Die Grundrisse im Maßstab 1 : 200 zeigen zwei Varianten der zweigeschossigen Einfamilienreihenhäuser. Sie sind aus dem traditionellen holländischen Haus mit einer Gesamtfrontbreite von 6 m (zwei ungleiche »Schiffe«) entwickelt. Das schmälere Schiff enthält Eingang, WC, Wendeltreppe und die Küche. Parallel zu dieser Raumgruppe ist das breitere Schiff mit durchgehendem Wohnzimmer angeordnet. Das Obergeschoß enthält drei Schlafräume und ein Bad. Typ B: Bei gleicher Frontbreite ist dieser Typ jedoch tiefer und hat daher im Obergeschoß vier Schlafräume mit innenliegendem Bad. Der zusätzliche fünfte Schlafraum im Erdgeschoß wäre günstiger an der Eingangsseite gelegen.

4. Part of the estate, with two-storey terrace houses. The existing trees have been carefully preserved.

4. Blick auf einen Teil der Siedlung mit den zweigeschossigen Einfamilienreihenhäusern. Die vorhandenen Bäume wurden sorgfältig geschont.

Terrace houses at Kaarela, near Helsinki (1960)
Architects: Kaija and Heikki Siren

Einfamilienreihenhäuser in Kaarela bei Helsinki (1960)
Architekten: Kaija und Heikki Siren

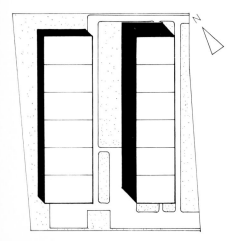

In its simplicity, and with its expert use of materials, this small housing scheme, consisting of two rows of six terrace houses, appears to be one of the most interesting attempts in Finnish housing to try out a new approach. The architects developed two types, viz. a single-storey house (type B) and a two-storey house (type A), juxtaposed to emphasize the gentle slope of the ground. None of the houses have basements. The two-storey type is designed as a hillside house with entrance from the higher ground. The layout is not only extremely economic; it also looks remarkably spacious. This intrinsic clarity is matched by the well balanced exterior design. Construction: with the exception of the pile-based concrete walls and the solid floor slabs above the ground floor of type A houses, all the structural elements are prefabricated timber units. Type A: gross floor area 124 sq. metres (1330 sq. ft.); floor space index 0.6. Type B: gross floor area 88 sq. metres (940 sq. ft.); floor space index 0.4.

Die kleine Siedlung von zwei Zeilen mit je sechs Einfamilienreihenhäusern erscheint in ihrer Schlichtheit und der sachgemäßen Materialverwendung als einer der interessantesten Versuche des finnischen Wohnbaues, neue Wege zu gehen. Die Architekten entwickelten zwei Typen, ein eingeschossiges (Typ B) und ein zweigeschossiges Haus, deren räumliche Folge die schwache Neigung des Hanges betont. Beide sind nicht unterkellert. Der zweigeschossige Typ A ist als Hanghaus mit dem Zugang auf der Bergseite entworfen. Die Grundrißdisposition ist nicht nur äußerst ökonomisch, sondern auch von einer beachtlichen räumlichen Wirkung. Dieser inneren Klarheit entspricht die Ausgewogenheit der äußeren Gestaltung. Konstruktion: Mit Ausnahme der pfahlgegründeten Brandmauern aus Beton und der Massivdecken über dem Erdgeschoß (bei Typ A) sind alle übrigen Elemente aus Holz vorgefertigt. Typ A: Bruttogeschoßfläche 124 qm, GFZ 0,6, Typ B: Bruttogeschoßfläche 88 qm, GFZ 0,4.

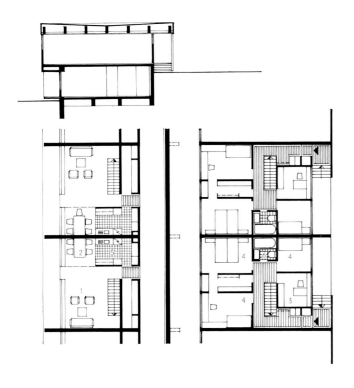

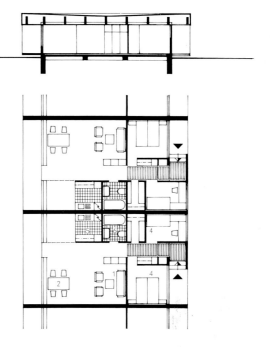

1. South-west side of the two-storey house, type A. Sitting room windows on the ground floor, bedroom windows on the upper floor.
2. Site plan, 1 in 1000.

1. Die zweigeschossige Südwestseite des Typs A. Im Erdgeschoß die Wohnraumfenster, im Obergeschoß die Fenster der Schlafräume.
2. Lageplan 1 : 1000.

3. Plans and sections, 1 in 300. Type A (left): As with type B, the hall is reached by a few canopied steps. In this case, however, the hall is on the upper floor which contains two bedrooms on the east side and two on the west side, with cupboard room and bathroom between them. A flight of stairs leads to the ground floor sitting room which, together with kitchen and dining area, forms a single unit. Behind the stairs is a storage room. Type B: Through the entrance, which is protected by a canopy, one enters a small hall giving access to all the rooms with the exception of the kitchen. The bedrooms face east; cupboard room, bathroom and kitchen are on the inside. The sitting room, with a dining area close to the kitchen, faces west.
4. Entrance side of type A house. The white concrete of the cross-walls and floor slabs forms an effective contrast to the dark timber units.

3. Grundrisse und Schnitte 1 : 300. Typ A (links): Wie bei Typ B gelangt man über einige überdachte Stufen in die Diele, in diesem Fall jedoch in das Obergeschoß. Es enthält je zwei nach Osten und Westen orientierte Schlafräume. Dazwischen liegen Schrankraum und Bad. Eine Treppe führt in den Wohnraum im Erdgeschoß, der mit Küche und Eßnische eine Einheit bildet. Hinter der Treppe befindet sich ein Vorrats- und Abstellraum. Typ B: Alle Räume, mit Ausnahme der Küche, werden über die kleine Diele erschlossen. Die beiden Schlafräume liegen nach Osten, Schrankraum, Bad und Küche im Hausinnern. Der Wohnraum, mit einer Eßnische vor der Küche, ist nach Westen orientiert.
4. Eingangsseite Typ A. Der weiße Beton der Brandmauern und Geschoßdecken steht in wirkungsvollem Kontrast zu den dunklen Holzteilen.

Lafayette Park housing scheme, Detroit (from 1955 onwards)
Architects: Ludwig Mies van der Rohe and Ludwig K. Hilberseimer

Siedlung Lafayette-Park, Detroit (ab 1955)
Architekten: Ludwig Mies van der Rohe und Ludwig K. Hilberseimer

This housing scheme covers a former slum area of 720 acres (290 ha) redeveloped by the architects. 225 acres (91 ha) are designated for multi-storey housing, 270 acres (109 ha) for single-storey and two-storey houses, 42 acres (17 ha) for shopping centres, community centre and public bath, and 140 acres (57 ha) for open spaces, including a school. Access to the area is from peripheral roads and internal loop roads forming lengthy-one-way streets with car parks and turning facilities. All the car parks are surrounded by lawn and trees. Traffic has thus been largely excluded, giving way to pedestrian precincts. The space effect of this generously designed housing scheme is governed by the contrast between several twenty-one-storey blocks of flats on the one hand, and the single-storey and two-storey terrace houses on the other hand. Construction: with both rows of terrace houses, the load bearing elements are steel columns. External and party walls are of brick. Gross floor area, type A: 140 sq. metres (1500 sq. ft.), type B: 124 sq. metres (1330 sq. ft.); floor space index 0.5.

Bei dieser Siedlung handelt es sich um ein ehemaliges Slumgebiet von 290 ha, das die Architekten neu erschließen und bebauen. Für Wohnhäuser wurden 91 ha, für ein- und zweigeschossigen Flachbau 109 ha, für Ladenzentren, Klubhaus mit Bad 17 ha und für Grünanlagen, einschließlich einer Schule, 57 ha vorgesehen. Die Erschließung der Siedlung erfolgt durch Randstraßen, von denen Stichstraßen in das Innere führen. Diese bilden langgestreckte Einbahnschleifen mit Parkplätzen und Wendemöglichkeit. Alle Abstellplätze liegen im Grünen und sind mit Blumen umpflanzt. Auf diese Weise werden die Gefahren des Verkehrs weitgehend von der Siedlung ferngehalten und reine Fußgängerbereiche geschaffen. Die räumliche Wirkung der großzügigen Anlage wird durch den Gegensatz von mehreren einundzwanziggeschossigen Hochhäusern und ein- und zweigeschossigen Einfamilienreihenhäusern bestimmt. Konstruktion: Die tragenden Elemente sind bei beiden Wohnhauszeilen Stahlstützen. Die Außen- und Zwischenwände bestehen aus Backstein. Bruttogeschoßfläche Typ A 140 qm, Typ B 124 qm, GFZ 0,5.

1. Part of the estate, with two-storey terrace houses and, in
the background, a row of single-storey houses.
2. Site plan, 1 in 5000.

1. Ein Teil der Siedlung mit zweigeschossigen Zeilen und
einer eingeschossigen Zeile im Hintergrund.
2. Lageplan 1 : 5000.

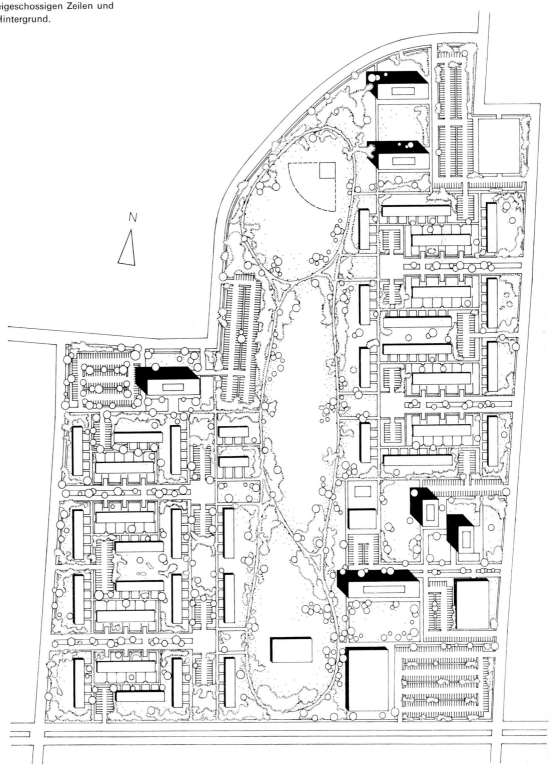

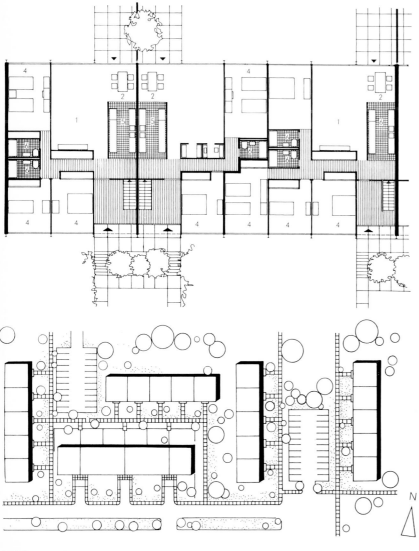

3. Plan, 1 in 300. The single-storey houses (type A) have three, four or five rooms and basement. A recessed entrance leads to a spacious hall giving access to very narrow corridors which are, however, enlarged at the doors leading to the rooms.

4. This section from the site plan, 1 in 2000, shows the juxtaposition of the rows of single-storey and two-storey houses.

3. Grundriß 1:300. Die eingeschossigen Wohnzeilen (Typ A) enthalten Drei-, Vier- und Fünfzimmerwohnungen und sind ganz unterkellert. Vom nischenartig zurückgesetzten Eingang gelangt man in eine weiträumige Diele, von der sehr schmale, vor den Zimmertüren jedoch verbreiterte Flure ausgehen.

4. Der Ausschnitt aus dem Lageplan, 1:2000, zeigt die Zuordnung der ein- und zweigeschossigen Hauszeilen zueinander.

5. Single-storey type A. To prevent the parked car from spoiling the view, the carports are placed on a lower level.
6. Owing to the alternation of low-height and multi-storey buildings, the housing scheme is lively and interesting.
7. The approximately 6 ft. high brickwall provides seclusion for a garden and an effective contrast to the aluminium-framed windows.

5. Der eingeschossige Typ A. Damit das vor der Haustür abgestellte Auto nicht den Ausblick behindert, sind die Autoabstellplätze vertieft angelegt.
6. Der Wechsel von Flach- und Hochbau ergibt eine höchst lebendige und abwechslungsreiche Gestaltung der Siedlung.
7. Die 2 m hohe Backsteinmauer schließt einen intimen Gartenbereich ein. Sie steht in wirkungsvollem Kontrast zu den Rauchglasfenstern in Aluminiumrahmen.

8. Plan, 1 in 200. Like type A, the two-storey terrace houses (type B) have three to five rooms. The ground floor hall is combined with a dining area. The stairs leading to the upper floor, cantaining all the bedrooms, have been placed in the sitting room which may well be a drawback. Kitchen, bathroom and W.C. form a central unit. All the houses are air-conditioned from a district heating plant.

8. Grundrisse 1:200. Die zweigeschossigen Wohnzeilen (Typ B) enthalten wie Typ A Drei- bis Fünfzimmerwohnungen. Im Erdgeschoß ist die Diele mit einem Eßplatz kombiniert. Daß der Aufgang zum Obergeschoß, in dem alle Schlafräume liegen, vom Wohnraum aus erfolgt, kann zu Störungen führen. Küche, Bad und WC bilden einen Installationskern im Hausinnern. Alle Wohnungen sind mit einer Klimaanlage versehen, die an eine Fernheizung angeschlossen ist.

6

7

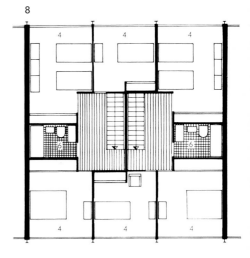

8

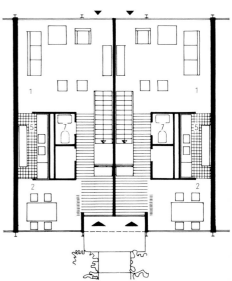

Paquetá Island housing scheme, Brazil (1954)
Architect: Francisco Bolonha

Siedlung auf der Insel Paquetá, Brasilien (1954)
Architekt: Francisco Bolonha

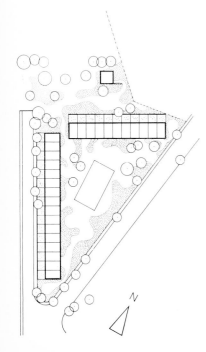

The erection of this group of 27 two-storey houses for workers in the low-income groups has been sponsored by the government of the Brazilian State of Guanabara. The occupiers were selected by the social welfare authorities. A representative of this office lives in the estate and is in charge of social welfare arrangements. Bolonha placed the houses in two rows at right angles to each other. The triangular space thus created contains a sports-ground and gardens. In both rows of houses, sitting rooms and patios face north and west, whilst the bedrooms and entrances face south and east. The lucid architectural design of this estate and the sub-tropic vegetation of the island are well attuned to each other. Construction: solid walls with steel stanchions at the covered walkway; timber lattice screens serving as wind protection; two-layer roof with asbestos cement roofing. Gross floor area: 78 sq. metres (830 sq. ft.); floor space index: 0.5.

Die Regierung der brasilianischen Provinz Guanabara ließ diese Gruppe von 27 zweigeschossigen Einfamilienhäusern für Arbeiter mit niedrigem Einkommen errichten. Die Bewohner wurden von der Sozialfürsorge ausgesucht. Ein Beauftragter dieses Amtes wohnt in der Siedlung und kümmert sich um die soziale Betreuung. Bolonha setzte die Häuser in zwei Zeilen rechtwinklig zueinander. In dem dadurch geschaffenen dreieckigen Raum fanden ein Sportplatz und Grünanlagen Platz. Beide Zeilen sind mit ihren Wohnräumen und Höfen nach Norden und Westen gerichtet, mit den Schlafräumen und der Eingangsseite nach Süden und Osten. Die klare Architektur dieser Siedlungsgruppe und die subtropische Vegetation der Insel ergänzen einander vorzüglich. Konstruktion: Massivbau mit Stahlstützen am Laubengang, transparente Windschirme aus Holz, doppelschaliges Dach mit Welleternitdeckung. Bruttogeschoßfläche 78 qm, GFZ 0,5.

56

1. View from the garden court on the entrance side of one of the rows of houses.
2. Site plan, 1 in 2000.
3. Plans and section, 1 in 200. The very simple but excellently conceived plan of the 5 metres (16′5″) wide two-storey terrace house contains, in the smaller bay of the ground floor, the dining area, kitchen and patio and, in the larger bay, the sitting room, stairs and entrance. On the upper floor are two bedrooms and a shower bath with W. C. The main purpose of the staggered two-way roof is to ensure a good ventilation of the house. Very attractive features are the covered walkway providing access at ground floor level, and the walled patio.
4. Outside the sitting room of each house is a small secluded patio.

1. Blick von der zentralen Grünfläche auf die Zugangsseite einer der Zeilen.
2. Lageplan 1 : 2000.
3. Grundrisse und Schnitt 1 : 200. Der sehr einfache, aber ausgezeichnet durchdachte Grundriß des 5 m breiten zweigeschossigen Reihenhauses enthält im »Seitenschiff« des Erdgeschosses Eßplatz, Küche und Gartenhof und im »Hauptschiff« Wohnraum, Treppe und Eingang. Im Obergeschoß befinden sich zwei Schlafräume und Duschraum mit WC. Das versetzte Dach dient in erster Linie einer guten Durchlüftung des Hauses. Sehr reizvoll ist die Erschließung durch einen ebenerdigen Laubengang und der ummauerte Gartenhof von rund 40 qm vor dem Wohnraum.
4. An den Wohnraum jedes Hauses schließt sich ein kleiner, abgeschlossener Hof.

Søholm housing estate, Klampenborg, Gentofte, Denmark (1950 and 1955)
Architect: Arne Jacobsen

Siedlung Søholm, Klampenborg, Gentofte, Dänemark (1950 und 1955)
Architekt: Arne Jacobsen

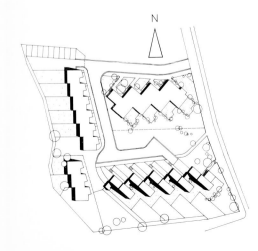

The Klampenborg area, situated in a particularly attractive seaside position north of Copenhagen, can be regarded as a kind of experimental workshop for the architect Arne Jacobsen. As early as 1933, Jacobsen built, in this area, the "Bellavista" apartments. This was followed, in 1950 and 1955, by the erection of chain type and terrace houses on the site of a manor house which had been demolished. In this way, Klampenborg not only provides excellent examples for urban housing; it also demonstrates the transition, after the Second World War, of the gifted Danish architect from a highly dynamic, emotional approach to a strictly rational, chilled design. Since both approaches are of such architectural quality that they can co-exist, an older example of staggered chain type houses may well be shown together with a more recent example of patio houses (page 108). The "Søholm No. I" project consists of five terrace houses with 1½ storeys and nine terrace houses with two storeys. The two-storey chain houses shown here are highly unconventional angular buildings. But the construction is conventional, with bright facing bricks, timber beam floors, and tiled roof. Gross floor area: 128 sq. metres (1380 sq. ft.); floor space index 0.4.

Das Gebiet Klampenborg – ein im Norden Kopenhagens günstig gelegenes Gelände am Meer – kann als eine Art Experimentierwerkstatt des Architekten Jacobsen angesehen werden. Bereits 1933 baute er hier die »Bellavista Appartements«, und 1950 und 1955 errichtete er auf dem Grundstück eines abgebrochenen Landhauses Ketten- und Reihenhäuser. Klampenborg enthält daher nicht nur hervorragende Beispiele für urbanes Wohnen, es zeigt auch die nach dem Zweiten Weltkrieg erfolgte Wandlung im Stil des dänischen Architekten von einer stark dynamischen, gefühlsbetonten Formgebung zu einer streng rationalen, unterkühlten Auffassung. Da beide Haltungen, was die architektonische Qualität angeht, nebeneinander bestehen können, wird ein älteres Beispiel gestaffelter Kettenhäuser und eine neuere Anlage von Atriumhäusern (Seite 108) gezeigt. Das Projekt »Søholm I« besteht aus fünf eineinhalbgeschossigen und neun zweigeschossigen Einfamilienreihenhäusern. Die zweigeschossigen hier abgebildeten Kettenhäuser sind sehr eigenwillige Bauten in Winkelform. Sie wurden in traditioneller Bauweise errichtet: außen heller Klinker, innen Holzbalkendecken und Schieferdach. Bruttogeschoßfläche 128 qm, GFZ 0,4 .

58

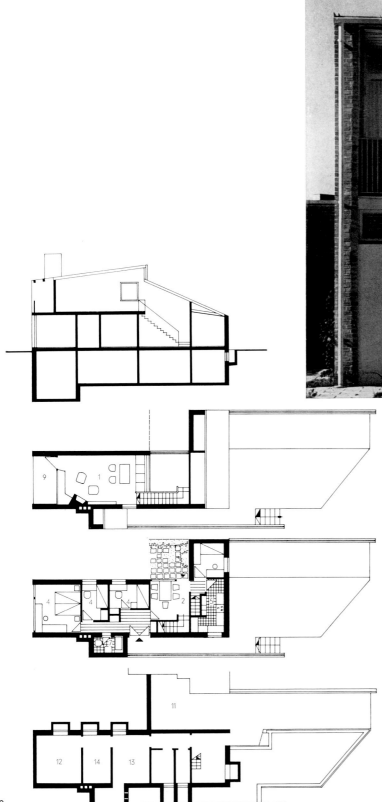

1. View from north-east.
2. Site plan, 1 in 2000.
3. View of chain type house from south-east.
4. Plans and section, 1 in 300. Apart from kitchen and dining room which open up to a kind of patio, the ground floor contains all the bedrooms and the bathroom. The roof storey forms a single long sitting room terminating in a loggia with a magnificent view across the Sound. Patio, main bedroom and sitting room face south-east, the kitchen has windows on the east side and the entrance is placed on the north-east side.

1. Ansicht von Nordosten.
2. Lageplan 1 : 2000.
3. Ansicht eines Kettenhauses von Südosten.
4. Grundrisse und Schnitt 1 : 300. Das Erdgeschoß enthält außer der Küche und dem Eßraum, der sich zu einer Art Atrium öffnet, sämtliche Schlafzimmer und das Bad. Das Dachgeschoß bildet einen langgestreckten Wohnraum. Er endet in einer Loggia mit einem prachtvollen Blick auf das Meer, den Öresund. Atrium, Hauptschlafraum und Wohnraum sind nach Südosten orientiert, die Küche mit Ostfenster und der Eingang liegen auf der Nordostseite.

5. View from south-west.
6. A glimpse of Arne Jacobsen's own garden.
7. One of the loggias, seen from the south.

5. Ansicht von Südwesten.
6. Blick in den Garten des Hauses Arne Jacobsen.
7. Eine Loggia, von Süden gesehen.

8 · Dining area, seen from the upper floor living room.
9. Sitting room in Jacobsen's own house.

8. Blick vom Wohnraum im Obergeschoß auf den Eßplatz.
9. Wohnraum des Hauses, das Jacobsen selbst bewohnt.

"Tall Oaks" housing scheme, Saconnex, Geneva (1959)
Architects: F. Maurice, J. Duret and J. P. Dom

Siedlung »Die großen Eichen« in Genf-Saconnex (1959)
Architekten: F. Maurice, J. Duret und J. P. Dom

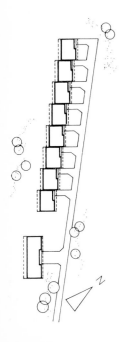

On gently sloping ground studded with old trees, the architects erected a group of eight terrace houses and one semi-detached pair. Access is provided by a spur road. The houses are slightly staggered so as to emphasize the individuality of each unit and, at the same time, to improve view and orientation. The houses are placed diagonally, with the living rooms on the south-west side and the bedrooms on the north-east side. The terrace houses have a frontage of 11 metres (36′1″) and a depth of 8 metres (26′3″). The well designed plan and the economic solution adopted for the stairs have resulted in an interesting interlinking of the spaces and a diversified facade. Construction: Bearing walls as well as structural floors and roof are 18 or 12 cm (7″ or 4.3/4″) thick concrete slabs. Non-bearing outer walls consist of a timber frame with a cladding of enamelled asbestos cement boards. Gross floor area 132 sq. metres (1420 sq. ft.); floor space index (with a plot size of 400 sq. metres, i.e. 4300 sq. ft.) 0.3.

Die Architekten errichteten auf einem von alten Bäumen bestandenen, leicht geneigten Hang eine Gruppe von acht Einfamilienreihenhäusern und ein Doppelhaus. Eine Stichstraße erschließt das Gelände. In der Aneinanderreihung sind die Häuser leicht gestaffelt, wodurch die Individualität jeder Wohneinheit hervorgehoben wird, aber auch Sicht und Orientierung eine Verbesserung erfahren. Die Diagonallage der Zeile ergibt für das Wohnen Südwest-, für das Schlafen Nordostlage. Der Reihenhaustyp hat eine Frontbreite von 11 m und eine Tiefe von 8 m. Der gut durchdachte Grundriß und die ökonomische Treppenlösung ließen eine interessante räumliche Durchdringung und eine bewegte Fassade entstehen. Konstruktion: Die tragenden Wände sind aus 18 bzw. 12 cm starken Betonscheiben, ebenso die Geschoßdecken und das Dach. Nichttragende Außenwände bestehen aus einem Holzskelett mit emaillierten Asbestzementplatten verkleidet. Bruttogeschoßfläche 132 qm, GFZ (bei 400 qm Grundstücksfläche) 0,3.

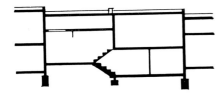

1. View from the east. The semi-detached pair is on the left.
2. Site plan, 1 in 2000.
3. Plans and section, 1 in 300. Because of the half-storey stagger, the house has four levels, viz. the entrance level with garage, laundry and cellar; the living room floor with sitting room, kitchen and a small bedroom at garden level; the bedroom floor with three bedrooms, bathroom and W.C., and finally, forming a fourth level above the kitchen, a 4 ft. high "creeping height" attic.
4. View of the housing project. Entrance side.
5. Garden side. Outside the sitting room, at garden level, is a covered sitting place.

1. Blick aus Osten. Links das Doppelhaus.
2. Lageplan 1:2000.
3. Grundrisse und Schnitt 1:300. Aus der Versetzung der Geschosse gegeneinander um jeweils ein halbes Geschoß ergeben sich vier Ebenen: die Eingangsebene mit Garage, Waschküche und Keller; das Wohngeschoß mit Wohnraum, Küche und Schlafnische auf der Ebene des Gartens; das Schlafgeschoß mit drei Schlafräumen, Bad und WC und schließlich als vierte Ebene über der Küche: ein »Kriechboden« von 1,2 m Höhe.
4. Ansicht der Eingangsseite.
5. Die Gartenseite. Vor dem Wohnzimmer eine Terrasse.

Berchtoldhof housing estate near Innsbruck (1962)
Architect: Hubert Prachensky

Siedlung Berchtoldhof bei Innsbruck (1962)
Architekt: Hubert Prachensky

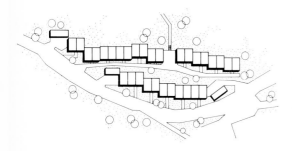

1. South side of one of the row of houses.
2. Site plan, 1 in 3000.

1. Die Südfassade der talseitigen Hauszeile.
2. Lageplan 1:3000.

In a low-density residential area on the mountain slopes on the north side of Innsbruck, the architect was able to secure permission for low-rise housing of higher density. The small estate comprises 31 terrace houses of 2½ storeys height, grouped in three units of irregular shape and unequal size which enclose a common open space. Near the main road, each row of houses terminates in a garage building. The individual houses are accessible by footpath only. The two-bay house built into the slope has a frontage of 6 metres (19′8″) and a depth of 10 metres (32′10″). Particularly adroit is the adaptation of the houses to the irregular contour lines. Construction: Brick masonry and reinforced concrete floors. Thermopane windows, built-up roof. Gross floor area: 134 sq. metres (1440 sq. ft.); floor space index: 0.7.

In einem Siedlungsgebiet mit offener Bebauung am Hang der Nordkette bei Innsbruck konnte der Architekt eine geschlossene Bebauung durchsetzen. Die kleine Siedlung umfaßt 31 zwei-einhalbgeschossige Einfamilienreihenhäuser, verteilt auf drei unregelmäßig gegliederte und ungleich große Gruppen, die einen angerförmigen Raum umschließen. Den Abschluß der Zeilen zur Straße bildet jeweils ein Garagenbau. Die einzelnen Häuser sind über Fußwege zugänglich. Das in den Hang gefügte zweischiffige Haus hat eine Frontbreite von 6 m und eine Tiefe von 10 m. Besonders geschickt erscheint die Anpassung der Baukörper an die ungleichmäßig geschwungenen Höhenlinien des Geländes. Konstruktion: Ziegelmauerwerk und Stahlbetondecke. Thermopanverglasung, Kiespreßdach. Bruttogeschoßfläche 134 qm, GFZ 0,7.

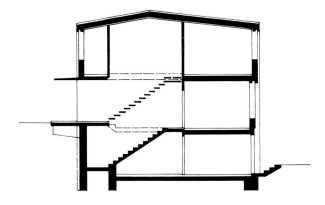

3. Plans and section, 1 in 200. From the north side, one enters the hall on the upper ground floor which comprises porch, kitchen, W. C., and the sitting room which extends, together with the dining recess, over the entire south front. On the upper floor are three bedrooms, the bathroom with W. C., and a cupboard room. Because of the sloping ground, it was possible to utilise the front part of the basement as a workroom. Adjacent to this additional room is a tool room with the garden exit, behind it the boiler room and storage cellar. The large windows of the sitting room provide a magnificent view over Innsbruck and the mountain ranges.
4. Detail of the south facade. The stairs provide a direct link between sitting room and garden. Below the stairs is the door leading to the tool room.

3. Grundrisse und Schnitt 1 : 200. Von der Nordseite gelangt man in den Flur des Erdgeschosses, das Windfang, Küche, WC und den die ganze Südseite einnehmenden Wohnraum mit Eßnische umfaßt. Im Obergeschoß befinden sich drei Schlafräume, das Bad mit WC und ein Schrankraum. Die Hanglage des Hauses ermöglichte den Ausbau des vorderen Teils des Kellergeschosses als Arbeitsraum. Neben diesem zusätzlichen Zimmer liegt der Geräteraum mit dem Gartenausgang, dahinter Heizungs- und Vorratskeller. Vom Wohnraum hat man durch die großen Glasfenster eine prachtvolle Aussicht auf Innsbruck und die Bergketten.
4. Detailansicht der Südfassade. Die Treppe stellt eine direkte Verbindung zwischen Wohnraum und Garten her. Unter der Treppe die Tür zum Geräteraum.

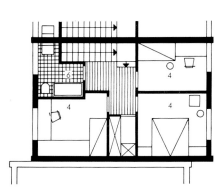

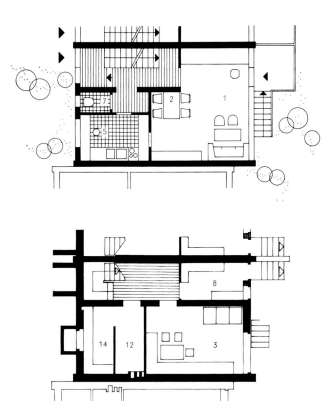

Terrace houses at Flamatt near Berne (1957 and 1960)
Architects: Atelier 5

Einfamilienreihenhäuser in Flamatt bei Bern (1957 und 1960)
Architekten: Atelier 5

On this site, situated between two rivers, one row of terrace houses was erected in 1957 and another in 1960, forming together with a garage building a group around a common garden. The interesting 1960 building, though 3½ storeys high, still conforms to the definition of "urban low-rise housing" given in the Introduction, as the four dwellings are directly connected with a private garden. The building contains three two-storey four-room maisonettes and a 2½-storey studio type maisonette with two rooms. On the roof is an excellently appointed roof garden. The four-room maisonettes face south, whilst the studio maisonette faces west. The living rooms are on the first floor. The strongly featured building, with its structure of untreated concrete, has a forceful, almost monumental effect. Construction: Reinforced concrete. Non-bearing walls of 4 cm (1½") precast concrete slabs. Thermal insulation of the outer walls by glass fibre boards inserted between concrete slabs. Flat roof: cork, three layers of felting, covering layer of concrete, top soil. Gross floor area: 114 sq. metres (1220 sq. ft.), studio maisonette 124 sq. metres (1330 sq. ft.); floor space index 0.3.

Auf dem zwischen zwei Flußläufen gelegenen Grundstück wurden 1957 und 1960 je ein Einfamilienreihenhaus errichtet und mit einem Garagengebäude um einen gemeinschaftlich genutzten Garten gruppiert. Der neuere interessante dreieinhalbgeschossige Bau ist nach der in der Einleitung gegebenen Definition durchaus ein »urbaner Flachbau«, da die vier Wohnungen unmittelbar mit einem der privaten Sphäre zugehörigen Grund verbunden sind. Das Gebäude enthält drei zweigeschossige Vierzimmerwohnungen und eine zweieinhalbgeschossige Atelierwohnung mit zwei Zimmern. Über den Wohnungen liegt ein ausgezeichnet bepflanzter Dachgarten. Während die Vierzimmerwohnungen nach Süden orientiert sind, ist die Atelierwohnung nach Westen ausgerichtet. Das Wohngeschoß liegt im ersten Stock. Der plastisch gestaltete Baukörper, mit der Struktur roher Betonschalung, hat eine kräftige, fast monumentale Wirkung. Konstruktion: Stahlbeton. Nichttragende Wände in 4 cm vorfabrizierten Betonplatten. Wärmeisolierung der Außenwände durch Glasseidenplatten zwischen Betonschalen. Flachdach: Kork, dreilagige Pappe, Überbeton, Humusschicht. Bruttogeschoßfläche 114 qm (Atelier 124 qm), GFZ 0,3.

1. View from south-west. On the left, the group erected in 1960; on the right that erected in 1957.

1. Blick aus Südwest. Links das 1960 und rechts das 1957 erbaute Haus.

2. Plans and section, 1 in 300. The ground floor with the access stairs is left open. The large space thus obtained can be utilised for many different purposes. On the first floor are the large living-cum-dining room, kitchen, hall and logia. On the second floor are the main bedroom and two of the children's rooms which are separated from each other by a panel-type sliding wall.
3. South and east side.

2. Grundrisse und Schnitt 1:300. Das Erdgeschoß mit den Zugangstreppen ist nicht ausgebaut. Der so entstandene große Raum läßt sich für verschiedenste Zwecke verwenden. Im ersten Stock befinden sich der große Wohn-Eßraum, Küche, Eingangsflur und Loggia; im zweiten Stock das Elternschlafzimmer und zwei Kinderzimmer, die durch eine als Tafel ausgebildete Schiebewand getrennt sind.
3. Die Süd- und Ostseite.

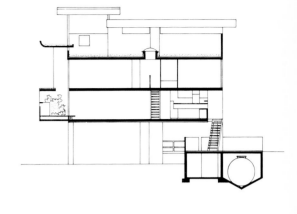

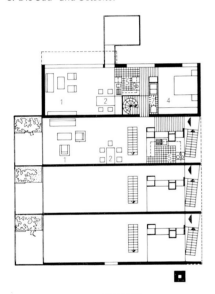

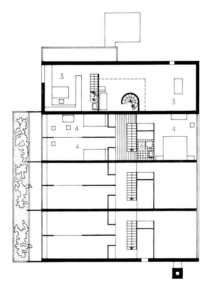

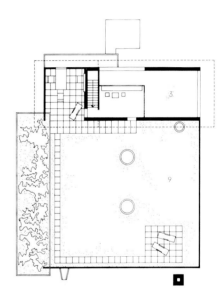

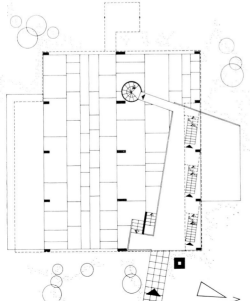

4. View from south-west.
5. Stairs leading to the four-room maisonettes.
6. The stairwell leading to the studio maisonette provides the direct link with the private garden.
7, 8. Living room of a four-room maisonette, with stairs leading to the bedroom floor.
9. Roof garden.

4. Südwestansicht.
5. Die Zugangstreppen zu den Vierzimmerwohnungen.
6. Der Treppenturm zur Atelierwohnung gibt die unmittelbare Verbindung zum privaten Grund.
7, 8. Blick in den Wohnraum einer Vierzimmerwohnung mit Treppe zum Schlafgeschoß.

9. Der Dachgarten.

Halen housing estate, near Berne (1961)
Architects: Atelier 5

Siedlung Halen bei Bern (1961)
Architekten: Atelier 5

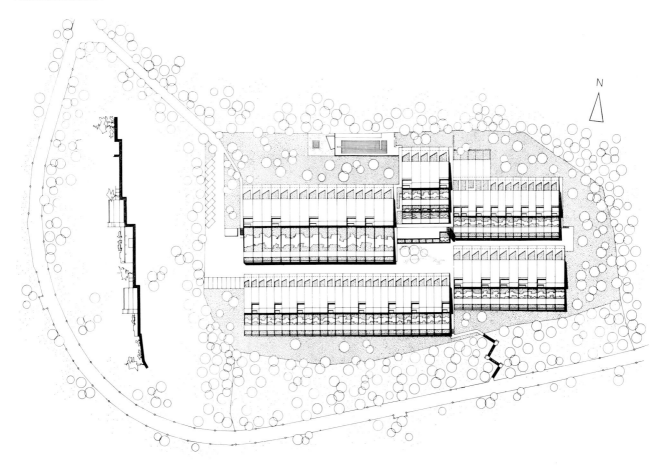

The Halen housing estate represents one of the most logical attempts at putting the idea of urban low-rise housing into practice. There are altogether 79 dwelling units, viz. 33 larger and 41 smaller three-storey terrace houses and 5 studio maisonnettes. The concentrated group of buildings on the very economically utilised south slope is in contrast to the wide, undulating and almost unspoilt landscape. Because of the difference in levels, each house has a free view across the grass-covered flat roof of the lower group. Privacy is preserved by secluded gardens and loggias. The economic spacing of the houses leaves sufficient space for playgrounds and sports. The plot sizes range from 200 to 230 sq. metres (2150 to 2470 sq. ft.). The garden covers an area of approx. 30 to 45 sq. metres (320 to 480 sq. ft.). The front parts of walls, floors and roof are exposed concrete. Type A: gross floor area 168 sq. metres (1800 sq. ft.); floor space index 0.9. Type B: gross floor area 215 sq. metres (2300 sq. ft.); floor space index 1.0.

Die Siedlung Halen verkörpert einen der konsequentesten Versuche, den Gedanken des urbanen Flachbaus zu realisieren. Die insgesamt 79 Wohneinheiten verteilen sich auf 33 größere und 41 kleinere dreigeschossige Einfamilienreihenhäuser sowie fünf Studios. Die verdichtete Anlage auf dem äußerst rationell genutzten Südhang steht im Gegensatz zu der weiten, bewegten, nahezu unberührten Landschaft. Durch den Geländeunterschied ist für jedes Wohnhaus freie Sicht über die grasbewachsenen Flachdächer der unteren Häusergruppen gegeben. Intime Gärten und Loggien wahren das Eigenleben. Die ökonomische Bebauung schafft der Wohngemeinschaft Raum für Spiel und Sport. Die Grundstücksgrößen liegen zwischen 200 und 230 qm. Der Gartenraum hat Ausmaße von rund 30 bis 45 qm. Wände, Decken und Dach sind an den Außenfronten aus unverputztem Beton. Typ A: Bruttogeschoßfläche 168 qm, GFZ 0,9. Typ B: Bruttogeschoßfläche 215 qm, GFZ 1.0.

1. Aerial photograph. View from north-west. The estate is surrounded by a sportsground with swimming pool, children's playgrounds and lawns.
2. Site plan and section, 1 in 2000.

1. Luftaufnahme. Blick aus Nordwest. Ein Sportplatz mit Schwimmbassin, Kinderspielplätze und Liegewiesen umgeben die Siedlung.
2. Lageplan und Schnitt 1 : 2000.

3. South side of the top row. Storey-high concrete walls ensure privacy.

4, 5. "As in small medieval towns, the houses are arranged in chains, forming groups, village streets, alleyways and small courtyards." Around the "village square" are the shops, a café, the central heating plant, electric substation and laundries.

6. All the residents enjoy the calmness, the fresh air, and the sun.

7. At the end of the over 300 ft. long access road, at the entrance to this "village," are the car parks, and a garage building placed below the gardens of the top row of houses.

8. Shops at the "village square." On the left, behind the trees, is the café.

3. Die Südseite der oberen Reihe. Geschoßhohe Betonwände sichern die Intimität.

4, 5. Wie in mittelalterlichen Kleinstädten reiht sich Haus an Haus, bilden sich Gruppen, Dorfstraßen, Gäßchen und kleine Plätze. Um den Dorfplatz gruppieren sich die Läden, ein Café, die Zentrale für Heizung und Waschküchen.

6. Alle Bewohner genießen die Ruhe, die gute Luft und die Sonne.

7. Am Ende der rund 100 m langen Zubringerstraße, am Eingang dieses »Dorfes«, befinden sich die Parkplätze und eine Sammelgarage unter den Gärten der oberen Häuserreihe.

8. Läden am Dorfplatz. Links, von den Bäumen verdeckt, das Café.

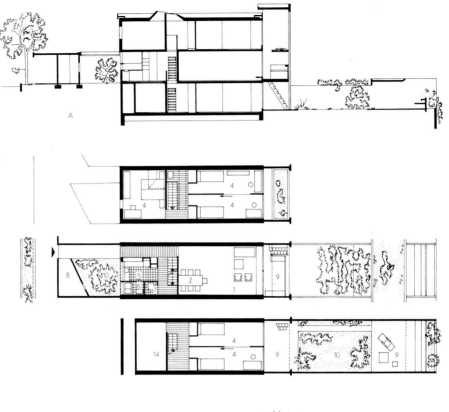

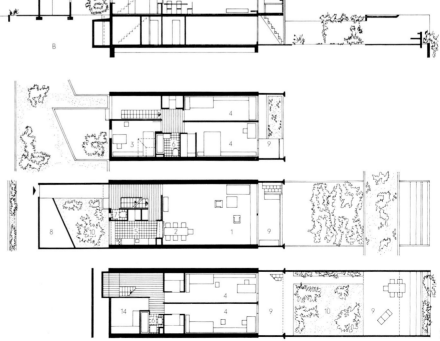

A

B

9. Stairs in type B house. View from upper floor towards the entrance.

10. Interior of a three-storey maisonette at night.

11. Plans and sections, 1 in 300. The design of the two single-bay types (A and B) is based on the same principle: From a path on the north side, one enters the intermediate floor containing the living rooms. The bedrooms are partly on the garden floor below, and partly on the upper floor above. The main bedrooms extend over the entire width of the house, the children's bedrooms over half the width. An interesting feature is the "interception" of the south sun for the north side bedrooms on the upper floor. All the dwellings face south. Type A: frontage 4 metres (13′1″), depth 14 metres (46″), transverse stairs. The arrangement of the bathroom and the connection from the kitchen to the living room are somewhat problematic. Type B: frontage 5 metres (16′5″), depth 14.5 metres (47′7″), longitudinal stairs. With this type, the kitchen has a direct connection to the living room. The bathroom is on the upper floor.

12. A private garden.

13, 14. Garden-side room of type A. The rooms can be separated by a sliding door. An additional external flight of stairs leads to the living room at street level.

9. Treppe im Haus des Typs B. Blick vom Obergeschoß auf den Eingang.

10. Blick in eine dreigeschossige Wohnung bei Nacht.

11. Grundrisse und Schnitte 1:300. Die beiden einschiffigen Typen A und B sind nach dem gleichen Prinzip entwickelt: Von einem auf der Nordseite gelegenen Wohnweg gelangt man jeweils in das mittlere, das Wohngeschoß. Das darunter befindliche Gartengeschoß sowie das darüberliegende Obergeschoß enthalten die Schlafräume. Für die Elternschlafräume ist die ganze Breite des Hauses, für die Kinderschlafräume die halbe Breite verwendet. Interessant ist das »Hereinholen« der Südsonne in den auf der Nordseite gelegenen Schlafraum des Obergeschosses. Sämtliche Wohnungen sind südgerichtet. Typ A: Frontbreite 4 m, Tiefe 14 m, Quertreppe. Die Anordnung des Bades und die Verbindung von der Küche zum Wohnraum ist etwas problematisch. Typ B: Frontbreite 5 m, Tiefe 14,5 m, Längstreppe. Die Küche hat bei diesem Typ unmittelbare Verbindung mit dem Wohnraum. Das Bad befindet sich im Obergeschoß.

12. Ein privater Garten.

13, 14. Gartenseitige Zimmer des Typs A. Durch eine Schiebetür können die Räume getrennt werden. Eine zusätzliche Außentreppe führt zum Wohnraum im Straßengeschoß.

South Hill Park terrace houses, Hampstead, London (1956)
Architects: Stanley Amis and William Howell

Einfamilienreihenhäuser South Hill Park in London-Hampstead (1956)
Architekten: Stanley Amis und William Howell

1, 2. Because of the sloping ground, the houses have three complete storeys facing the road, and four storeys on the opposite side.

1, 2. Die Hanglage ließ an der Straßenseite drei, an der offenen, fallenden Seite des Grundstücks vier Vollgeschosse entstehen.

This group of six terrace houses represents an extreme case of "low-rise housing" of the kind hitherto mainly encountered in North-West Europe. The site was originally occupied by four Victorian houses which were destroyed during the war. By erecting six houses with narrower frontages, including the houses for the two architects, it was possible to make up for the increased cost of the land. In their external and internal design, these six attractive and congenial terrace houses are so unmistakably English that they might be regarded as a straight continuation of the old Anglo-Saxon dwelling culture. But this effect has been achieved without the slightest compromise with conventional form. Construction: Facing masonry, reinforced concrete floors, and flat timber framed roof. Each house has its own anthracite boiler. Hot-water heating pipes are embedded in the floors (radiation heating). Gross floor area: 192 sq. metres (2080 sq. ft.); floor space index 1.0 (net).

Die Gruppe von sechs Einfamilienreihenhäusern zeigt einen extremen Fall von »Flachbau«, wie er bisher vorwiegend im Nordwesten Europas entstanden ist. Auf dem Grundstück standen ursprünglich vier viktorianische Häuser, die während des Krieges zerstört wurden. Durch die Errichtung von sechs Häusern mit schmaleren Fronten, in denen auch die beiden Architekten ihre Wohnung einrichteten, konnten die gestiegenen Grundstückspreise ausgeglichen werden. In ihrer äußeren und inneren Gestaltung sind diese sympathischen und wohnlichen sechs Reihenhäuser so unverwechselbar englisch, daß man von einer Fortsetzung der alten angelsächsischen Wohnkultur sprechen kann. Sie sind dies aber ohne den mindesten Kompromiß an traditionelle Formen. Konstruktion: Die Häuser wurden in sichtbarem Ziegelmauerwerk mit Eisenbeton-Plattendecken und Holzkonstruktion des Flachdaches errichtet. Jedes Haus hat seinen eigenen Boiler. Warmwasserheizkörper liegen in den Decken. Bruttogeschoßfläche 192 qm, GFZ 1,0.

3. Plans and section, 1 in 300. All the plumbing units, including the kitchen, are placed adjacent to the stairwell so that the facades can be entirely opened up to windows. On the ground floor at street level, each house has a garage. On the garden side is the split-level living room, extending into the floor above. On the upper floors are the bedrooms and studies.

4. Interior of first floor bedroom.

5. Dining area, seen from the sitting room gallery.

3. Grundrisse und Schnitt 1:300. Alle Installationen der Naßgruppe sind neben dem Treppenhaus angelegt, so daß die Außenfronten ganz zur Belichtung verfügbar werden. Im Straßengeschoß kann je ein Wagen eingestellt werden. Der teilweise zweigeschossige Wohnraum liegt auf der Gartenseite. In den oberen Stockwerken befinden sich Schlaf- und Arbeitsräume.

4. Blick in den Schlafraum im ersten Obergeschoß.

5. Blick vom Wohnraum hinab auf den Eßplatz.

3

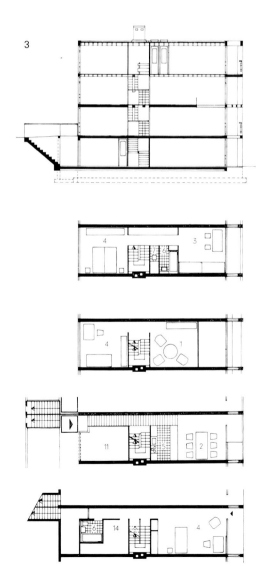

4

5

Terrace houses at Niedergösgen, Switzerland (1954–1956)
Architect: Alfons Barth

Einfamilienreihenhäuser in Niedergösgen, Schweiz (1954–1956)
Architekt: Alfons Barth

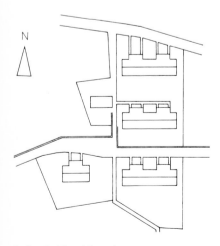

1. South side, with gardens.
2. Site plan, 1 in 2000.

1. Blick auf die Südseite mit den Wohngärten.
2. Lageplan 1 : 2000.

On this south slope, it was originally intended to build detached houses. But the architect was able to convince his four private clients of the advantages of adopting the principle of low-rise high-density housing. That the objections against this project were overcome is due to the support given by the Solothurn Association for the Protection of Amenities. The housing scheme consists of three rows of four terrace houses on different levels; each house has a frontage of 8 metres (26′3″), and there are two different types of plans. In addition, there is a semi-detached pair. Garages are provided at the approach to the estate. By staggering the floors, it was possible to give both the living room and the bedrooms a south orientation, with a view of the Alps. Construction: Brick walls, rendered; reinforced concrete roof with Durisol cavity slabs, gravel-covered asphalt and inside drainage; reinforced concrete slabs for floors and stairs. All the houses are let. Gross floor area 112 sq. metres (1200 sq. ft.), floor space index 0.4.

Auf dem geneigten Südhang sollten ursprünglich freistehende Einfamilienhäuser errichtet werden. Der Architekt konnte die vier privaten Bauherren jedoch von den Vorzügen einer Lösung im urbanen Flachbau überzeugen. Bemerkenswert ist die Tatsache, daß nur mit Hilfe der Solothurnischen Heimatschutz-Kommission die Widerstände gegen das Bauvorhaben überwunden wurden. Die Bebauung gliedert sich in drei übereinanderliegende Zeilen mit je vier Reihenhäusern von 8 m Frontbreite in zwei Grundrißvariationen und ein Doppel-Einfamilienhaus. Am Zugang der Siedlung wurden Sammelgaragen angelegt. Durch die Geschoßversetzung konnten Wohn- und Schlafräume nach Süden, mit dem Blick auf die Alpen, orientiert werden. Konstruktion: Ziegelwände, verputzt; Dach Stahlbeton mit Durisol-Hohlkörpern, Asphalt mit Kies und Innenentwässerung; Gesims in Sichtbeton; Decke und Treppe Betonplatte mit Linoleum. Alle Wohnungen werden vermietet. Bruttogeschoßfläche 112 qm, GFZ 0,4.

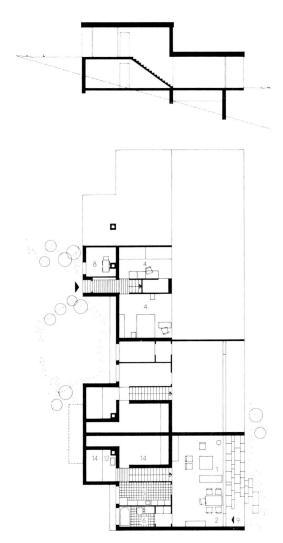

3. Plans and section, 1 in 300. Access is from the high ground in the north through a porch leading to the upper floor which contains two bedrooms and a store room. From this level, a flight of stairs leads down to the main floor which contains the living room, possibly a third bedroom and, on the north side, kitchen, bathroom, boiler room and cellars.

4. General view of the estate, from the south.

5. Street frontage of one row of houses.

6. View from the porch down the stairs to the living room. On the left the children's room.

3. Grundrisse und Schnitt 1:300. Der Zugang erfolgt von Norden über einen Windfang in das Obergeschoß, das die beiden Schlafräume und eine Abstellmöglichkeit enthält. Von dieser Ebene führt eine Treppe in das Hauptgeschoß, in dem Wohnraum (eventuell ein dritter Schlafraum) und auf der Nordseite Küche, Bad, Heizung und Kellerräume liegen.

4. Gesamtansicht der Siedlung von Süden.

5. Die Zugangsseite einer Zeile.

6. Blick vom Windfang über die Treppe in den Wohnraum; links das Kinderzimmer.

Terrace house estate at Sandviken, Sweden (1955/56)
Architects: Fritz Jaenecke and Sten Samuelson

Einfamilienreihenhaus-Siedlung in Sandviken, Schweden (1955/56)
Architekten: Fritz Jaenecke und Sten Samuelson

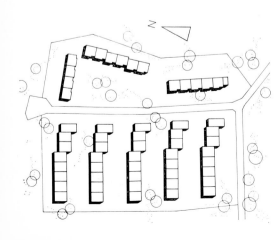

This estate of fifty terrace houses was built for the employees of a large steelworks in Northern Sweden. Five east-west orientated rows of houses of one type, together with one east-west and two north-south orientated rows of houses of the second type, are grouped around a common open space. The architects have made skilful use of the contours of the rocky, wooded site. The lively buildings with their diversified plans convincingly match the contours of the slope. The two types, which differ from each other by the position of the roof in relation to the front, have terraces on the south or west side, with projecting partitions to ensure privacy. Construction: Walls of lightweight concrete blocks, brightly rendered. All the timber parts are painted with the well-known red paint normally used for Swedish timber houses. The estate has central heating. Gross floor area: type A 160 sq. metres (1720 sq. ft.), type B 154 sq. metres (1550 sq. ft.); floor space index 0.4.

Die Siedlung von fünfzig Einfamilienreihenhäusern wurde für die Angestellten eines großen Stahlwerks im nördlichen Schweden errichtet. Fünf in Ost-West-Richtung gestellte Zeilen des gleichen Wohnungstyps sind zusammen mit einer kleinen ostwest- und zwei nordsüd-gerichteten Zeilen des zweiten Typs um einen Anger gruppiert. Die Architekten haben die Bewegung des felsigen, bewaldeten Geländes geschickt ausgenutzt: Lebendige Baukörper mit differenziertem Grundriß drücken die Gegenbewegung zum Hang überzeugend aus. Die beiden Typen, die sich durch Traufen- oder Giebelstellung unterscheiden, haben auf der Süd- bzw. Westseite Terrassen, deren Seitenwände vorgezogen sind, um gegenseitige Störungen zu vermeiden. Konstruktion: Wände aus Leichtbetonblocksteinen, hell verputzt. Alle Holzteile sind mit der bekannten roten schwedischen Holzhausfarbe gestrichen. Die Siedlung wird zentral beheizt. Bruttogeschoßfläche: Typ A 160 qm, Typ B 154 qm, GFZ 0,4.

1. Two rows of type A houses. In the background, type B. The south frontage is wide open to the sun.

2. Site plan, 1 in 3000. Access is from a spur road; at the top the three rows of type B houses, below the five rows of type A houses.

3. Plans, 1 in 300. Type A, with a frontage of approx. 26 ft., has one storey on the entrance side (north side) but two storeys on the south side. Hall, toilet, dining recess and kitchen are thus placed on an intermediate level from which five steps lead down to the living room at south side ground level. Connection with the top floor, which contains three bedrooms, bathroom and W.C., is provided by a flight of stairs leading up from the hall at intermediate level.

4. The movement of the roofs in relation to the slope is a distinct design feature.

1. Zwei Zeilen des Typs A. Im Hintergrund Typ B. Weit öffnet sich die Südseite zur Sonne.

2. Lageplan 1:3000. Eine Stichstraße erschließt die Siedlung; oben die drei Zeilen des Typs B, unten die fünf Zeilen des Typs A.

3. Grundrisse 1:300. Typ A, mit einer Frontbreite von rund 8 m, ist auf der Nord-, der Eingangsseite, eingeschossig und auf der Südseite zweigeschossig. Diele mit Toilette, Eßplatz und Küche befinden sich so in einem Zwischengeschoß, von dem fünf Stufen zum ebenerdigen, auf der Südseite gelegenen Wohnzimmer hinunterführen. Die Verbindung zum darüberliegenden Obergeschoß mit drei Schlafräumen und Bad mit Toilette stellt eine Treppe her, die von der Diele im Zwischengeschoß ausgeht.

4. Die Bewegung der Dächer gegen den Hang ist deutlich als gestaltendes Element erkennbar.

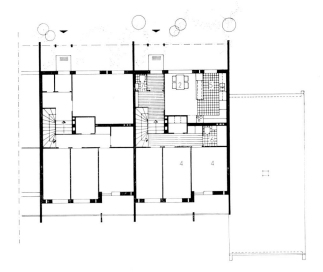

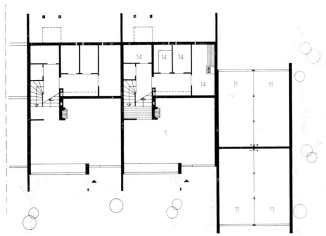

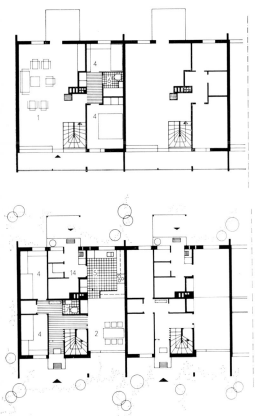

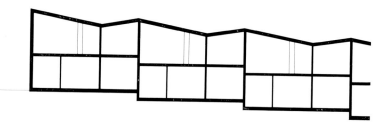

5. Plans and section, 1 in 300. Type B, with a frontage of approx. 29 ft., is a two-storey terrace house. The houses of this type have no basement at all. On the ground floor are the entrance, kitchen, storage rooms, dining room and two bedrooms, on the upper floor a large living room, the bathroom and two further bedrooms.

6. One row of type B terrace houses under construction. The broken line of the roofs avoids the monotonous impression often associated with terrace houses.

5. Grundrisse und Schnitt 1:300. Typ B, mit einer Frontbreite von knapp 9 m, ist ein zweigeschossiges Reihenhaus. Die Häuser dieses Typs haben im Gegensatz zu den halbunterkellerten des Typs A keinen Keller. Im Erdgeschoß befinden sich Eingang, Küche, Vorratsräume, Eßzimmer und zwei Schlafkammern, im Obergeschoß Wohnraum, Bad und zwei weitere Schlafräume.

6. Eine Zeile des Typs B im Rohbau. Die Faltung der Dächer vermeidet den häufig langweiligen Eindruck von Reihenhäusern.

"Omega" terrace houses, Vällingby, Sweden (1958)
Architect: Ragnar Uppman

Terrassenhäuser »Omega« in Vällingby, Schweden (1958)
Architekt: Ragnar Uppman

Situated on a plateau covering approximately 10 acres, the "Omega" housing project comprises 24 terrace houses of three types, A, B, C, where type B is but a slight variation of type A. The stony, steeply sloping site, covered with heather and studded with fir trees, has been skilfully utilised. Living room and study, enjoying a free view over the landscape, are on the lower floor. The centre of the estate is formed by a small communal space with a children's playground which is within view from the private gardens as well as from the kitchens. A typically Scandinavian feature of the plan is the spacious hall serving as a dining area, and as a link between all the other rooms. The hall is connected with the living rooms in the lower floor by a straight flight of stairs. Owing to the ample dimensions and adequate storage space, the dwellings offer a high standard of comfort. Attractive features are the well conceived and clear design and the contrast between raw concrete and timber. Particularly pleasing is the integration of the small group of houses with the landscape. Type A: Gross floor area 144 sq. metres (1550 sq. ft.). Type C: 158 sq. metres (1700 sq. ft.). Floor space index 0.3.

Die Siedlung »Omega« umfaßt auf einem Gelände von rund 4 ha 24 Einfamilienreihenhäuser in drei Typen A, B, C, wobei Typ B nur eine unwesentliche Variante des Typs A ist. Das steil abfallende, mit Kiefern und Heide bewachsene Felsgrundstück ist auf geschickte Weise ausgenutzt: Wohn- und Arbeitsraum mit freiem Blick in die Landschaft liegen im Untergeschoß. Den Mittelpunkt der Siedlung bildet eine kleine Grünfläche mit Kinderspielplatz. Dieser kann sowohl vom Wohnhof als auch von der Küche aus überblickt werden. Eine skandinavische Eigenheit der Grundrisse ist die geräumige Diele als Eßplatz und als Verbindungsglied zu allen übrigen Räumen. Mit den im Untergeschoß liegenden Wohnräumen wird sie durch eine gradläufige Treppe verbunden. Die Weite der Grundrisse und ausreichender Abstellraum geben den Charakter einer bequemen Wohnlichkeit. Sympathisch wirkt die straffe, klare Gestaltung und der Gegensatz von rohem Beton und Holz. Besonders erfreulich ist die Verbindung der kleinen Gruppe mit der Landschaft. Typ A: Bruttogeschoßfläche 144 qm, Typ C: 158 qm, GFZ 0,3.

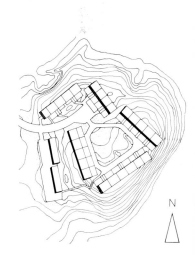

1. View from the east across the communal open space, with two rows of houses in the background.
2. Site plan, 1 in 3000.

1. Blick aus Osten über die gemeinsame Grünfläche auf zwei Häuserzeilen.
2. Lageplan 1:3000.

3. View of the two-storey living room side.
4. Entrance side. The small private gardens are screened by wooden fences.

3. Blick auf die zweigeschossige Wohnseite.
4. Die Eingangsseite. Die kleinen Privatgärten sind mit einem Holzzaun eingefriedet.

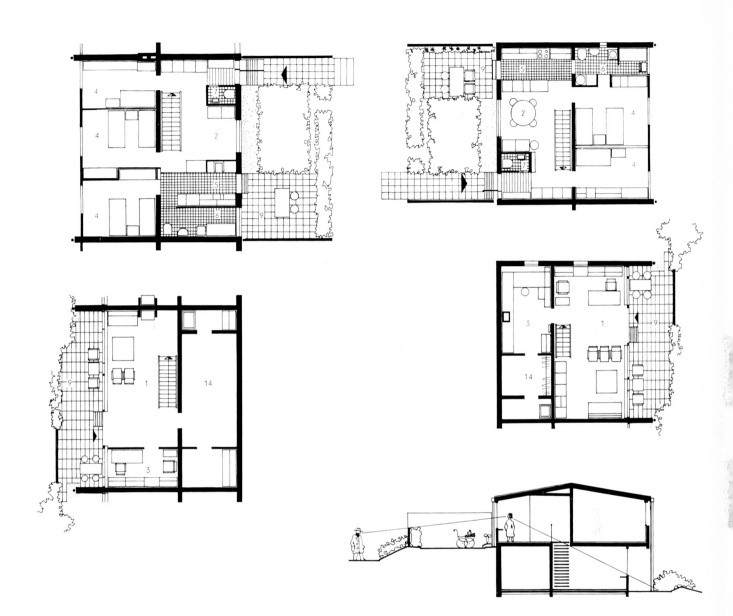

5. Plans, type C, 1 in 200. With a frontage of 10.5 metres (34'5'') and a depth of 8.4 metres (27'7''), type C is somewhat larger than type A. The greater width has made it possible to accommodate a third room on the ground floor. Admittedly, the arrangement of the bathroom opening from the kitchen does not seem to be quite felicitous.

6. Plans and section, type A, 1 in 200. Frontage 9.5 metres (31'2''), depth 8.4 metres (27'7''). The entrance is from the central open space to which each house is linked by a small garden patio, surrounded by a wooden fence. From the hall, which has a separate W. C., the kitchen is reached across the dining area. The two bedrooms and the bathroom occupy the second half of the ground floor. Both the kitchen and the main bedroom have direct doors to the bathroom-cum-W. C. In the lower floor are, in addition to living room and study, some store rooms and a partially covered terrace.

5. Grundrisse Typ C 1:200. Typ C ist mit einer Frontbreite von 10,5 m und Tiefe von 8,4 m etwas umfangreicher als Typ A. Die größere Breite macht es möglich, im Erdgeschoß ein drittes Zimmer unterzubringen. Die Anordnung des Bades in der Eingangshälfte neben der Küche scheint allerdings nicht ganz geglückt.

6. Grundrisse und Schnitt Typ A 1:200. Frontbreite 9,5 m, Tiefe 8,4 m. Der Eingang erfolgt von der zentralen Grünfläche, an die sich jedes Haus mit einem kleinen mit Holzplanken umschlossenen Gartenhof anschließt. Von der Diele mit separatem WC gelangt man über den Eßplatz in die Küche. Die beiden Schlafzimmer und das Bad nehmen die zweite Hälfte des Erdgeschosses ein. Küche und Elternschlafzimmer haben einen direkten Zugang zum Bad mit WC. Im Untergeschoß befinden sich neben dem Wohn- und Arbeitsraum Abstellräume und ein teilüberdeckter Sitzplatz im Freien.

Nonnenbusch housing estate, Marl, Germany (1956)
Architect: Heinrich Bormann

Siedlung Nonnenbusch in Marl, Deutschland (1956)
Architekt: Heinrich Bormann

This small group of prefabricated houses was erected by the architect on his own initiative and for his own purpose. He wanted to prove that low-rise dwellings need not be more expensive than flats, his ultimate intention being to secure, for low-rise housing, a greater share in the social housing programme. The experiment must be regarded as successful as the cost per house is no more than 10 per cent higher than that of an equally large flat in multi-storey housing. The houses which, without garage, have a frontage of approximately 42 ft. are erected on plots of approximately 300 sq. metres (3200 sq. ft.). For commercial reasons, some of them had to be built as detached houses. Construction: Walls and floors are of prefabricated light-weight concrete units. The foundation consists of a concrete slab about 1 ft. thick. Floors and walls have no interior rendering; the outside is rendered with a coating permeable to water vapour. The roof, which has central drainage, consists of Siporex or Ytong slabs and plastic sheet ("Acella-krep"). Oil-fired central heating will be provided. Gross floor area 104 sq. metres (1118 sq. ft.); floor space index 0.4.

Der Architekt errichtete die kleine Gruppe vorfabrizierter Einfamilienhäuser auf eigene Initiative und in eigener Regie. Er wollte mit diesem Unternehmen beweisen, daß Wohnungen im Flachbau nicht teurer sein müssen als Wohnungen im mehrgeschossigen Haus und damit im Endeffekt erreichen, daß in die Programme des Sozialen Wohnungsbaues ein höherer Anteil an flachgebauten Wohnungen aufgenommen wird. Das Experiment darf als gelungen angesehen werden, da die Kosten je Haus nur um 10% höher liegen als die für eine gleichgroße Wohnung im Stockwerksbau. Die Häuser – Frontbreite ohne Garage etwa 13 m – sind auf Grundstücken von rund 300 qm errichtet. Sie mußten aus verkaufstechnischen Erwägungen zum Teil freistehend angeordnet werden. Konstruktion: Wände und Decken bestehen aus vorfabrizierten Gasbetonelementen. Als Fundament dient eine rund 30 cm starke Betonplatte. Decken und Wände sind innen unverputzt; außen wurde eine wasserdampfdurchlässige Spachtelschicht aufgetragen. Das innenentwässerte Dach besteht aus Siporex- oder Ytongplatten und einer Kunststoffolie (Acellakrep). Vorgesehen ist eine Ölzentralheizung. Bruttogeschoßfläche 104 qm, GFZ 0,4.

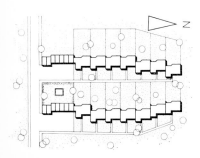

1. Entrance side, view from the east.
2. Site plan, 1 in 3000. If built as terrace houses, each row would be headed by a garage.
3. West side, with covered terrace and living room window.
4. Plan, 1 in 200. From the entrance, one enters a spacious hall giving access to kitchen, bathroom, living room and two bedrooms. A third bedroom is accessible through the living room. A noteworthy feature is the dining recess which is inserted between kitchen and living room and connected with a covered terrace. There is no basement except for a small storage cellar below the kitchen.

1. Eingangsseite, Blick von Osten.
2. Der Lageplan 1 : 3000 zeigt die Reihungsmöglichkeit. Am Anfang der Zeilen sind Sammelgaragen vorgesehen.
3. Die Westseite mit überdecktem Sitzplatz und Wohnraumfenster.
4. Grundriß 1 : 200. Vom Eingang gelangt man in einen geräumigen Flur, der Küche, Bad, Wohnraum und zwei Schlafräume aufschließt. Ein dritter Schlafraum wird durch den Wohnraum zugänglich gemacht. Beachtenswert ist die zwischen Küche und Wohnraum geschaltete Eßnische in Verbindung mit einem überdeckten Freiraum. Das Haus ist nicht unterkellert, lediglich unter der Küche befindet sich ein niedriger Abstellraum.

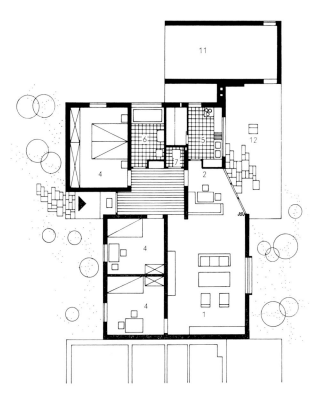

Veterans' Housing Project, Wellesley, Mass., USA (1951)
Architect: Hugh Stubbins

Veteranen-Siedlung in Wellesley, Mass., USA (1951)
Architekt: Hugh Stubbins

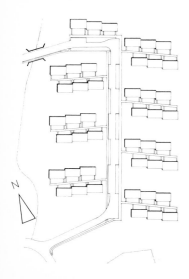

This state-subsidized housing project for veterans comprises 90 dwelling units. The houses are asymmetrically arranged in groups of three on either side of a cul-de-sac. At the access road, which is at right angles to the cul-de-sac, a car space is reserved for each dwelling. Both plan variations provide for single-storey houses with open-plan living rooms. Notwithstanding strict economy measures, the houses are comfortable owing to their felicitous layouts and the lively juxtaposition of high-quality building materials. In spite of certain shortcomings, this housing project is superior in many respects to low rent housing in Germany, owing to its imaginative and lucid planning standard. Type A: Gross floor area approx. 95 sq. metres (1020 sq. ft.), floor space index 0.5. Type B: Gross floor area approx. 93 sq. metres (1000 sq. ft.), floor space index 0.5.

Die staatlich subventionierte Siedlung für Veteranen umfaßt 90 Wohneinheiten. Je drei spiegelbildlich angelegte Wohnhäuser bilden eine Gruppe um einen Wohnweg. Die rechtwinklig dazu liegende Aufschließungsstraße enthält für jede Wohnung einen Autoabstellplatz. Beide Varianten des Grundtyps sind eingeschossig und haben einen durchgehenden Wohnraum. Bei sehr starker Rationalisierung ist der Typ wohnlich durch gute Raumverhältnisse und in lebendigen Gegensatz gebrachte Baustoffe guter Qualität. Trotz mancher Mängel ist diese Siedlung in ihrer großzügigen und klaren Gesamthaltung den Erzeugnissen unseres Sozialen Wohnungsbaues in vieler Hinsicht überlegen. Typ A: Bruttogeschoßfläche rund 95 qm, GFZ 0,5. Typ B: Bruttogeschoßfläche rund 93 qm, GFZ 0,5.

1. View of the Veterans' Housing Project from the south.
2. Site plan, 1 in 5000.
3, 4. Entrance side, with details of the entrance, courtyard and clothes-drying area near the kitchen. By staggering the houses in pairs and extending the party walls, covered terraces are created on the garden side. In addition, each dwelling unit has a garden covering some 26 sq. metres (280 sq. ft.), enclosed by a pierced wall.

1. Ansicht der Siedlung aus Süden.
2. Lageplan 1:5000.
3, 4. Eingangsseite und Details des Zugangs mit Wirtschaftshof und Wäschetrockenplatz vor der Küche. Durch die Versetzung von je zwei Häusern und das Vorziehen der Haustrennwände ergeben sich gedeckte Sitzplätze auf der Gartenseite. Zu jeder Wohneinheit gehört außerdem ein mit einer transparenten Mauer eingefaßter Gartenhof von rund 26 qm.

5. Plans, 1 in 300. Type A contains two bedrooms. In the case of type B, which has about the same floor area, space for a third bedroom has been created by reducing the size of the dining area and the other two bedrooms, and re-arranging the bathroom. As with many American houses, the entrance hall is combined with the dining area. The reduction in living room space for a greater number of beds is questionable; so is the north-north-east orientation of every other bedroom.

5. Grundrisse 1:300. Bei nahezu gleicher Grundfläche beider Typen enthält Typ A zwei Schlafräume. Bei Typ B ist durch Verkleinerung des Eßplatzes, der beiden Schlafzimmer und die Umstellung des Bades Platz für ein drittes Schlafzimmer geschaffen. Der Eingang ist, wie bei vielen amerikanischen Wohnungen, mit der Eßnische kombiniert. Die Verringerung des Wohnraums bei größerer Bettenzahl ist fragwürdig und ebenso die Orientierung der Hälfte aller Schlafräume nach Nord-Nord-Ost.

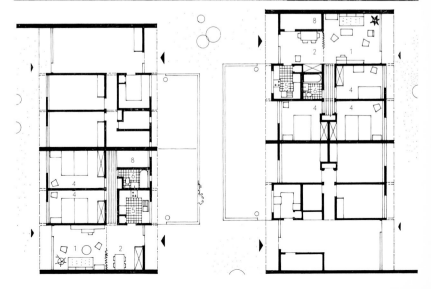

Terrace houses at Coventry, England (1962)
Architects: John M. Austin Smith, P. J. Lord and Geoffrey Salmon

Einfamilienreihenhaus in Coventry, England (1962)
Architekten: John M. Austin-Smith, P. J. Lord und Geoffrey Salmon

This interesting single-storey terrace house was awarded a prize in the RIBA Ideal Home competition. The architects were particularly concerned with the problem of the growing family; they solved the problem by combining kitchen, bathroom and W.C. in a single unit which is placed in a central position and at the same time creates a clear separation between living room and bedrooms. Flexibility is ensured by using non-bearing partitions which permit changes in layout. With the exception of the main bedroom to which the parents can retire, all the rooms are in open connection. They can, however, easily be partitioned by sliding doors so that they can meet different functional needs at one and the same time. Construction: Facing brickwalls with timber frames and timber roof structure. All the internal partitions consist of specially soundproofed prefabricated plastic units; parts of the front and rear are fully glazed or are equipped with sliding doors. The oil-fired boiler is installed in a cupboard recess by the side of the entrance. Gross floor area 156 sq. metres (1670 sq. ft.); floor space index 0.5.

Das interessante Einfamilienreihenhaus ist ein preisgekröntes Ergebnis des RIBA-Wettbewerbs »The Ideal Home«. Die Architekten beschäftigten sich besonders mit dem Problem der wachsenden Familie und lösten es, indem sie Küche, Bad und WC zu einem Naßkern zusammenfaßten. Er liegt zentral und schafft gleichzeitig eine klare Trennung zwischen Wohn- und Schlafteil. Nichttragende Innenwände ermöglichen räumliche Veränderungen und somit Flexibilität. Mit Ausnahme des Hauptschlafraumes, dem Rückzugsgebiet der Eltern, fließen alle Räume ineinander. Andererseits können sie durch Schiebetüren leicht voneinander getrennt werden und auf diese Weise verschiedene Funktionen (Gesellschaften) zur gleichen Zeit erfüllen. Konstruktion: Sichtbare Ziegelwände mit Holzrahmenabschluß und Holzdach. Sämtliche Innenwände bestehen aus besonders schallisolierten, vorfabrizierten Kunststoffelementen. Vorder- und Rückseite haben zum Teil Vollverglasung oder Schiebetüren. Der Boiler der Ölheizung ist in einer Schranknische neben dem Eingang installiert. Bruttogeschoßfläche 156 qm, GFZ 0,5.

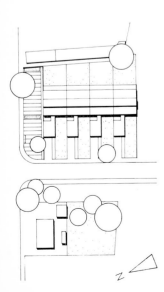

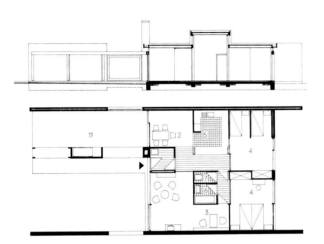

1. Living room side, seen from south-west. The canopy entrance is flanked by the American type carport. Because of the adjacent terrace, this solution must be regarded as less ideal.

2. Site plan, 1 in 1500.

3. Plan and section, 1 in 300.

4, 5. View of entrance, and part of bedroom. The partition between kitchen and hall provides for a breakfast bar. The housewife can keep an eye on all the parts of the house as well as the garden and front door so that visitors and children can be observed. The inside rooms receive their daylight through a raised roof.

1. Blick aus Südwest auf die Wohnfront. Der aus Amerika übernommene »carport« flankiert den überdeckten Eingang. Diese Lösung ist allerdings in Anbetracht der danebenliegenden Wohnterrasse weniger »ideal«.

2. Lageplan 1:1500.

3. Grundriß und Schnitt 1:300.

4, 5. Blick von der zentralen Diele aus auf Eingang und Schlafteil. Die Wand der Küche zur Diele ist als Frühstücksbar ausgebildet. Der Hausfrau ist es möglich, alle Bereiche der Wohnung zu übersehen und auch den Garten und die Haustür, so daß Besucher und Kinder beobachtet werden können. Belichtet und belüftet werden die innenliegenden Räume durch Höherführen des Daches.

Housing estate at Denickestrasse, Hamburg-Harburg (1958)
Architects: Ingeborg and Friedrich Spengelin and Otto Kindt

Siedlung an der Denickestraße, Hamburg-Harburg (1958)
Architekten: Ingeborg und Friedrich Spengelin und Otto Kindt

1. View from the south.
2. Site plan, 1 in 3000.

1. Ansicht der Siedlung von Süden.
2. Lageplan 1:3000.

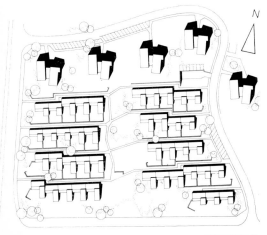

The centre of the estate, situated on an extensive south slope, is taken up by a school which is surrounded, at an appropriate distance, by houses of different height and design, forming lively groups. On the higher part of the ground are three- and four-storey blocks of flats and tower blocks with four or five storeys or with nine storeys whilst the lower ground is occupied by one-storey and two-storey low-rise houses. Two examples of the latter are shown here. The single-storey and one-and-a-half-storey L-type terrace houses on the east and west side were designed by Professor Spengelin, the two-storey terrace houses in the centre of the estate by Kindt. Construction: Brick walls (facing bricks alternating with rendered walls). Low-pitch timber roof with asbestos cement roofing. Type A: Gross floor area 87 or 101 sq. metres (930 or 1090 sq. ft.); floor space index 0.4–0.5. Type D: Gross floor area 102 sq. metres (1100 sq. ft.); floor space index 0.7.

Im Mittelpunkt der Siedlung auf einem langgestreckten Südhang liegt eine Schule, um die sich Wohnbauten verschiedener Höhe und Form zu lebendigen Gruppen zusammenfügen: Auf dem höher gelegenen Teil des Geländes stehen drei- und viergeschossige Mehrfamilienhäuser, vier- bis fünf- und neungeschossige Punkthäuser, auf dem unteren Teil ein- und zweigeschossige Flachbauten, von denen zwei Beispiele hier gezeigt werden. Die gereihten ein- und eineinhalb-geschossigen L-Typen im östlichen und westlichen Teil errichtete Professor Spengelin, die zweigeschossigen Reihenhäuser im mittleren Teil der Siedlung Dr. Kindt. Konstruktion: Ziegel-wände, wobei Sichtmauerwerk mit verputzten Teilen wechselt. Flach geneigte Dächer in Holzkonstruktion mit Welleternit. Bruttogeschoßfläche: Typ A 87 und 101 qm, GFZ 0,4–0,5; Typ D 102 qm, GFZ 0,7.

3. Plan, types D and E, 1 in 300 (Architect O. Kindt). The houses of one row are staggered. The kitchen, connected with a spacious dining area in the hall, is on the entrance side. The three bedrooms on the upper floor are separated by a cross corridor. The house at the end of the row is of a modified type E, facing south.

4. Plan and section type A, 1 in 300. Bedrooms and kitchen are on the entrance side. A noteworthy feature is the grouping of the rooms around a hall which serves as a play room but can also be used as a dining area and, like the third bedroom, faces the garden. The living room, at right angles, faces west. The modified type shown here differs from the basic type in that it contains a fourth bedroom or study adjacent to the living room. A disadvantage is the north position of two bedrooms.

5. Entrance side of type A house.

6. Private garden.

3. Grundriß Typ D und E 1:300 (Architekt O. Kindt). Die Häuser sind in der Reihe gegeneinander versetzt. Die Küche liegt in Verbindung mit einer großen Eßdiele auf der Eingangsseite. Die drei Schlafräume im Obergeschoß sind durch einen Querflur getrennt. Am Ende der Zeilen als Variante ein südgerichteter Endtyp E.

4. Grundriß und Schnitt des Typs A 1:300. Schlafräume und Küche liegen auf der Eingangsseite. Bemerkenswert ist die Gruppierung der Räume um einen Spielflur, der auch als Eßdiele benutzt werden kann und wie der dritte Schlafraum zum Gartenhof orientiert ist. Der abgewinkelte Wohnraum richtet sich nach Westen. Die hier gezeigte Variante unterscheidet sich vom Grundtyp durch den vierten, an den Wohnraum anschließenden Schlafraum bzw. Studio. Ein Nachteil ist die Nordlage von zwei Schlafräumen.

5. Zugangsseite des Typs A.

6. Blick in einen Gartenhof.

Saga estate, Hamburg-Lurup (1962)
Architects: Bernhard Hermkes and Gerhart Becker

Saga estate, Hamburg-Lurup (1962)
Architects: Bernhard Hermkes and Gerhart Becker

Saga-Siedlung, Hamburg-Lurup (1962)
Architekten: Bernhard Hermkes und Gerhart Becker

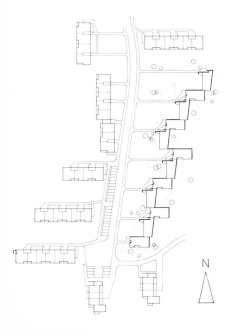

In a housing unit with approx. 1000 dwellings, forming part of a social housing programme, two types of houses are of the low-rise type. They form informally arranged rows placed in a large open space which is surrounded by blocks of flats with two, three or six storeys. The two slightly different types of low-rise houses are placed at right angles and staggered in relation to each other, one of them facing west, the other south, so that sufficient sunlight is ensured and congenial and secluded garden courts are created. Each house has hot water central heating and a ventilated creep cellar accessible from the boiler room. Construction: Concrete foundations and lime-brick walls with water-repelling external rendering; reinforced concrete floor, PVC floorings. Roof: wooden panels with boarding and 2'' thick ''Sürofa'' boards. Type 1: Gross floor area 92 sq. metres (990 sq. ft.); floor space index 0.3. Type 2: Gross floor area 98 sq. metres (1060 sq. ft.); floor space index 0.3.

Innerhalb einer Stadteinheit von rund 1000 Wohnungen, geplant im Rahmen des Sozialen Wohnungsbaues, wurden auch zwei Typen im Flachbau errichtet. Sie sind in gelockerten Zeilen in einen größeren Grünraum eingebettet, der durch zwei-, drei- und sechsgeschossige Mehrfamilienhäuser begrenzt wird. Die beiden geringfügig variiierten Flachbautypen sind rechtwinklig aneinandergestellt und jeweils gegeneinander versetzt. Dabei ist der eine Typ nach Westen und der zweite nach Süden orientiert, so daß ausreichende Besonnung und ruhige, abgeschlossene Wohnhöfe gewährleistet sind. Jedes Haus hat eine eigene Warmwasserheizung und einen vom Heizraum aus zugänglichen, belüfteten Kriechkeller. Konstruktion: Betonfundament, Kalksandsteinmauerwerk mit wasserabweisendem Außenputz, Stahlbetondecke, PVC-Bodenbeläge. Dach: Holzplatten mit Brettschalung. Bruttogeschoßfläche Typ 1: 92 qm, GFZ 0,3; Typ 2: 98 qm, GFZ 0,3.

1. Entrance side, seen from north.
2. Site plan, 1 in 3000.
3. South-east side.
4. Terrace and covered sitting place on the south-west side of a house.

1. Eingangsseite, von Norden gesehen.
2. Lageplan 1 : 3000.
3. Südostseite.
4. Terrasse und überdeckter Sitzplatz eines Hauses auf der Südwestseite.

5. Plans, 1 in 300. Through a canopied entrance, one enters a hall giving access to kitchen, living room, ancillary and storage rooms. The bedrooms, with bathroom, separate W. C. and cupboard room or an additional spare room, are accessible from the centrally placed living room so that the plan is particularly economic in corridor space. The plan of the bedroom wing is made flexible by placing a wooden sliding wall between the children's bedrooms. This wall can also be wholly removed.

5. Grundrisse 1 : 300. Durch einen überdeckten Eingang gelangt man zum Vorplatz, von dem aus Küche, Wohnraum sowie die Neben- und Abstellräume erschlossen werden. Die Schlafraumgruppe mit Bad, getrenntem WC und Schrankraum oder einem zusätzlichen Zimmer ist von dem zentral gelegenen Wohnraum aus zugänglich, wodurch die Aufschließungsflächen besonders sparsam bemessen werden konnten. Eine Holzschiebewand zwischen den Kinderzimmern macht den Grundriß im Schlafteil flexibel. Die Wand kann auch ganz entfernt werden.

This estate, built on a site of 130 acres at the fringe of London, is among the best examples of modern town planning in England. The beautiful parkland of the manor houses and villas previously occupying this site, which has a very high residential value, has been largely preserved. Groups of high and low buildings between the old trees are extremely skilfully adapted to the local topography. The requirements of the residents have been taken into account in many respects: 15 twelve-storey point blocks, 5 eleven-storey slab blocks, 1 ten-storey and 26 four-storey maisonette blocks, and finally, the low-rise houses shown here which comprise six rows of three-storey and 14 rows of two-storey terrace houses as well as 49 houses for old people. With a net density of 100 persons to the acre, the estate has accommodation for some 10,000 people. Type A: Gross floor area 112 sq. metres (1900 sq. ft.); floor space index 0.5. Type B: Gross floor area 132 sq. metres (1420 sq. ft.); floor space index 0.7. Type C: Gross floor area 48 sq. metres (520 sq. ft.), floor space index 0.4.

Die auf einem Gelände von 52 ha am Rande Londons errichtete Wohnstadt gehört zu den besten städtebaulichen Beispielen Englands. Die wundervollen Parks der früheren Herrschaftshäuser und Villen in diesem Gebiet mit hervorragendem Wohnwert wurden weitgehend geschont. Gruppen hoher und niedriger Bauten zwischen alten Bäumen passen sich geschickt der Topographie an. Den Wohnwünschen der Bewohner wird vielfältig Rechnung getragen: In 15 zwölfgeschossigen Punkthäusern, in 5 elfgeschossigen Scheibenhäusern, einem zehngeschossigen und 16 viergeschossigen Maisonetteblocks und schließlich im hier gezeigten Flachbau: in sechs dreigeschossigen und in 14 zweigeschossigen Zeilen sowie 49 ebenerdigen Wohnungen für alte Leute. Bei einer Dichte von 250 Einwohner/ha netto bietet die Siedlung rund 10000 Menschen Unterkunft. Typ A: Bruttogeschoßfläche 112 qm, GFZ 0,5. Typ B: Bruttogeschoßfläche 132 qm, GFZ 0,7. Typ C: Bruttogeschoßfläche 48 qm, GFZ 0,4.

1. Two rows of type C single-storey houses. Because of the irregular staggering, protected terraces are created on either side of the houses.

1. Zwei Zeilen des eingeschossigen Typs C. Durch die unregelmäßige Staffelung entstehen geschützte Sitzplätze vor oder hinter den Häusern.

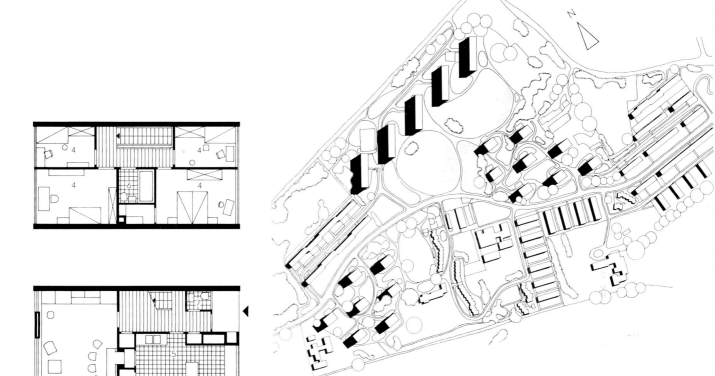

2. Plans, 1 in 200, of type A house. This house has a frontage of approx. 17 ft. and a depth of 36 ft. On the ground floor, the living room occupies the whole of the south or west side and opens on to a garden of over 500 sq. ft., terminated by a shed. A good solution is provided by the recessed entrance and the consequently small hall. Parallel to the latter are kitchen and dining room. On the upper floor are four bedrooms and centrally placed bathroom. This type of house is economic and, in common with the entire estate, of particularly high architectural and technical standard.
3. Site plan of Alton Estate (West), 1 in 7500.
4. One row of the two-storey type A house.

2. Grundrisse Typ A 1:200. Das Haus hat rund 5 m Frontbreite und 11 m Tiefe. Im Erdgeschoß nimmt der Wohnraum auf der Süd- oder Westseite die ganze Front ein und öffnet sich in einen rund 50 qm großen Gartenhof mit einem Abstellschuppen als Abschluß. Eine gute Lösung ist der zurückgesetzte Eingang und der hierdurch sparsame Flur. Parallel dazu liegen Küche und Eßraum. Das Obergeschoß enthält vier Schlafräume und ein innen liegendes Bad. Der Typ ist ökonomisch und wie die gesamte Siedlung architektonisch und technisch von besonderer Qualität.
3. Lageplan Alton West 1:7500.
4. Eine Zeile des zweigeschossigen Typs A.

5. Plan and section, 1 in 300, of type C house. In contrast to the rigid rows of terrace houses and the geometrical pattern of the other buildings, the two single-storey rows of houses for old people have been designed informally and in a particularly congenial way. The small dwellings have a frontage of 20 ft. and a depth of 26 ft. A sitting-out porch leads to a hall which contains, on one side, a small kitchen and, and on the other side, a bathroom and a storage room. The bed-sitting room occupies the entire width of the house.

6. The rows of terrace houses have been placed deliberately and in highly diversified layouts between the existing trees of the old park.

7. Plan, 1 in 200, of type B house. Type B is a three-storey terrace house with narrow frontage (approx. 13 ft.) and great depth (36 ft.). With its centrally placed two-flight stairs, the house is in principle reminiscent of the terrace houses designed by Amis and Howell. From the entrance, one enters a hall giving access to W.C., storage rooms, stairs, and a spacious dining kitchen. The west side of the first floor is occupied by a living room, the east side by a bedroom. On the second floor are two further bedrooms with built-in cupboards, and a bathroom.

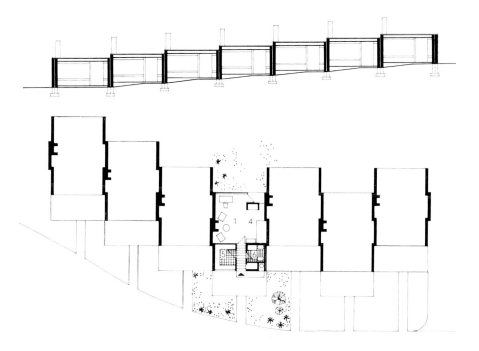

5. Grundriß und Schnitt Typ C 1:300. Im Gegensatz zu den strengen Zeilen und geometrischen Rastern der übrigen Bauten sind die beiden eingeschossigen Reihen der Wohnungen für alte Leute bewegt und besonders liebenswürdig gestaltet. Die kleinen Häuser haben eine Frontbreite von 6 m und eine Tiefe von 8 m. Über einen gepflasterten Vorplatz gelangt man in einen Flur, der auf der einen Seite eine kleine Küche, auf der anderen das Bad und einen Abstellraum enthält. Der Wohnraum nimmt die ganze Breite des Hauses ein.

6. Die stark gegliederten Zeilen wurden überlegt zwischen die vorhandenen alten Parkbäume gesetzt.

7. Grundriß 1:200. Typ B ist ein dreigeschossiges Einfamilienreihenhaus mit schmaler Front (rund 4 m) und großer Tiefe (11 m). Es ähnelt mit seiner im Kern gelegenen doppelläufigen Treppe im Prinzip den von Amis und Howell gestalteten Reihenhäusern. Vom Eingang gelangt man in einen Flur, an dem WC, Vorratsräume, Treppe und eine geräumige Eßküche liegen. Das erste Obergeschoß enthält auf der Westseite einen Wohnraum, auf der Ostseite einen Schlafraum. Im zweiten Obergeschoß befinden sich zwei weitere Schlafräume mit Einbauschränken und das Bad.

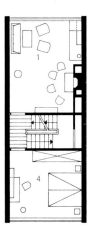

Demonstration housing projects at Wolfsburg and Hanover (1963/64)
Planning: "Niedersächsische Heimstätte"; Architects: Dellemann, Günschel

Demonstrativbauvorhaben in Wolfsburg und Hannover (1963/64)
Planung: Niedersächsische Heimstätte; Architekten: Dellemann, Günschel

The demonstration housing projects sponsored by the German authorities are primarily intended to promote family housing and house ownership. The Wolfsburg-Detmerode estate is part of major building project which provides for the construction of 3800 dwelling units within the next years. The first phase of the programme includes 85 houses, the second 130. Apart from medium-high and multi-storey buildings, the project includes single-storey and two-storey chain type houses, single-storey terrace houses, and patio houses. In the case of the terrace houses, the privacy of each unit is ensured by the projection of the living room into the garden. The position of the Hanover-Marienwerder estate in the middle of an old copse near the river Leine provides all the conditions for healthy housing. The development plan envisages three characteristic types of houses, viz. a carpet-like tissue of low-rise houses, three-storey blocks of flats, and eight-storey blocks with flatlets. The low-rise housing programme comprises 114 terrace houses in groups of three to nine units including a one-and-a-half storey-type, and two single-storey types. Construction: the outer walls are of 36½ cm (14.3/8'') thick red bricks without rendering. Floors and roof are of reinforced concrete with vapourproof thermal insulation consisting of glass foam panels. Floor coverings are of linoleum or plastic on floating floors or cork bricks. Double-pane windows and insulation type glazing. Heating: partly by gas. Type A: Gross floor area 136 sq. metres (1460 sq. ft.); floor space index 0.4–0.6. Type B: 135 sq. metres (1450 sq. ft.); floor space index 0.5. Type C: 130 sq. metres (1400 sq. ft.), floor space index 0.4. Type D: 138 sq. metres (1490 sq. ft.); floor space index 0.8. Type E: 133 sq. metres (1440 sq. ft.), floor space index 0.6. Type F: 157 sq. metres (1680 sq. ft.), floor space index 0.7.

Im Rahmen eines Demonstrativprogrammes werden in erster Linie Familieneigenheime und Eigentumswohnungen gefördert. Die Siedlung Wolfsburg-Detmerode ist der Beginn eines Bauvorhabens, das im Laufe der nächsten Jahre die Errichtung von 3800 Wohnungen vorsieht. Im ersten Abschnitt werden 85 Eigenheime, im zweiten 130 gebaut. Außer Mittel- und Hochbau gibt es ein- bis zweigeschossige Kettenhäuser, eingeschossige Reihenhäuser und Atriumhäuser. Bei den Reihenhäusern schirmt der in den Gartenteil vorspringende Wohnraum jede Einheit gegen den Nachbarn ab.
Die Lage der Siedlung Hannover-Marienwerder inmitten eines alten Waldbestandes nahe der Leineniederung bietet alle Voraussetzungen für ein gesundes Wohnen. Der Bebauungsplan sieht drei Haustypen in der ihnen eigentümlichen Form vor: das teppichartige Gewebe der Einfamilienhäuser, dreigeschossige Häuser mit Familienwohnungen und achtgeschossige mit Kleinwohnungen. Der flach gebaute Teil enthält 114 Einfamilienreihenhäuser in Gruppen von drei bis neun Einheiten eines eineinhalbgeschossigen Typs und zwei eingeschossiger Typen. Konstruktion: Die unverputzten Außenwände bestehen aus 36,5 cm starkem Ziegelmauerwerk. Für Decken und Dach wurde Stahlbeton mit diffusionsdichter Wärmeisolierung durch Glasschaumplatten verwendet. Die Böden haben Linoleum oder Kunststoffbelag auf Estrich oder Korkplatten. Verbundfenster und Isolierungsverglasung. Heizung: zum Teil Gasthermenheizung. Bruttogeschoßfläche: Typ A 136 qm, GFZ 0,4–0,6; Typ B 135 qm, GFZ 0,5; Typ C 130 qm, GFZ 0,4; Typ D 138 qm, GFZ 0,8; Typ E 133 qm, GFZ 0,6; Typ F 157 qm, GFZ 0,7.

1. Model photograph, type A. Garden side.

1. Modellphoto Typ A, Gartenseite.

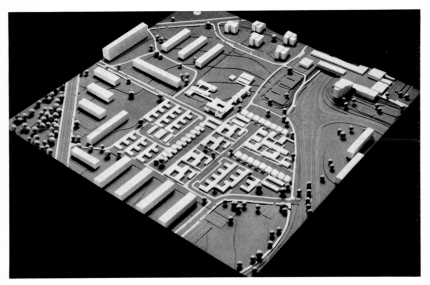

2. Model photograph of the Wolfsburg-Detmerode project. View from north-west.

3. Site plan, Wolfsburg-Detmerode, 1 in 3000.

4. Plan and section, type A house, 1 in 300. The approx. 11.2 metres (37 ft.) wide chain house comprises a two-storey and a single-storey part which are staggered in level by half-a-storey height. This plan results in lively space effects. It is particularly suited for a duplex house with separate entrance for retired parents or for lodgers.

2. Modellphoto des Bauvorhabens Wolfsburg-Detmerode. Blick aus Nordwest.

3. Lageplan Wolfsburg-Detmerode 1:3000.

4. Grundriß und Schnitt Typ A 1:300. Das 11,20 m breite Kettenhaus enthält einen zwei- und einen eingeschossigen Teil, die um ein halbes Geschoß gegeneinander versetzt sind. Der Grundriß ergibt lebendige räumliche Wirkungen. Er ist besonders für ein Duplex-Haus mit eigenem Eingang für den Altenteil oder Einliegerfamilie geeignet.

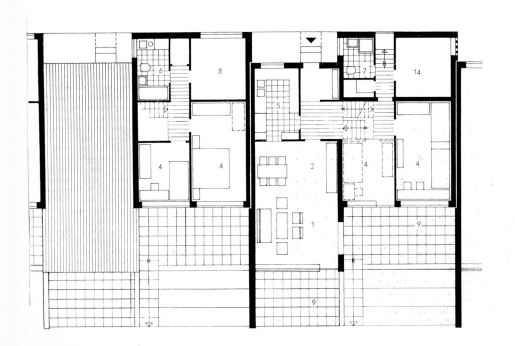

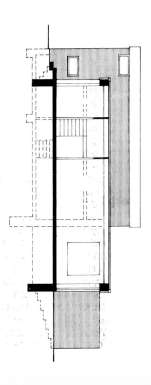

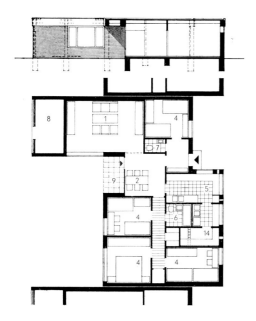

5. Plan and section, type B house, 1 in 300. The single-storey chain-type house has a frontage of nearly 50 ft. The entrance leads to a hall which is used as dining room and is extended by a covered terrace. This plan, too, is well thought out and very economic.

6. Model photograph, type B.

7. Plan and section, type C house, 1 in 300. Type C represents the I-type of a patio house, covering an area of approx. 54×26 ft. with a patio of approx. 33×46 ft. and an additional covered terrace. There is ample ancillary space. This plan, too, shows new ideas.

8. Model photograph, type C.

5. Grundriß und Schnitt Typ B 1:300. Das ebenerdige Reihenhaus hat 15 m Frontbreite. Vom Eingang gelangt man in eine Eßdiele, die durch einen überdeckten Sitzplatz erweitert ist. Auch dieser Grundriß ist in seinen Funktionen gut durchdacht und sehr ökonomisch.

6. Modellphoto Typ B.

7. Grundriß und Schnitt Typ C 1:300. Typ C stellt den I-Typ eines Hofhauses dar, mit einer Grundfläche von rund 16,5×7,9 m, einem Atrium von rund 10x14 m und einem zusätzlichen überdeckten Freisitz. Für reichlich Nebenraum ist gesorgt. Auch diese Anordnung zeigt neue Gedanken.

8. Modellphoto Typ C.

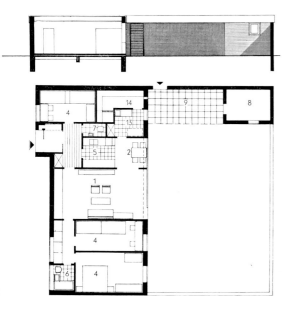

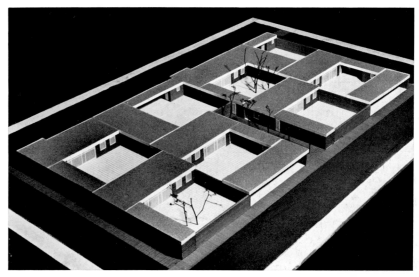

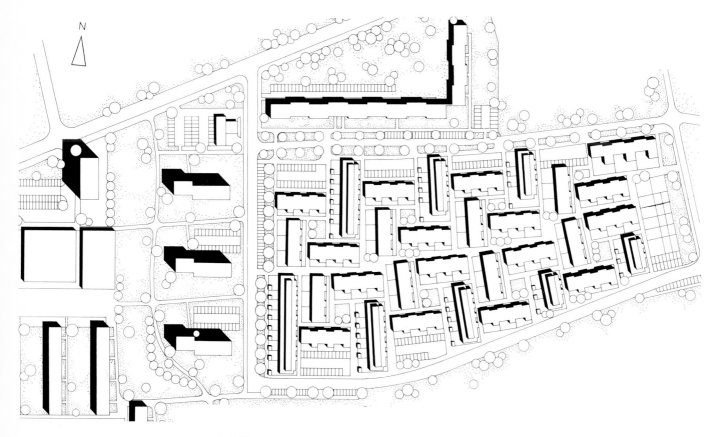

9. Part of site plan, Hanover-Marienwerder, 1 in 3000.

9. Lageplan Marienwerder 1 : 3000. Ausschnitt.

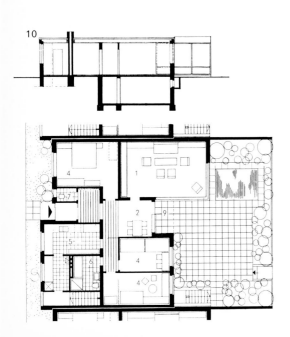

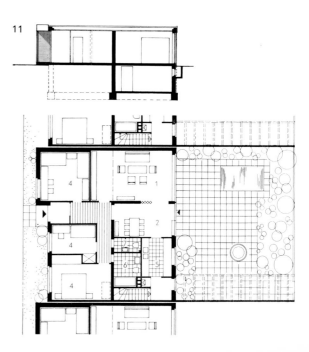

10. Plan and section, type F, 1 in 300. Type F may be regarded as an L-type house. This house is approximately 44 ft. wide and 33 ft. deep and contains a bedroom, kitchen and ancillary rooms on the entrance side, and two bedrooms on the garden side. The dining area serves as linking passage whilst the living room projects into the garden, thus screening the latter (which covers approx. 1000 sq. ft.) against view from outside.

11. Plan and section, type E, 1 in 300. The plan of type E, 11.4×12 metres (37½×39½ ft.), is nearly square. On the entrance side are three bedrooms; on the garden side, facing the approx. 1300 sq. ft. garden, are living room, dining room and kitchen. A clear and economic solution.

13. Plan and section, type D, 1 in 300. The approx. 26 ft. wide one-and-a-half-storey type has a depth of approx. 42 ft. Two bedrooms are placed on the entrance side whilst kitchen, dining area and living room face the garden court which covers an area of 100 to 120 sq. metres (1080 to 1280 sq. ft.). Stairs and spare rooms are placed in the centre. The upper floor contains two bedrooms and a bathroom. The type shows some variations in floor area utilisation inasmuch as the corners are designed in several different ways.

10. Grundriß und Schnitt Typ F 1:300. Typ F kann man als L-Typ bezeichnen. Bei dem rund 13,4 m breiten und rund 10 m tiefen Haus liegen ein Schlafraum, Küche und Nebenräume auf der Eingangsseite und zwei Schlafräume zum Garten hin. Der Eßplatz ist Verbindungsglied und Durchgang, während der Wohnraum in den Gartenraum vorspringt und damit den Gartenhof von rund 100 qm gegen Nachbarn abschirmt.

11. Grundriß und Schnitt Typ E 1:300. Typ E hat mit 11,4×12 m einen fast quadratischen Grundriß. Auf der Eingangsseite liegen drei Schlafräume, auf der Gartenseite an einem rund 120 qm großen Gartenhof Wohn- und Eßraum und Küche. – Eine klare und sparsame Lösung!

13. Grundriß und Schnitt Typ D 1:300. Der rund 8 m breite eineinhalbgeschossige Typ hat eine Tiefe von rund 13 m. Zwei Schlafräume liegen auf der Eingangsseite; Küche, Eßplatz und Wohnraum öffnen sich gegen den 100–120 qm großen Gartenhof. Im Hausinnern befinden sich Treppe und Nebenräume. Das Obergeschoß enthält zwei Schlafräume und das Bad. Der Typ variiert in der Wohnfläche, indem er die Möglichkeiten der Eckausbildungen nutzt.

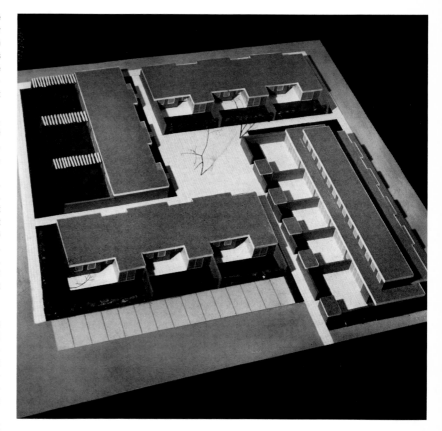

12. Marienwerder. Models of the three types.

12. Marienwerder. Die drei Typen im Modell.

13

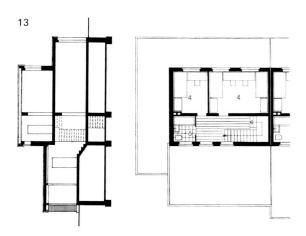

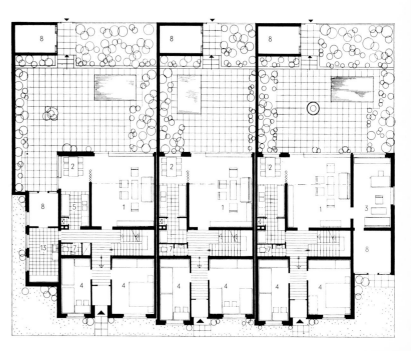

103

**"In den Gartenhöfen" and "Im Pfeiffengarten" housing schemes,
Reinach near Basle (1959/60 and 1961)**
Architects: Ulrich Löw and Theodor Manz; Landscape gardening: Wolf Hunziker and
Meinrad Löw

1. Patio seen from the garden. If desired, the open fourth side of the patio can be screened by shrubs, blinds or, as in this case, by a curtain.
2. "In den Gartenhöfen." View from the east.
3. Model photograph of "Im Pfeiffengarten" scheme, seen from south-west. A feature common to both projects is a centre with market square, shopping parade, children's playground and garage buildings.
4. Site plan of "In den Gartenhöfen" scheme, 1 in 3000.

The two estates of patio houses in the vicinity of Basle were erected in rapid succession by the same architects, partly making use of the same house type. The first-named scheme comprises, on an area of 1.32 hectare (3.25 acres), 30 patio houses of the four-and-a-half room type. The second scheme, with approx. 50 dwelling units, additionally comprises a three-room type for single persons and childless couples as well as a six-and-a-half room type for larger families. In the centre are two two-storey blocks of flats. Owing to the understanding attitude of the cantonal and local authorities, bye-laws were relaxed to permit very economic access facilities with paths of no more than 1 metre (3'3") width. The smallest plot size is 244 sq. metres (2610 sq. ft.), the largest (at the corner) 473 sq. metres (5100 sq. ft.). The plots are, to a great extent, screened by hedges. Ancillary rooms and kitchen are on the north side, facing the path. Cellars extend under approx. one-half of the house. Coke or oil fired central heating is provided. The architects have deliberately adhered to the use of well-tried materials in order to keep the design as simple as possible. Foundations, basements, the low garden walls and the floors above the basements are of concrete or reinforced concrete. The ground floor outer walls are of the sandwich type, consisting of 12 cm (4³/₄") facing brick, 2 cm (³/₄") rockwool sheets, and 10 cm (4") insulating brick, except for the outer walls of the bedrooms which, like the roofs, are of timber. The roofing is of the three-layer built-up type, forming a level trough with central drainage. Gross floor areas of the three types: 6½ rooms 144 sq. metres (1540 sq. ft.), floor space index 0.4; 4½ rooms 115 sq. metres (1230 sq. ft.), floor space index 0.4; 3 rooms 94 sq. metres (1010 sq. ft.), floor space index 0.5.

**Siedlungen »In den Gartenhöfen« und »Im Pfeiffengarten«, Reinach bei Basel
(1959/60 und 1961)**
Architekten: Ulrich Löw und Theodor Manz; Gartenarchitekten: Wolf Hunziker und Meinrad Löw

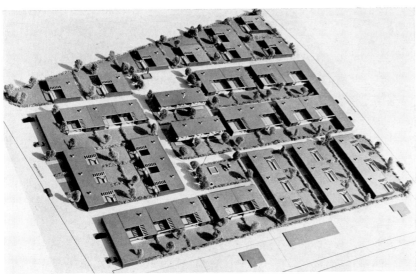

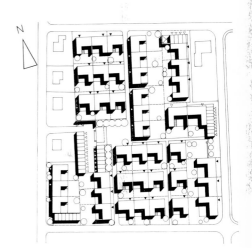

Die Architekten errichteten in der Nähe von Basel zwei Siedlungen mit Atriumhäusern unmittelbar nacheinander und teilweise unter Verwendung des gleichen Typs. Die erste Siedlung enthält auf 1,32 ha 30 Atriumhäuser des Viereinhalbzimmertyps. Bei der zweiten Siedlung mit rund 50 Wohneinheiten wurden zusätzlich ein Dreizimmertyp für Ledige und kinderlose Ehepaare sowie ein Sechseinhalbzimmertyp für größere Familien erstellt. Im Zentrum stehen zwei zweigeschossige Mehrfamilienhäuser. Mit Hilfe der einsichtsvollen Kanton- und Gemeindebehörden konnte das sparsame Aufschließungssystem mittels nur einen Meter breiter Wohnwege entgegen den gesetzlichen Bestimmungen durchgesetzt werden. Die kleinsten Parzellen umfassen 244 qm, die größte (Eck-)Parzelle 473 qm. Die einzelnen Grundstücke sind durch Hecken weitgehend gegeneinander abgeschirmt. Die nach Norden liegenden Nebenräume und die Küche sind dem Wohnweg zugewandt. Die Häuser sind etwa zur Hälfte unterkellert. Zentrale Koks- bzw. Ölheizung ist vorgesehen. Von den Architekten wurde die Konstruktion unter Verwendung bewährter Baustoffe so einfach wie möglich gehalten. Fundamente, Keller, Gartensitzmauern und Kellerdecken bestehen aus Beton bzw. Stahlbeton. Die Umfassungswände im Erdgeschoß bilden ein Zweischalenmauerwerk, bestehend aus 12-cm-Sichtbackstein, 2-cm-Steinwollplatten und 10-cm-Isolierbackstein, während die Außenwände des Schlafteils sowie die Dächer in Holz konstruiert wurden. Als Dachhaut dient ein dreilagiges Kiesklebedach, das als gefällelose Wanne mit innerem Ablauf ausgebildet wurde. Bruttogeschoßfläche der drei Typen: sechseinhalb Zimmer 144 qm, GFZ 0,4; viereinhalb Zimmer 115 qm, GFZ 0,4; drei Zimmer 94 qm, GFZ 0,5.

1. Blick vom Garten in einen Atriumhof. Je nach Bedarf kann die vierte offene Seite des Atriums durch Bepflanzung, Lamellen oder – wie in diesem Fall – durch einen Vorhang geschlossen werden.
2. »In den Gartenhöfen«. Ansicht von Osten.
3. Modellphoto »Im Pfeiffengarten« aus Südwesten. Beiden Siedlungen gemeinsam ist ein ausgeprägter Mittelpunkt mit Dorfplatz, Läden, Kinderspielplatz und Sammelgarage.
4. Lageplan 1:3000 »In den Gartenhöfen«.

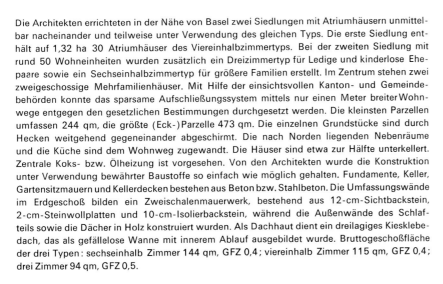

5–7. "In den Gartenhöfen."
5. View from the east. In the background is the shopping parade.
6. View along the northern access road.
7. Patio with pool of water. With all three house types, the living and bedrooms have an east, south or west orientation, facing a paved garden court of some 320 to 430 sq. ft.
8–10. Through a recessed entrance, one enters a hall from which a corridor leads to the bedrooms. This corridor, with side entrance, cupboard walls and working area, represents a particularly well thought out feature of an otherwise conventional type of house.
8. Plan, 1 in 300, of the four-and-a-half room type at "In den Gartenhöfen."
9, 10. Plans at "Im Pfeiffengarten," 1 in 300, three room and six-and-a-half room types.
11. Living room. The open fireplace separates the dining area from the sitting room proper.

5–7. »In den Gartenhöfen«.
5. Blick von Osten. Im Hintergrund das Ladengebäude.
6. Blick durch die nördliche Wohnstraße.
7. Atriumhof mit Wasserbecken. Bei allen drei Typen öffnen sich die Wohn- und Schlafräume nach Osten, Süden oder Westen zu einem gepflasterten Gartenhof von 30 bis 40 qm Größe.
8–10. Über eine Eingangsnische erfolgt der Zugang zur Diele mit anschließendem Flur zu den Schlafräumen. Eine besonders sorgfältige Durcharbeitung des an sich konventionellen Typs ist der Flur des Schlafteiles mit dem Wirtschaftseingang, Schrankteil und Arbeitsplatz.
8. Grundriß 1:300 des Viereinhalbzimmertyps »In den Gartenhöfen«.
9, 10. Grundrisse »Im Pfeiffengarten« 1:300. Dreizimmer- und Sechseinhalbzimmertyp.
11. Wohnraum mit offenem Kamin als Trennung von Eßplatz und Wohnraum.

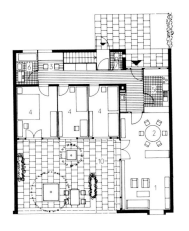
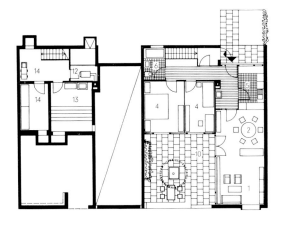
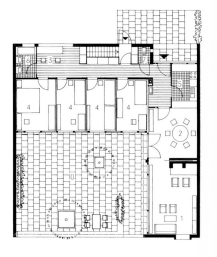

Patio houses at Bellevue Bay, Klampenborg, Gentofte, Denmark (1960/61)
Architect: Arne Jacobsen

Atriumhäuser Bellevue Bugt in Klampenborg, Gentofte, Dänemark (1960/61)
Architekt: Arne Jacobsen

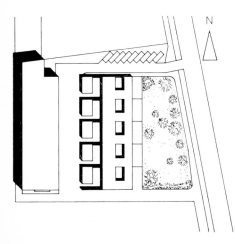

A group of five houses with fully enclosed patios was erected, in 1960/61, together with a four-storey block of luxury flats. In this case, the combination of low-rise and medium-rise housing has been successful as the disadvantages, especially the lack of privacy in the patios, are mitigated by the intermediate garage building. The U-shaped patio with an inner and outer garden represents a slight variation of the patio houses designed by Jacobsen for the Hansa District, Berlin, in 1957. At Klampenborg, a second courtyard was created by the garages. An interesting feature is the combination of facing bricks with the asbestos cement fascia boards, resulting in an aesthetic and tidy appearance of the roof. Gross floor area 145 sq. metres (1560 sq. ft.), floor space index 5.5.

Eine Gruppe von fünf Häusern mit geschlossenen Atrien wurde 1960/61 zusammen mit einem viergeschossigen Block Luxuswohnungen errichtet. Die Kombination von Flachbau und mittelhohem Bau ist in diesem Fall gut gelungen, wobei die Nachteile, vor allem der Einblick in die Wohnhöfe, durch den zwischengeschalteten Garagenstreifen erschwert wird. Der U-förmige Atriumtyp mit einem Innen- und einem Außengarten stellt eine geringe Variation jener Hofhäuser dar, die Jacobsen 1957 im Hansaviertel in Berlin baute. In Klampenborg entstand ein zweiter Innenhof durch die vorgelagerten Garagen. Interessant ist die Kombination von Sichtmauerwerk mit Eternitschürzen des Dachgesimses, durch die eine ästhetische und saubere Dachaufsicht erreicht wird. Bruttogeschoßfläche 145 qm, GFZ 5,5.

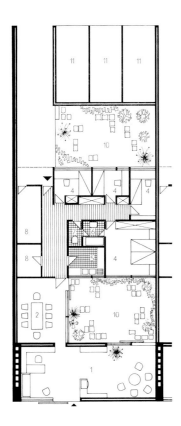

1. Patio houses seen from north-east. Storey-high window units permit an unobstructed sea view from the living room. In the background, the four-storey block of flats.
2. Site plan, 1 in 2000.
3. Plan, 1 in 300. The western part of the building, with entrance and a spacious storage room, contains the kitchen and all the bedrooms. The eastern part forms the living room which also opens westwards towards the patio whilst the dining room serves as a link between the two parts. Despite this clearly conceived plan, the access by the side of the garages is problematic; so is the placing of all the children's bedrooms on the west side.
4. Patio.
5. Garages and patio, seen from the four-storey block of flats.

1. Die Atriumhäuser von Nordosten. Raumhohe Fensterelemente geben den Blick vom Wohnraum auf das Meer frei. Im Hintergrund der viergeschossige Wohnblock.
2. Lageplan 1 : 2000.
3. Grundriß 1 : 300. Der nach Westen gelegene Bautrakt mit Eingang und geräumigem Abstellraum enthält die Küche und alle Schlafräume. Der nach Osten gelegene Trakt bildet den Wohnraum, der sich auch nach Westen in das Atrium öffnet, während der Speiseraum das Zwischenglied beider Baukörper ist. Trotz dieser klar durchdachten Konzeption ist der Zugang neben den Garagen problematisch, ebenso die Lage aller Kinderschlafräume nach Westen.
4. Blick in einen Innenhof, der mit sparsamen Mitteln sorgfältig gärtnerisch gestaltet ist.
5. Blick vom viergeschossigen Wohnblock auf Garagen und Innenhof.

Patio house shown at the Brussels World Exhibition (1958)
Architect: Eduard Ludwig; Landscape gardening: Walter Rossow

Haus mit Wohnhof auf der Weltausstellung in Brüssel (1958)
Architekt: Eduard Ludwig; Gartenarchitekt: Walter Rossow

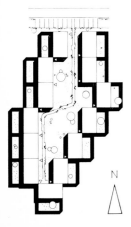

The architect responsible for this particularly carefully conceived patio house was the late Eduard Ludwig. It was erected on the ground of the German Pavilon and designed as a bungalow or terrace house for a household of two persons. A 6½ ft. high wall of bright yellow facing bricks encloses bungalow and patio in a kind of "angular spiral." On the three other sides, a continuous ribbon of high-level windows provides access for light and air, permitting a room height of 2.35 metres (7′9″). The flat roof, consisting of a reinforced concrete slab, is supported by tubular units of steel. Gross floor area 59 sq. metres (630 sq. ft.), floor space index 0.4.

Dieses besonders sorgfältig durchgeplante Atriumhaus verdanken wir dem verstorbenen Architekten Eduard Ludwig. Es wurde auf dem Gelände des deutschen Pavillons errichtet und als ebenerdiges, reihungsfähiges Hofhaus für einen Zweipersonenhaushalt entworfen. Eine zwei Meter hohe unverputzte Mauer aus hellgelbem Klinker umschließt Wohnung und Wohnhof in einer Art »rechteckigen Spirale«. An den drei übrigen Seiten gibt ein umlaufendes Fensterband Licht und Luft und erlaubt eine lichte Raumhöhe von 2,35 m. Das Flachdach – eine Stahlbetonplatte – wird von Gußstahlrohren getragen. Bruttogeschoßfläche 59 qm, GFZ 0,4.

1. Bedroom, with the patio in the background.
2. Site plan, 1 in 2000. The plan shows how the bungalows can be linked.
3. Section and plan, 1 in 300. One-third of the patio, which covers an area of 106 sq. metres (1140 sq. ft.), is taken up by a paved terrace, the remaining two-thirds being lawn. Kitchen and bathroom are placed in the centre of the bungalow, sharing a wall with the plumbing installations. Living room and bedroom are separated by sliding doors from kitchen and corridor.
4. Entrance side.
5. The south side, facing the garden is all glazed.
6. Living room, with the continuous ribbon of windows.

1. Der Schlafraum mit Blick in den Wohnhof.
2. Lageplan 1:2000. Der Lageplan zeigt die Reihungsmöglichkeit des Atriumhauses.
3. Schnitt und Grundriß 1:300. Der 106 qm große Wohnhof ist in ein Drittel plattenbelegte Terrasse und zwei Drittel Rasenfläche unterteilt. Küche und Bad sind im Mittelpunkt des Hauses an eine gemeinsame Installationswand angeschlossen. Wohnraum und Schlafraum werden durch Schiebetüren von Küche und Flur getrennt.
4. Eingangsseite.
5. Die Gartenhoffront ist an der Südseite ganz verglast.
6. Der Wohnraum mit dem umlaufenden Fensterband.

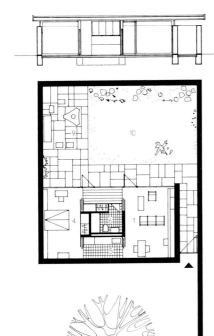

Five bungalows in the Hansa District, Berlin (1957)

Architect: Eduard Ludwig

Fünf Einfamilienhäuser im Hansa-Viertel, Berlin (1957)

Architekt: Eduard Ludwig

The so-called "Ring Project," one of the numerous town planning solutions proposed for the resurrection of the Hansa District in Berlin, provided for more than 50 per cent of the residents to live in low-rise houses. Of this and other projects, no more than a few came to pass. Among them were the interesting experimental houses designed by Eduard Ludwig. Room and patio layouts of the five bungalows are adapted to the requirements of families of different sizes. Apart from the patio, each house has a small utility courtyard (which also serves as entrance), a garage and a hobby room. There are no basements. Heating is by storage units built into the walls beneath windows which are heated overnight by cheap electric current. Particularly praiseworthy is the modesty and human scale of this group of prototype houses where nothing can be seen from the road except a few walls and flowers whilst the interior provides the calm privacy needed by an urban family to compensate for the continuous "contacts" and ever changing impressions associated with life in a great city. The patio has a size of approx. 150 sq. metres (1610 sq. ft.). Type A: Gross floor area 119 sq. metres (1280 sq. ft.), floor space index 0.3. Type B: Gross floor area 148 sq. metres (1590 sq. ft.), floor space index 0.4. Type C: Gross floor area 158 sq. metres (1700 sq. ft.), floor space index 0.5. Type D: Gross floor area 124 sq. metres (1330 sq. ft.), floor space index 0.3.

Das »Ringprojekt«, eine unter den zahlreichen städtebaulichen Lösungen für das Hansa-Viertel, sah für mehr als 50% der Einwohner urbanen Flachbau vor. Von diesen und anderen Vorschlägen wurde nur ein kleiner Rest verwirklicht. Darunter auch die interessanten Versuchsbauten von Eduard Ludwig. Die fünf eingeschossigen Hofhäuser sind in der Raumkombination und Freiraumgestaltung den jeweiligen Bedürfnissen unterschiedlich großer Familien angepaßt. Außer dem Wohnhof hat jedes Haus einen kleinen Wirtschaftshof, der gleichzeitig den Eingang bildet, eine Garage und einen Bastelraum. Die Häuser sind nicht unterkellert. Sie werden durch Nachtstromspeicheröfen beheizt, die in die Fensterbrüstungen eingebaut sind. Ganz besonders hervorgehoben werden soll die bescheidene und humane Haltung dieser Musterhausgruppe, bei der an der Wohnstraße nur ein paar Wände und Blumen sichtbar werden, im Innern aber jene Ruhe einer privaten Sphäre erreicht wird, die eine Großstadtfamilie als Gegensatz zu ständigen »Kontakten« im Beruf und ununterbrochen wechselnden Eindrücken benötigt. Wohnhof: Größe rund 150 qm. Typ A: Bruttogeschoßfläche 119 qm, GFZ 0,3. Typ B: Bruttogeschoßfläche 148 qm, GFZ 0,4. Typ C: Bruttogeschoßfläche 158 qm, GFZ 0,5. Typ D: Bruttogeschoßfläche 124 qm, GFZ 0,3.

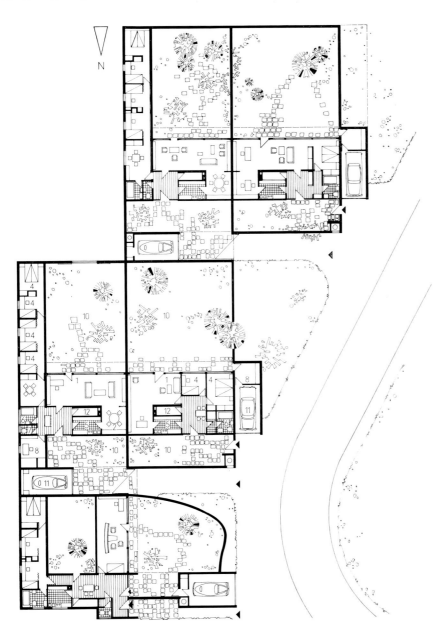

1. General view from north-west. The different patios are enclosed by storey-high walls of corrugated asbestos cement boards.

2. Plan, 1 in 400. Because of the staggering of the entrances along a curve of the road, the plots in the rear are hardly noticeable. Compared with the generous design of the group of buildings as a whole, the bedrooms with their bunk-like arrangement seem to be rather small. But the access to the last bedroom directly from the patio does not appear to be a drawback. By comparison, the unit formed by living room, kitchen and dining recess, skilfully integrated yet with effective functional segregation, conveys an impression of spaciousness. This impression is reinforced by the complete glazing of the side facing the patio.

3. Livingroom, with the patio in the background.

4. Entrance and garage drive.

1. Gesamtansicht aus Nordwest. Raumhohe Spundwände aus profilierten Asbestzementplatten begrenzen die einzelnen Wohnhöfe.

2. Grundriß 1:400. Durch die Staffelung der Eingänge an einer Straßenkurve wird die Hintereinanderschaltung der Grundstücke kaum spürbar. Gegenüber der großzügigen Planung der ganzen Anlage sind die Schlafräume in ihrer kojenartigen Anordnung etwas zu sparsam bemessen. Der Zugang zum letzten Schlafraum unmittelbar über den Wohnhof erscheint jedoch nicht als Mangel. Um so großräumiger wirkt in ihrem Ineinanderfließen, bei guter funktioneller Trennung, die Gruppe Wohnraum-Küche-Eßnische. Dieser Eindruck wird durch eine Ganzverglasung der den Wohnhöfen zugekehrten Seite verstärkt.

3. Blick aus dem Wohnraum in den Wohnhof.

4. Eingang und Garagenzufahrt.

Kingö near Elsinore and Bakke draget, Fredensborg, housing schemes (1958/59, 1963)
Architect: Jörn Utzon

Siedlungen Kingö bei Helsingör und Bakke draget in Fredensborg (1958/59 und 1963)
Architekt: Jörn Utzon

The Kingö housing scheme comprises 63 patio houses which, on undulating ground, are combined in three groups so as to enclose garden courts or lawns of different size and shape. The focus of the estate is a pond at the bottom of a meadow.

A very similar picture is provided by the Bakkedraget housing scheme near Fredensborg which is designed for Danish citizens who have returned from long residence abroad. The centre of this estate is a clubhouse where the residents, mainly elderly couples, take their main meals. The congenial atmosphere is created by a successful mixture of Danish dwelling culture with well-nigh Japanese austerity. An attractive feature is the deliberate renunciation of technical perfection, reflected, e.g. in the use of raw ceiling boards, unconcealed rainwater drainage along channels, bright brick walls. Gross floor area 98 and 102 sq. metres (1060 and 1090 sq. ft.), floor space index 0.5.

Die Hofhaussiedlung Kingö umfaßt 63 Einfamilienhäuser, die auf einem stark bewegten Gelände in drei Gruppen so untergliedert wurden, daß sie Höfe oder Rasenflächen unterschiedlicher Größe und Form umschließen. Schwerpunkt der Anlage ist der in einer Wiesenmulde gelegene Teich.

Fast das gleiche Bild bietet die für heimgekehrte Auslandsdänen errichtete Siedlung Bakke draget bei Fredensborg. Hier bildet den Mittelpunkt der Anlage ein Klubhaus, in dem die Bewohner der Siedlung, vorwiegend ältere Ehepaare, ihre Hauptmahlzeiten einnehmen. Die wohnliche Atmosphäre entsteht aus der gelungenen Mischung dänischer Wohnkultur mit fast japanischer Schlichtheit. Sympathisch ist der Verzicht auf technische Perfektion: ungehobelte Bretter für die Deckenuntersicht, an Ketten ablaufendes Regenwasser und helle Backsteinmauern. Bruttogeschoßfläche 98 und 102 qm, GFZ 0,5.

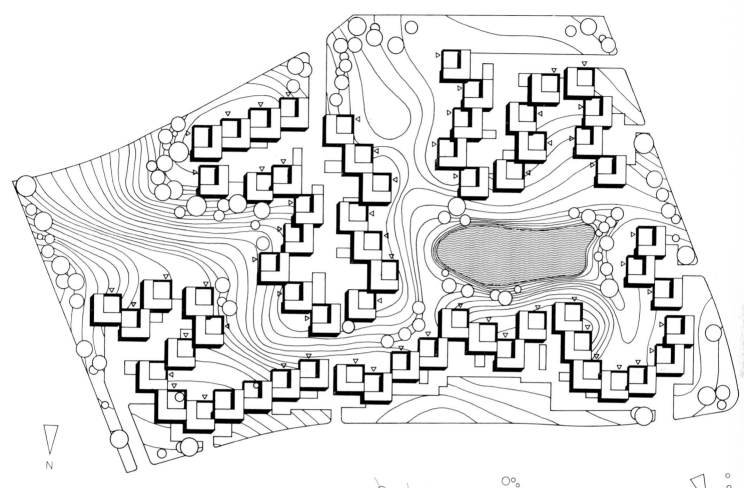

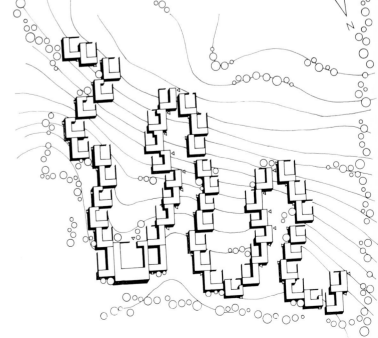

1. View of one of the rows of houses. The estate is organically integrated with the landscape.
2. Site plan of Kingö housing estate, 1 in 2000.
3. Site plan of Bakke draget housing estate, 1 in 3000.

1. Ansicht einer der Hauszeilen. Die Siedlung fügt sich organisch in die Landschaft.
2. Lageplan Kingö 1 : 2000.
3. Lageplan Bakke draget 1 : 3000.

4

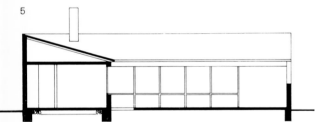

5

4, 6–8. The relatively small openings, the walled courtyards and the skilful adaptation of the houses to the undulating ground create a distinctly plastic effect. By using the same material (yellow bricks) for walls, roofs and the paving of the terraces, the architect has achieved a strong effect of homogeneity which is accentuated by the contrast with the exact concrete lintels above doors and windows.

4, 6–8. Sparsame Öffnungen und die Umschließung der Höfe mit Mauern bewirken bei geschickter Ausnutzung des bewegten Geländes eine stark plastische Erscheinung. Die Verwendung des gleichen Materials, gelbe Ziegel für Wände, Dächer und den Bodenbelag der Sitzplätze, läßt eine starke einheitliche Wirkung entstehen, die durch den Kontrast exakter Betonstürze über den Öffnungen gesteigert wird.

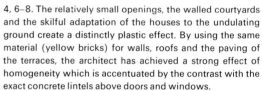

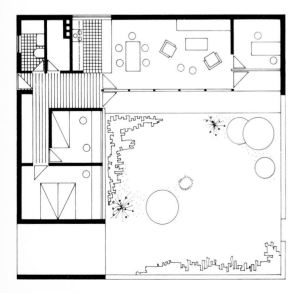

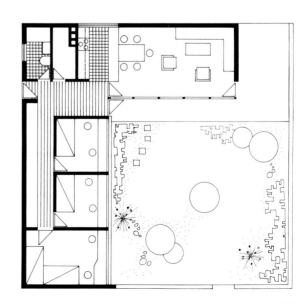

6

7

8

5. Plans and section, 1 in 200. The architect makes use of two L-type plans of almost equal size and similar basic layout. They differ by the arrangement of the garage which, with one variant, is placed at the end of the living room wing and, with the other variant, at the end of the bedroom wing. Accordingly, type A has a somewhat larger bedroom wing, with three bedrooms, whilst type B, with two bedrooms, has a larger living room wing, with an additional study. Kitchen, bathroom and boiler room are concentrated at the entrance hall at the intersection of the two wings. But, in view of the otherwise rather generous design, the W. C. should have been separated from the bathroom. Living and bedrooms face the patio. The bedroom corridor also serves as cupboard room.

5. Grundrisse und Schnitt 1 : 200. Der Architekt verwendet zwei L-Typen nahezu gleicher Größe und Grundrißbildung. Sie unterscheiden sich durch die Anordnung der Garage, die bei der einen Variante in der Verlängerung des Wohntraktes, bei der anderen in der Verlängerung des Schlafteiles liegt. Dementsprechend ist bei Typ A der Schlaftrakt mit drei Zimmern um einen Raum größer und bei Typ B, mit zwei Schlafräumen, ein Arbeitsraum dem Wohnteil angegliedert. Naßgruppe und Heizung sind an der Eingangsdiele, der Überschneidung beider Trakte, konzentriert. Bei der sonst recht opulenten Anlage hätte jedoch eine Trennung von Bad und WC erfolgen sollen. Wohn- und Schlafräume öffnen sich zum Wohnhof. Der Flur des Schlafraums ist gleichzeitig Schrankraum.

"Haka" patio houses, Tapiola near Helsinki (1963–1965)
Architect: Pentti Ahola

Atriumhäuser »Haka«, Tapiola bei Helsinki (1963–1965)
Architekt: Pentti Ahola

Tapiola, the garden suburb of Helsinki, represents a kind of exhibition ground of modern Finnish architecture. Here, many of the features advocated in the present book have been realized in an exemplary manner. Within the general development plan, architect Ahola was responsible for a project of some 20 patio houses which, informally grouped, are adapted to the slightly undulating ground. A point was made of preserving the old trees. Footpaths of up to 330 ft. in length connect the houses with the carriageway and a garage building. The architect has developed a U-shaped plan with unequal sides, enclosing a spacious patio. By extending a subsidiary wing, an unconventional and lively solution has been obtained inasmuch as the visual enclosure of the patio ensures privacy without severing the link with the surroundings. The open plan comprising the sitting and utility rooms is generous without being wasteful. Another noteworthy feature is the vertical differentiation between the rooms; parts of the living room are raised above normal storey height whilst the subsidiary wing is kept lower. Construction: Rendered brickwork, built-up roof timber beam supports. The timber cladding forms an effective contrast to the white plaster facing. Gross floor area 120 sq. metres (1290 sq. ft.), floor space index 0.3.

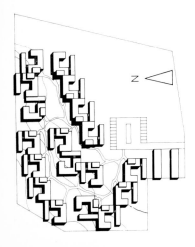

Tapiola, die Gartenvorstadt Helsinkis, stellt eine Art Beispielsammlung neuer finnischer Architektur dar. Hier sind viele der Forderungen dieses Buches vorbildlich erfüllt. Innerhalb des Generalbebauungsplanes errichtet auch der Architekt Ahola eine Siedlung von rund 20 Atriumhäusern, die in lockerer Gruppierung dem leicht bewegten Gelände angepaßt werden. Dabei wurde besonderer Wert darauf gelegt, den Baumbestand zu erhalten. Maximal 100 Meter lange Fußwege verbinden die Wohnbauten mit der Fahrstraße und einer Sammelgarage. Der Architekt entwickelte einen U-Typ mit ungleichen Seitentrakten, der ein geräumiges Atrium einschließt. Durch das Vorsetzen eines Nebenflügels entsteht eine unkonventionelle und räumlich lebendige Lösung: einerseits wird so der optische Abschluß des Atriums, der Intimsphäre, erreicht und andererseits bleibt gleichzeitig die Verbindung mit der Umgebung gewahrt. Der Grundriß mit den ineinanderfließenden Wohn- und Verkehrsräumen ist großzügig, ohne verschwenderisch zu sein. Beachtlich auch die vertikale Differenzierung der Räume: Teile des Wohnraums sind höher als das Normalgeschoß. Konstruktion: Ziegelmauerwerk verputzt, Kiespreßdach auf Holzbalken. Die Holzverschalung steht in wirksamem Gegensatz zu den weißen Putzflächen. Bruttogeschoßfläche 120 qm, GFZ 0,3.

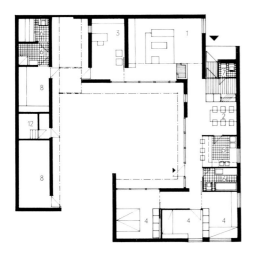

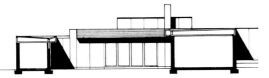

1. One of the patio houses, not yet occupied. The photograph clearly demonstrates the care with which the existing trees have been preserved.
2. Site plan, 1 in 3000.
3. Section and plan, 1 in 300. The entrance is accentuated by recessing the corner. Hall, dining area and kitchen form a unit, flanked by the bedroom wing. On the opposite side are the living room and study. A covered passage connects with the subsidiary wing which contains a spare bedroom, a cellar, a hobby room and a sauna.
4. A view from the subsidiary wing across the patio towards the bedroom and utility wings.
5. A glimpse of the patio. On the right, the "corridor" serving the dining area and kitchen. In the background, a corner of the living room.

1. Eines der noch nicht bezogenen Atriumhäuser. Deutlich ist zu erkennen, wie rücksichtsvoll man mit dem vorhandenen Baumbestand umgeht.
2. Lageplan 1 : 3000.
3. Grundriß und Schnitt 1 : 300. Der Zugang wird betont durch Einziehen der Ecke. Vorraum, Eßplatz und Küche bilden eine Einheit, an die sich der Schlafzimmertrakt anschließt. Auf der gegenüberliegenden Seite befinden sich Wohnraum und Studio. Ein überdeckter Gang schafft die Verbindung zu dem Nebengebäude, das Gastzimmer, Keller, Bastelraum und Sauna enthält.
4. Blick vom Nebengebäude in den Wohnhof auf Hauswirtschafts- und Schlafzimmertrakt.
5. Blick in das Atrium. Rechts der Flur vor Eßplatz und Küche. Im Hintergrund eine Ecke des eineinhalbgeschossigen Wohnraumes.

"Mäntykallio" patio houses, Matinkylä, Espoo, Finland (1963)
Architect: Toivo Korhonen

Atriumhäuser »Mäntykallio«, Matinkylä bei Espoo, Finnland (1963)
Architekt: Toivo Korhonen

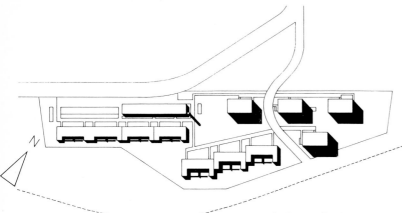

In the woodlands near Espoo, about 7 miles west of Helsinki, the architect has erected a housing unit of composite type, comprising six concatenated patio houses, eight terrace houses, and a cluster of point blocks. All the houses face south-south-east and are erected from prefabricated units. The rigidly formal design is in effective contrast with the virgin countryside where birch trees and granite rock are conspicuous. Construction: The outer walls are reinforced concrete slab walls with rockwool insulation. Gross floor area 123 sq. metres (1320 sq. ft.), floor space index 0.5.

1. The housing estate seen from south-east. In the foreground, a semi-detached patio house. In the background, two of the point blocks.
2. Site plan, 1 in 3000.

1. Blick aus Südost auf die Wohngruppe. Im Vordergrund ein Atriumdoppelhaus. Im Hintergrund zwei der Punkthäuser.
2. Lageplan 1:3000.

Auf einem Waldgelände bei Espoo, rund 11 km westlich von Helsinki, hat der Architekt eine Wohngruppe in gemischter Bebauungsweise errichtet. Sie besteht aus sechs gereihten Atriumhäusern, acht Reihenhäusern und einer Gruppe von Punkthäusern. Alle Wohnbauten sind nach Südsüdost gerichtet und wurden aus vorfabrizierten Elementen erstellt. Die streng formale Haltung der Siedlung steht in einem wirkungsvollen Gegensatz zu der unberührten Natur mit Birken und Granitfelsen. Konstruktion: Stahlbeton-Plattenwände mit Steinwollisolierung bilden die Außenwände. Bruttogeschoßfläche 123 qm, GFZ 0,5.

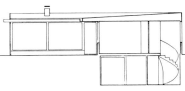

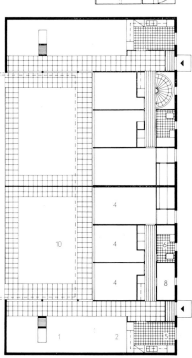

3. Section and plan, 1 in 300. The semi-detached patio house is accessible from the north side through a porch and a hall which leads, without doors, to the living room. The three bedrooms and the living room face a patio of 7 × 9 metres (23 × 29½ ft.). The transverse position of the fireplace in the living room permits the provision of a separate study or a further bedroom. On the north side are the kitchen, the stairs to the cellar and a number of amply dimensioned ancillary rooms.

4. The staggering of the rows of houses matches the contour lines.

5. Entrance side: white facings alternate with black panels of anodised aluminium.

6. Patio seen from the living room. On the left the bedroom windows.

3. Schnitt und Grundriß 1 : 300. Das gereihte Atriumdoppelhaus wird von der Nordseite über einen Windfang und eine Diele erschlossen, die türenlos in den Wohnraum übergeht. Die drei Schlafräume und der Wohnraum öffnen sich zu einem Wohnhof von 7 × 9 m. Der quergestellte Kamin im Wohnraum ermöglicht die Abtrennung eines weiteren Arbeits- oder Schlafraumes. Auf der Nordseite liegen die Küche, Kellertreppe und eine Reihe reichlich bemessener Nebenräume.

4. Die Staffelung der Zeilen folgt der natürlichen Bewegung des Geländes.

5. Die Eingangsseite: weiß gehaltene Elemente wechseln mit schwarz galvanisierten Aluminiumplatten.

6. Blick in einen Wohnhof vom Wohnraum aus. Links die Fenster des Schlafteils.

Case Study Apartments No. 1, Phoenix, Arizona, USA (1963)
Architect: Alfred N. Beadle, Dailey Associates

Case Study Apartments Nr. 1, Phoenix, Arizona, USA (1963)
Architekt: Alfred N. Beadle, Dailey Associates

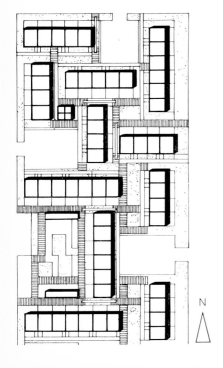

N

This cluster of terrace houses has been erected as part of a new Study Programme of the journal "Arts and Architecture." Similar to the objectives of the earlier programme for a "Case Study House" for one family, the aim of this programme is to stimulate and promote good and exemplary solutions in the sphere of houses for several families, including terrace houses. The architect of this project is trying to demonstrate, by architectural means, the principle of concentration and urban unity. The paths are no longer regarded as extraneous but already become part of the forecourt of a cluster of low-rise houses with dwelling units which are, nevertheless, more informally and independently arranged than in multi-storey housing. In addition to the private garden courts, which cover about the same area as the dwelling itself, the scheme also includes, for each cluster of dwellings, playgrounds with small open spaces and paddle pools as well as car parks. Both with the single-storey type and the two-storey type, the plan represents a very simple and conventional, yet well conceived solution. Construction: Bearing elements and roof consist of a timber framework (Douglas fir); the walls are of precast concrete blocks. The different rooms are separated by light plywood partitions. Sliding doors are of aluminium; white formica has been used in the corridor. All the vertical units, with the exception of the white doors and posts, are painted beige. Gross floor area: 82 sq. metres (880 sq. ft.), floor space index 0.5.

Diese Gruppe von Einfamilienreihenhäusern wurde im Rahmen eines neuen Studienprogramms der Zeitschrift Arts and Architecture errichtet. Man will damit, ähnlich wie es für das freistehende Einfamilienhaus mit dem Programm der »Case Study Houses« geschah, nun für gereihte und gruppierte Einfamilienhäuser gute und richtungweisende Lösungen anregen und fördern. Der Architekt dieses Projektes bemüht sich, mit architektonischen Mitteln Verdichtung und urbane Einheit sichtbar zu machen. Die Wohnwege, als Vorraum eines »flachgebauten« Mehrfamilienhauses, gehören nicht mehr zum Außenraum. Dennoch sind die einzelnen Wohnzellen freier und unabhängiger als die eines vertikal errichteten Gebäudes. Neben den privaten Gartenhöfen mit etwa der gleichen Fläche wie die Wohnung sind in der Gesamtanlage für jede Wohngruppe auch noch Spielplätze mit kleinen Grünanlagen und Wasserbecken sowie Autoabstellplätze vorgesehen. Der Grundriß ist bei den eingeschossigen und bei den zweigeschossigen Typen eine sehr einfache, traditionelle, aber gut durchdachte Lösung. Konstruktion: Tragende Elemente und Dach aus einem Holzskelett aus Douglasfichte, die Wände dagegen aus Betonsteinen. Leichte Sperrholzwände trennen die Innenräume. Schiebetüren aus Aluminium. Für den Flur fand weißes Formica Verwendung. Bruttogeschoßfläche 82 qm, GFZ 0,5.

1. General view of cluster No. 1, entrance side.
2. Site plan, 1 in 2000.
3. Plan, 1 in 300. The entrance, flanked by storage rooms, leads past the kitchen to a large living room. A short corridor leads to the two bedrooms and the bathroom which, together with the kitchen, forms a single installation unit. The plan is extremely economic if somewhat rigid and without due regard to orientation.
4. Covered walkway with the front gardens which can be screened off from each other.
5. A view of kitchen and living room. In the background, centre, the short corridor leading to the bedrooms.

1. Gesamtansicht der ersten Gruppe, Zugangsseite.
2. Lageplan 1:2000.
3. Grundriß 1:300. Der Eingang, neben dem Abstellräume liegen, erfolgt über die Küche in den Wohnraum. Über einen kleinen Flur gelangt man in die beiden Schlafräume und das Bad, das mit der Küche eine Installationseinheit bildet. Die Anlage ist außerordentlich ökonomisch, wenn auch etwas starr und ohne Rücksicht auf die Orientierung geplant.
4. Der innenliegende Wohnweg mit den Vorgärten, die gegeneinander abgeschirmt werden können.
5. Blick in Küche und Wohnraum. In Bildmitte der kleine Stichflur zu den Schlafräumen.

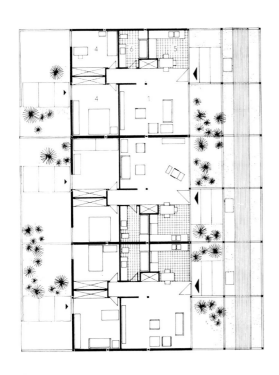

Patio houses in Chicago
Architect: Yau Chun Wong

Atriumhäuser in Chicago
Architekt: Yau Chun Wong

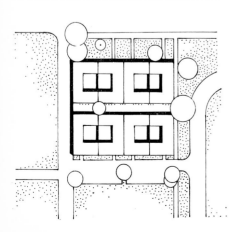

These eight patio houses were erected as part of an urban renewal plan for a somewhat blighted district of Chicago. Two rows of houses surround a narrow jointly used courtyard which provides access to the different houses. There are no doors or windows facing the roads. All the rooms are grouped around the patio. Despite the symmetric arrangement of the group as a whole, there are slight variations in the types of the different houses. The architect, himself a resident of one of the houses, was particularly concerned to provide effective soundproofing of all the partitions so as to ensure the privacy of each family. Gross floor area: 1400 sq. ft. In addition, the patio covers an area of 450 sq. ft. Floor space index 0.5.

Die acht Hofhäuser wurden im Zuge der Stadterneuerung innerhalb eines etwas »abgewohnten« Bezirks von Chicago errichtet. Zwei Reihen umschließen einen schmalen Gemeinschaftshof, der den einzelnen Häusern als Zugang dient. Die Straßenseiten sind völlig geschlossen. Alle Räume gruppieren sich um den innenliegenden Gartenhof. Trotz strenger Symmetrie und spiegelbildlicher Anordnung der gesamten Anlage ist der Typ des einzelnen Hauses leicht variiert. Besonderen Wert legte der Architekt, der eines der Häuser selbst bewohnt, auf gute Schallisolierung sämtlicher Trennwände und damit Schutz der privaten Sphäre der Bewohner der einzelnen Häuser. Die Bruttogeschoßfläche beträgt rund 130 qm. Der Gartenhof umfaßt zusätzlich rund 42 qm. GFZ 0,5.

1. A view from the living room across the sun-lit patio towards the bedrooms. By using storey-high windows and sliding doors, the patio becomes visually part of the dwelling.
2. Site plan, 1 in 1500.
3. Plans and section, 1 in 400. Access is, in each case, through a small hall leading to the living room which gives access to all the other rooms. Flanking the entrance in one wing are kitchen, bathroom and bedroom with cupboard room, and in the other wing a second bathroom, a storage room and either two smaller rooms or a large study. Daylight for all the rooms comes from the patio. There is accommodation for three to six beds.
4. One of the patios.
5. Entrance side with service road.

1. Blick vom Wohnraum über den Sonnenhof auf die Schlafzimmer. Der Gartenhof wird durch wandhohe Glaswände und Schiebetüren als zusätzlicher Raum in die Wohnung einbezogen.
2. Lageplan 1 : 1500.
3. Grundrisse und Schnitt 1 : 400. Der Zugang erfolgt jeweils über eine kleine Diele in den Wohnraum, von dem aus sämtliche anderen Räume erschlossen werden. Neben dem Eingang liegen im ersten Flügel Küche, Bad und Schlafzimmer mit begehbarem Schrankraum, im anderen ein zweites Bad, Abstellraum und zwei kleinere Zimmer oder ein großes Studierzimmer. Alle Räume werden über das Atrium belichtet. Bettenzahl: drei bis sechs.
4. Blick in ein Atrium.
5. Die Zugangsseite mit dem Wohnweg.

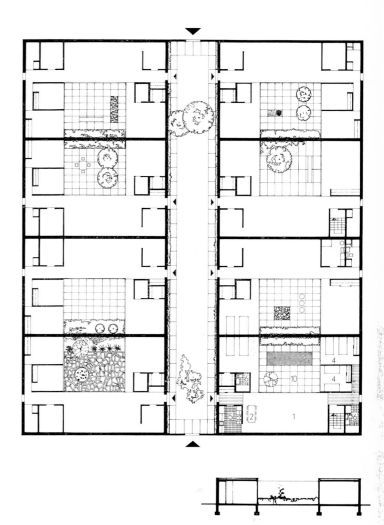

"Carpet-type" housing estate at Karlsruhe, Germany (1960/61)
Architect: Reinhard Gieselmann

Teppichsiedlung in Karlsruhe, Deutschland (1960/61)
Architekt: Reinhard Gieselmann

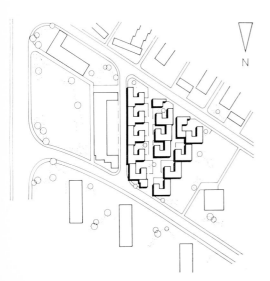

Twelve patio houses are grouped around a small piazza which, with its old limetree and a seat for old people, forms the focus of this small "neighbourhood unit." From the piazza, two service roads—one straight, the other with several right angles—lead to the houses. Although the houses are all of the same type, each has its own unmistakable character because of the different shape of the plots, the different positions and type of the entrances, and the different arrangement of the garages. The only exception is the Doctor's house which is extended by a surgery. The single-storey patio houses, which are of slightly modified L-type, have been created by adopting symmetric arrangements and certain off-sets in their layout. The size of the plots ranges from 277 to 521 sq. metres (2960 to 5580 sq. ft.). Construction: Perforated brick walls with limestone facing (1 ft.), box girder roof with exposed concrete fascia, built-up roof, double-glass thermopane windows. Gross floor area 132 sq. metres (1420 sq. ft.), floor space index 0.4.

Zwölf Hofhäuser sind um einen kleinen Platz komponiert. Mit einer Linde und einer Sitzbank für die Alten bildet er den Schwerpunkt dieser engeren »Nachbarschaft«. Zwei Wohnwege, ein gerader und ein verwinkelter, erschließen von diesem Zentrum ausgehend die Siedlung. Der ungleiche Zuschnitt der Parzellen, die unterschiedliche Art und Lage der Zugänge sowie die Anordnung der Garagen gibt den Häusern trotz ihrer Typengleichheit einen eigenen Charakter, etwas Unverwechselbares. Lediglich das Arzthaus bildet durch seinen Praxisanbau eine Ausnahme. Die eingeschossigen Hofhäuser, L-Typen mit geringfügigen Abweichungen, entstanden durch spiegelbildliche Anwendung und durch die unterschiedliche Situation. Die Größe der Grundstücke schwankt zwischen 277 und 521 qm. Konstruktion: Ziegelwände mit Kalksandsteinverblendung (30 cm), Hohlstegdach mit Sichtbetongesims, Dachhaut: Kiespreßdach, Verbundfenster mit Thermopane-Verglasung. Bruttogeschoßfläche 132 qm, GFZ 0,4.

1. Part of the housing estate, seen from the north.
2. Site plan, 1 in 3000.
3. One of the access roads.
4. Privacy is ensured by the sand-lime honeycomb brick walls with cappings of exposed concrete.

1. Teilansicht der Siedlung aus Norden.
2. Lageplan 1 : 3000.
3. Ein Wohnweg.
4. Mauern aus einem Kalksandstein-Luftziegelverband mit Sichtbetonkranz wahren den privaten Bereich.

5, 6. The gardens are not so large that the occupiers become the weekend slaves of the lawnmower. But the often irregular shape of the gardens provides welcome inspiration to the imaginative amateur gardener.

5, 6. Die Gärten sind so bemessen, daß die Bewohner des Hauses nicht zum Wochenendsklaven des Rasenmähers werden. Die oft verwinkelte Form ist dem phantasievollen Gartenenthusiasten willkommene Anregung zur Gestaltung.

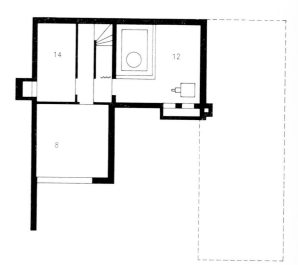

7. Plans, 1 in 200. The architect likens the plans to a "rectangular snail." Three rectangular wings of almost equal size all but enclose a square patio facing south. One of the wings, two steps higher than the others, contains dining area, kitchen, W.C., entrance and a spare room which may be used as another bedroom, a study or an office. On the opposite is the bedroom wing, the connection being provided by the wing containing the large living room. All the rooms face the garden or patio, the only exception being the kitchen window which faces outwards.
8. One of the patios.

7. Grundrisse 1:200. Der Architekt vergleicht den Grundriß mit einer »rechtwinkligen Schnecke«: Drei fast gleich große Rechtecke umschließen einen quadratischen, nach Süden liegenden Wohnhof. In dem einen befindet sich der zwei Stufen höher gelegene Teil mit Eßdiele, Küche, WC, Eingang und Gastzimmer, das auch als zweites Kinderzimmer, Arbeitszimmer oder Büro verwendet werden kann. Gegenüber liegt der Schlafzimmertrakt. Die Verbindung bildet das große Wohnzimmer. Alle Räume, mit Ausnahme der Küche, sind zum Gartenhof orientiert.
8. Blick in ein Atrium.

"Carpet-type" housing estate "Biserhof," St. Gall, Switzerland (1956–1960)
Architects: Heinrich Danzeisen and Hans Voser

Teppichsiedlung Biserhof in Sankt Gallen, Schweiz (1956–1960)
Architekten: Heinrich Danzeisen und Hans Voser

This group of twelve patio houses owes its existence to the initiative of its architects. In this case, the advantages of the L-type—secluded and wind-protected patios integrated with the dwelling proper—have been successfully combined with the advantages of a hillside position. By staggering the buildings on the westwards sloping ground, each house has obtained an unobstructed view on the landscape. The estate was built in two stages. There are slight variations in the basic type. At some points, the slope permitted the addition of a fourth bedroom at the end of the bedroom wing. With another variant, the living room is extended by a study. The size of the patios ranges from 80 to 120 sq. metres (860 to 1290 sq. ft.). For financial reasons, the originally planned construction of a central garage had to be omitted. The St. Gall planning authorities relaxed the bye-laws applicable to this area of approx. 2 acres so that the minimum distance between buildings could be reduced from 10 to 6 metres (32'10'' to 19'8''). Access to the four rows of houses and two detached houses is by footpaths and stairs from north and east. Gross floor area 125 sq. metres (1350 sq. ft.). Floor space index 0.3.

Die Wohngruppe von zwölf Hofhäusern verdankt ihr Entstehen der Initiative der Architekten. Die Vorteile des Winkeltyps, Schutz vor Einblick und windgeschützter intimer Wohnhof in unmittelbarem Zusammenhang mit den Wohnräumen, konnten bei dieser Anlage mit den Vorzügen der Hanglage verbunden werden. Durch Versetzen der Baukörper auf dem nach Westen geneigten Hang erhielt jedes Haus einen freien Ausblick in die Landschaft. Die Ausführung erfolgte in zwei Bauetappen. Der Grundtyp ist teilweise variiert. An einigen Stellen erlaubt die Hanglage, noch einen vierten Schlafraum anzufügen. Eine andere Variante ist die Erweiterung des Wohnraums durch einen Arbeitsraum. Die Wohnhöfe haben ein Ausmaß zwischen 80 und 120 qm. Eine ursprünglich geplante Sammelgarage ließ sich aus finanzierungstechnischen Gründen nicht verwirklichen. Durch das Entgegenkommen der Baubehörde St. Gallen konnte der für das 8200 qm große Gelände mit 10 m festgelegte Gebäudeabstand auf 6 m verringert werden. Vier Zeilen und zwei Einzelhäuser wurden durch Fußwege und Treppen von Norden und Osten erschlossen. Bruttogeschoßfläche 125 qm, GFZ 0,3.

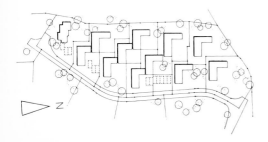

1. View from the west.
2. Site plan, 1 in 3000, of the estate as actually built.
3. Model photograph. Only twelve of the originally planned fourteen houses have been erected.
4. The lock-up garages are placed at the approach road and are built into the hillside. The original plan provided for a joint garage building only.

1. Ansicht von Westen.
2. Der Lageplan 1:3000 zeigt die Siedlung in ihrer endgültigen Ausführung.
3. Modellphoto. Von den ursprünglich geplanten vierzehn Häusern wurden nur zwölf errichtet.
4. Die Garagen liegen an der Erschließungsstraße und sind in den Hang hineingebaut. Die ursprüngliche Planung sah nur eine gemeinsame Einstellgarage vor.

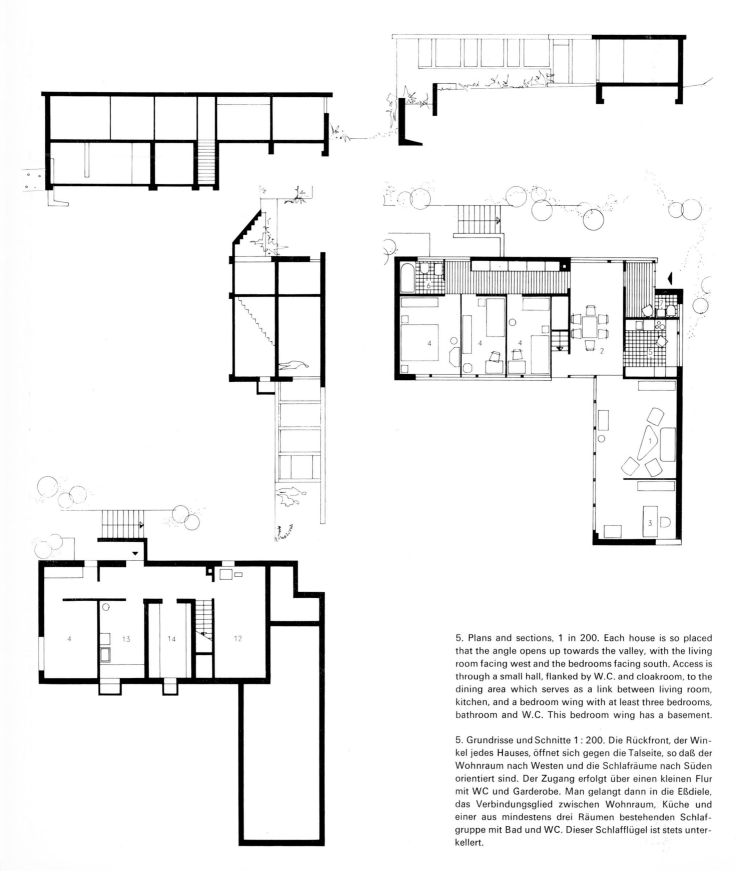

5. Plans and sections, 1 in 200. Each house is so placed that the angle opens up towards the valley, with the living room facing west and the bedrooms facing south. Access is through a small hall, flanked by W.C. and cloakroom, to the dining area which serves as a link between living room, kitchen, and a bedroom wing with at least three bedrooms, bathroom and W.C. This bedroom wing has a basement.

5. Grundrisse und Schnitte 1 : 200. Die Rückfront, der Winkel jedes Hauses, öffnet sich gegen die Talseite, so daß der Wohnraum nach Westen und die Schlafräume nach Süden orientiert sind. Der Zugang erfolgt über einen kleinen Flur mit WC und Garderobe. Man gelangt dann in die Eßdiele, das Verbindungsglied zwischen Wohnraum, Küche und einer aus mindestens drei Räumen bestehenden Schlafgruppe mit Bad und WC. Dieser Schlafflügel ist stets unterkellert.

6. View from the east, towards the city of St. Gall.
7. A terrace.
8. Dining room, with view towards living room and garden.

6. Ansicht von Osten mit Blick auf St. Gallen.
7. Eine Terrasse.
8. Eßzimmer mit Durchblick in Wohnzimmer und Garten.

"Back-to-back" houses "Im Ringelsacker," Duisdorf near Bonn (1964)
Architect: Karl Selg

Back-to-back-Eigenheime »Im Ringelsacker«, Bonn-Duisdorf (1964)
Architekt: Karl Selg

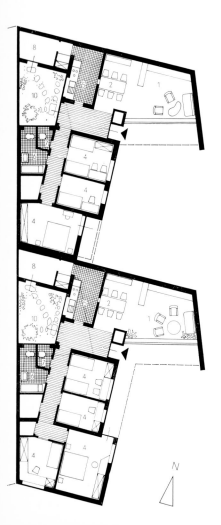

In 1956, Professor Selg was awarded the First Prize in an ideas competition for "Waldstadt," a satellite town some 4 miles from Karlsruhe. At the "Im Ringelsacker" estate at Duisdorf near Bonn, the same house type has again been used in a similar arrangement. Whilst at Karlsruhe, the architect's intentions had been considerably modified so that no more than the road network remained of his original plan, the Duisdorf estate represents a homogeneous design. However, there appears to be a need for softening and improving the transition between the four-storey blocks and the low-rise houses by leaving some open space between them. The four patio houses shown here are of particular interest inasmuch as the idea of the "back-to-back" house is resumed and skilfully modified. Altogether, 78 units of this type have been built. The orientation would not necessarily have called for the rigid arrangement of the rows apparent from the aerial photograph (Fig. 1). The space inside the estate is exclusively reserved for pedestrians. Construction: Walls erected of pumice concrete bricks measuring 11.5×24 cm (4½×9½''). The walls separating the houses are of 36.5 cm (14³/₈'') thick sand-lime brick. Reinforced concrete floors; ventilated two-ply built-up roof. Type A: Gross floor area 114 sq. metres (1230 sq. ft.), floor space index 0.6. Type B: Gross floor area 132 sq. metres (1430 sq. ft.), floor space index 0.5

Bei dem um 1956 veranstalteten städtebaulichen Ideenwettbewerb für den Trabanten Waldstadt, 6 km vor Karlsruhe, erhielt Professor Selg den Ersten Preis. In der Siedlung »Im Ringelsacker« bei Bonn-Duisdorf fand dieser Typ in ähnlicher städtebaulicher Anordnung wiederum Verwendung. Wurden in Karlsruhe die Absichten des Architekten ganz erheblich abgewandelt, so daß von der ursprünglichen Planung fast nur das Straßennetz übrigblieb, so gelang in Bonn-Duisdorf eine einheitliche Gestaltung. Es erscheint jedoch notwendig, den Übergang von den viergeschossigen Bauten zum Flachbau durch Grün zu mildern. Die hier gezeigten Atriumhäuser sind vor allem interessant, da sie den Gedanken des Back-to-back-Hauses aufnehmen und geschickt abwandeln. Im ganzen wurden 78 Wohneinheiten in dieser Art errichtet. Die Ausrichtung der Typen hätte nicht unbedingt eine so starre Anordnung der Zeilen erfordert, wie sie das Luftbild (Abb. 1) zeigt. Der innere Bereich der Siedlung ist ausschließlich den Fußgängern vorbehalten. Konstruktion: Wände aus Bimsbetonstein, 11,5 und 24 cm. Haustrennwände in Kalksandstein, 36,5 cm. Decken in Stahlbeton, zweischaliges belüftetes Dach mit Kiespreßdach. Typ A: Bruttogeschoßfläche 114 qm, GFZ 0,6. Typ B: Bruttogeschoßfläche 132 qm, GFZ 0,5.

1. Aerial photograph of the housing estate, seen from the south.
2. Plans, 1 in 300. The differences between the two types are mainly confined to their size. Type A: The house entrance is reached through a garden court of some 860 sq. ft. on the east or west side of the house. In each case, the living room faces south whilst the three bedrooms face east or west. Kitchen, bathroom and a storage room surround a small utility courtyard of 150 sq. ft. Type B houses are those at the end of a row; they contain an additional bedroom facing south. The estate is connected to a district heating plant.
3. Entrance and covered terrace outside the living room.
4. View of a house from south-east.
5. This photograph of a similar house at Karlsruhe shows how the houses will look when the lawn is in proper fettle.

1. Luftaufnahme der Siedlung, Blick aus Süden.
2. Grundrisse 1:300. Die beiden Typen unterscheiden sich im wesentlichen nur in der Größe. Typ A: Durch einen nach Osten bzw. Westen vorgelagerten Gartenhof von rund 80 qm gelangt man zum Hauseingang. Der Wohnraum ist grundsätzlich nach Süden gerichtet, die drei Schlafräume nach Osten bzw. Westen. Küche, Bad und Abstellraum liegen an einem 14 qm großen Wirtschaftshof. Typ B ergibt sich aus den jeweiligen Endbauten einer Zeile. Er hat einen zusätzlichen nach Süden orientierten Kinderschlafraum. Die Siedlung ist an eine Fernheizung angeschlossen.
3. Blick auf Zugang und überdeckten Sitzplatz.
4. Südostansicht eines Hauses.
5. Diese Ansicht eines Karlsruher Hauses vom gleichen Typ zeigt in etwa das Bild, das sich bei einer stärkeren Begrünung der Gärten bieten wird.

Per-Albin-Hanson housing estate, Vienna (1960)
Architects: Wolfgang and Traude Windbrechtinger-Ketterer

Per-Albin-Hanson-Siedlung, Wien (1960)
Architekten: Wolfgang und Traude Windbrechtinger-Ketterer

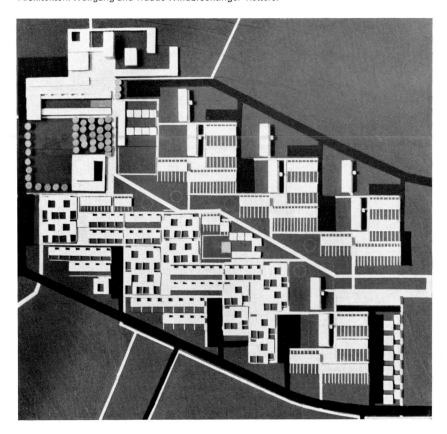

The architects' prize-winning design for the Per-Albin-Hanson housing estate makes an interesting contribution to the problem of arranging different types of patio houses in a carpet-like combination. In the present design, each cluster is a combination of three types, viz. two houses of type 1 (a I-shaped plan of great depth), one house of type 2 (with an L-shaped plan), and one house of type 3 (likewise with L-shaped plan). In the case of type 2, the living rooms face south and the bedrooms east whilst, in the case of type 3, in contrast to the other types, the living rooms face west and the bedrooms south. All three types have patios of some 540 to 650 sq. ft.; in addition, the houses of types 2 and 3 have a utility courtyard, combined with the entrance. A welcome feature is the provision by the architects of a shed of adequate size immediately adjacent to the joint entrance. The houses have no basements. Misgivings arise from the position of the main bedroom window which faces the utility courtyard of the adjacent house. With this exception, the plan creates intimate, diversified interiors well adapted to the functional requirements of a household. Type 1: Gross floor area 104 sq. metres (1120 sq. ft.), floor space index 0.7. Type 2: Gross floor area 109 sq. metres (1170 sq. ft.), floor space index 0.5. Type 3: Gross floor area 96 sq. metres (1030 sq. ft.), floor space index 0.5.

Der preisgekrönte Wettbewerbsentwurf der Architekten Windbrechtinger-Ketterer für die Per-Albin-Hanson-Siedlung bietet einen interessanten Beitrag zur Frage der Anordnung verschiedener Hofhaustypen zu einer teppichartigen Kombination. In dem vorliegenden Entwurf werden drei Typen miteinander verbunden, und zwar zweimal der Typ 1, ein tiefer I-Typ, einmal Typ 2, ein L-Typ, und einmal Typ 3, gleichfalls ein L-Typ. Bei Typ 2 sind die Wohnräume nach Süden und die Schlafräume nach Osten orientiert, bei Typ 3 sind im Gegensatz zu den benachbarten Typen die Wohnräume nach Westen und der Schlaftrakt nach Süden gerichtet. Alle drei Varianten haben Wohnhöfe von 50 bis 60 qm, Typ 2 und 3 zusätzlich einen mit dem Eingang kombinierten Wirtschaftshof. Erfreulich ist, daß die Architekten für jeden Typ einen Abstellraum in ausreichender Größe unmittelbar neben den Grundstückszugängen vorsehen. Die Bauten sind nicht unterkellert. Schwierigkeiten dürften sich durch das Fenster des Elternschlafzimmers zum Wirtschaftshof des Nachbarn hin ergeben. Davon abgesehen, entstehen intime räumliche Differenzierungen bei sorgfältigem Eingehen auf alle Funktionen einer Familie. Typ 1: Bruttogeschoßfläche 104 qm, GFZ 0,7. Typ 2: Bruttogeschoßfläche 109 qm, GFZ 0,5. Typ 3: Bruttogeschoßfläche 96 qm, GFZ 0,5.

1. In addition to the house types described here, this model photograph shows some further possible variants of these types, as well as terrace houses.
2. Plan and section, 1 in 300. Type 1: House for four persons, Type 2: House for five persons. Type 3: House for five. persons.
3. The garden of a terrace house. Drawing by Traude Windbrechtinger-Ketterer.

1. Das Modellphoto zeigt über die im Text erwähnten Typen hinaus noch weitere Varianten und Einfamilienreihenhäuser.
2. Grundriß und Schnitt 1 : 300. Typ 1 : Einfamilienhaus für vier Personen, Typ 2 : Einfamilienhaus für fünf Personen, Typ 3 : Einfamilienhaus für fünf Personen.
3. Der Garten eines Einfamilienreihenhauses. Zeichnung von Traude Windbrechtinger-Ketterer.

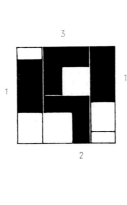

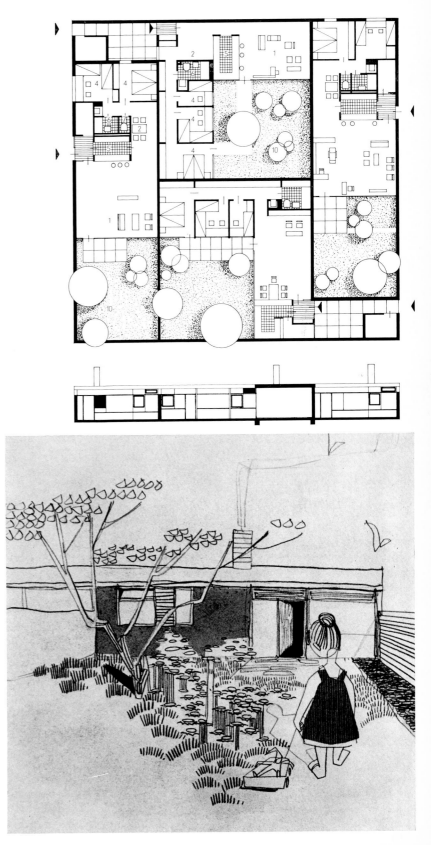

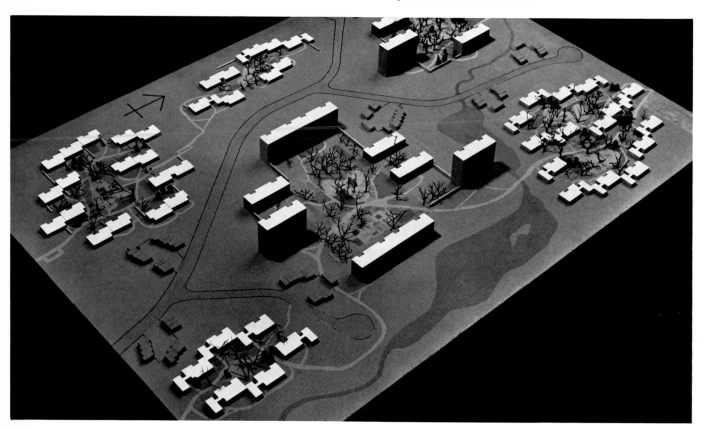

2

From among the extensive works of these architects whose efforts represent valuable contributions to the subject of urban low-rise housing, two typical projects have here been selected though none of them has been realised so far. Thus, a simple and economic solution, particularly relevant to our subject matter, has been found in response to a competition sponsored by the Ytong Works which called for a type of dwelling equally suitable for low-rise and multi-storey housing (cf. Fig. 1, 2). Similar types and clusters, but extended to include a garage courtyard, have also been suggested for Nordweststadt, Frankfurt. One of the proposed types (cf. Fig. 3, 4) is a patio house with a two-storey wing containing entrance, kitchen and one bedroom on the ground floor, and two further bedrooms on the upper floor. Above the large single-storey living room is a roof terrace. Another type (cf. Fig. 5, 6) represents a modification of the two-storey L-type house. Entrance is through a hall leading to a split-level living room. On the ground floor is the kitchen; on the upper floor, accessible from a gallery, are two bedrooms and the bathroom. Gross floor area: type A 135 sq. metres (1450 sq. ft.); type B 110 sq. metres (1180 sq. ft.); type C 92 sq. metres (990 sq. ft.). Floor space index: type A 0.6, type B 0.7, type C 0.6.

Aus dem umfangreichen Werk der Architekten, deren Arbeiten wertvolle Beiträge zum Thema des urbanen Flachbaus darstellen, werden zwei typische Projekte gezeigt, von denen jedoch keines verwirklicht werden konnte. So wurde im Rahmen eines von den Ytong-Werken ausgeschriebenen Wettbewerbs, der einen für Flachbau und Hochbau gleichermaßen geeigneten Wohnungstyp verlangte, eine für unser Thema besonders interessante, einfache und sparsame Lösung gefunden (siehe Abb. 1, 2). Ähnliche Typen und Gruppierungen, jedoch unter Einbeziehung eines Garagenhofes, wurden auch für die Nordweststadt-Frankfurt am Main vorgeschlagen. Einer der Typen (siehe Abb. 3, 4) ist ein Atriumhaus mit einem zweigeschossigen Flügel, der Eingang, Küche und Schlafraum im Erdgeschoß und zwei weitere Schlafräume im Obergeschoß enthält. Über dem großen eingeschossigen Wohnraum liegt eine Terrasse. Ein anderer Typ (siehe Abb. 5, 6) wandelt das zweigeschossige L-Haus ab. Der Eingang führt über eine Diele in den zweigeschossigen Wohnraum. Im Erdgeschoß liegt die Küche, im Obergeschoß befinden sich an einer Galerie zwei Schlafräume und das Bad. Bruttogeschoßfläche Typ A: 135 qm, Typ B: 110 qm, Typ C: 92 qm. GFZ Typ A: 0,6, Typ B: 0,7, Typ C: 0,6.

3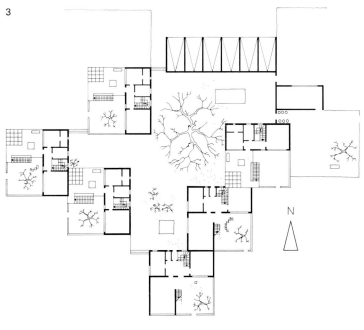

5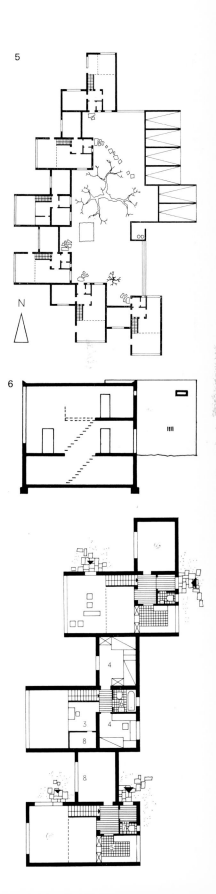

4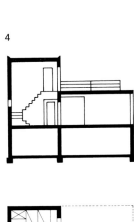
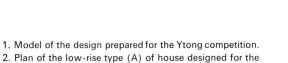

6

1. Model of the design prepared for the Ytong competition.
2. Plan of the low-rise type (A) of house designed for the Ytong competition, 1 in 300. Living and bedrooms are grouped around an all-purpose hall which serves as a dining area and playroom and connects the kitchen with the outdoor terrace. Kitchen, bathroom and W.C. form a single installation unit facing east. Together with a separate flatlet designed for elderly parents, this part of the building surrounds a smaller and a larger utility courtyard.
3–6. "Nordweststadt," Frankfurt-on-Main.
3. Draft site plan, 1 in 600.
4. Plans and section, 1 in 300, type B.
5. Draft site plan, 1 in 600.
6. Plans and section, 1 in 300, type C.

1. Modellphoto des Entwurfs für den Ytong-Wettbewerb.
2. Grundriß des Flachbautyps A im Ytong-Wettbewerb 1:300. Die Wohn- und Schlafräume sind um eine Eßdiele gruppiert, eine Art Allraum, der Küche und Freiraum verbindet, in dem gegessen wird und in dem die Kinder spielen können. Küche, Bad und WC liegen nach Osten um einen Installationskern. Dieser Baukörper umschließt mit dem abgetrennten Altenteil ein kleineres und ein großes Wohnhöfchen.
3–6. Frankfurt a. M. – Nordweststadt.
3. Lageplanentwurf 1:600.
4. Grundrisse und Schnitt 1:300, Typ B.
5. Lageplanentwurf 1:600.
6. Grundrisse und Schnitt 1:300, Typ C.

Cluster of houses at Stetten, Remstal, Germany (1962)
Architects: Hans Kammerer and Walter Belz

Wohnhausgruppe in Stetten im Remstal, Deutschland (1962)
Architekten: Hans Kammerer und Walter Belz

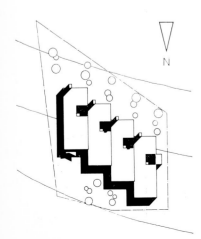

At Stetten, some 12 miles outside Stuttgart, the pooling of a number of minute agricultural plots yielded a redevelopment area of about half-an-acre where, in accordance with the bye-laws, no more than two houses could have been placed. The architects were, however, able to accommodate four houses, staggered in depth. The view from the north and the consistent adoption of the two-bay plan convey the impression that all the houses are of the same type. In fact, however, the standard plan as applied to the two houses in the centre has been modified for the two houses at the ends which are occupied by the architects themselves. Construction: The outer walls consist of 36.5 cm (14³/₈″) thick sand lime blocks. The houses are separated by double brick walls of 24 and 11.5 cm (9½″ and 4½″) thickness with 1 cm (³/₈″) glasswool insulation. Structural floors; reinforced concrete slabs and precast joists. The horizontal roof is a beam structure carrying square timbers on which a raw timber cladding is placed. The roof covering consists of four layers of felt covered by some 2½″ of gravel. Gross floor area 220 sq. metres (2380 sq. ft.); floor space index 0.4.

In Stetten, etwa 20 km von Stuttgart entfernt, entstand aus der Zusammenlegung landwirtschaftlicher Parzellen ein rund 2100 qm großes Gelände, auf dem nach der normalen Bebauungsvorschrift nur zwei Häuser Platz gefunden hätten. Den Architekten gelang es jedoch, vier gestaffelte, in den Grundrissen in die Tiefe entwickelte Häuser unterzubringen. Die Nordansicht und das Konstruktionsprinzip des zweischiffigen Grundrisses lassen *einen* Typ vermuten. In Wirklichkeit handelt es sich jedoch um einen »Grundtyp«, die beiden mittleren Häuser, und um zwei daraus entwickelte Varianten, die »Randhäuser«, in denen die Architekten wohnen. Konstruktion: Die Außenwände bestehen aus 36,5 cm starken Wandscheiben aus Kalksandsteinen. Zur Dämmung der Haustrennwände wurden 1-cm-Glaswollmatten zwischen 24 und 11,5 cm starken Mauern verwendet. Die Decken bestehen aus Stahlbetonplatten und Fertigbalkendecken. Die gefällelose Dachebene wird aus einer Balkenkonstruktion gebildet, mit einer Aufsattelung von Rahmenhölzern, um die rauhe Holzschalung zu befestigen. Die Dachhaut besteht aus vier Lagen Pappe mit einer rund 6 cm hohen Kiesschüttung. Bruttogeschoßfläche 220 qm, GFZ 0,4.

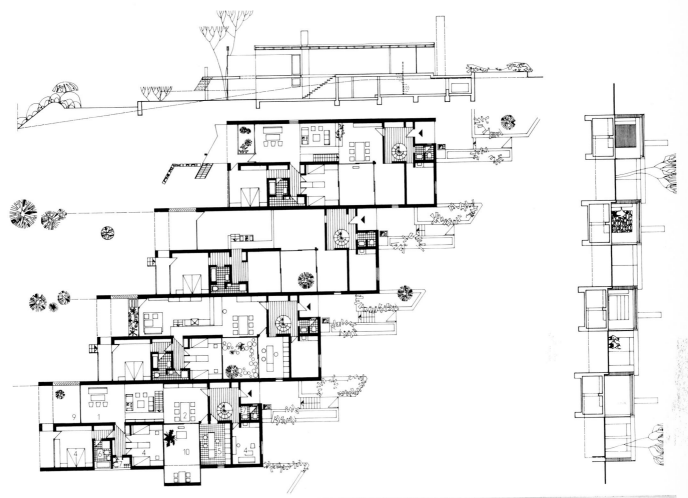

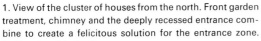

1. View of the cluster of houses from the north. Front garden treatment, chimney and the deeply recessed entrance combine to create a felicitous solution for the entrance zone.
2. Site plan, 1 in 1500.
3. Longitudinal section, cross-section and plan, 1 in 400. The slight south-eastward fall of the ground favoured the construction of houses with a single storey on the north side and two storeys on the south side.
4. The gardens are on the south side.

1. Nordansicht der Reihenhausgruppe. Die Bepflanzung, der Kamin und die tiefe Eingangsnische zeigen eine geglückte Lösung des Eingangs.
2. Lageplan 1 : 1500.
3. Längsschnitt, Querschnitt und Grundriß 1 : 400. Der leicht nach Südosten fallende Hang begünstigte die Kombination von auf der Nordseite eingeschossigen und auf der Südseite zweigeschossigen Baukörpern.
4. Auf der Südseite liegen die Gärten.

5. South side of the house at the western end. The living room is on two levels.
6. South side of standard house.
7. Patio of the house occupied by Belz, with view towards the nursery.
8. Night view of the split-level living room of the house at the eastern end.

5. Die Südfront des westlichen Endtyps. Der Wohnraum ist zweigeschossig.
6. Südfassade des Grundtyps.
7. Innenhof des Hauses Belz mit Blick auf das Kinderzimmer.
8. Zweigeschossige Wohnzone des östlichen Endtyps bei Nacht.

9. Patio of the house at the eastern end. View from the dining area on the covered terrace on the east side. On the right the nursery, on the left the kitchen. In this secluded zone, family life can be concentrated.

10. Living room with fireplace in the house occupied by Belz. The steps give access to a gallery leading to the dining area.

11. View from the raised dining area across the study to the living room.

9. Der Innenhof des östlichen Endtyps. Blick vom Eßplatz auf den überdeckten Sitzplatz im Osten. Rechts Kinderzimmer, links Küche. In diesem abgeschlossenen Bereich kann sich das Familienleben konzentrieren.

10. Wohnraum mit Kamin im Hause Belz. Die Stufen führen zu einer Galerie, auf der man zum Eßplatz gelangt.

11. Blick vom erhöhten Eßplatz über den Arbeitsplatz in den Wohnraum.

Torre Valentina, Costa Brava, Spain (1959)
Architects: José A. Coderch and Manuel Valls

Torre Valentina, Costa Brava, Spanien (1959)
Architekten: José A. Coderch und Manuel Valls

1. View from the east/Ansicht von Osten.

On a site of about 8½ acres on one of the most beautiful stretches of the Costa Brava, the architects have planned the construction of 300 houses and a hotel. Eleven rows of houses of different length run more or less parallel to the contour lines, broadly orientated north-to-south. All the living rooms face east; the sun on the west side would be intolerably hot in these latitudes. The houses have a width of about 15 ft. and are built into the slope. Living room and balcony are projected so that a covered arcade is created in which the entrance stairs are situated. This arcade is an ideal playground for children in rainy weather. Since the rows of houses are placed at different levels one above the other and since, moreover, each individual dwelling "climbs" the slope, there is a sea view from the living room, from one of the bedrooms, and from the terrace of each house. Construction: Brick walls and reinforced concrete beam floors; living rooms supported by columns. Gross floor area ranging from 63 to 160 metres (670 to 1730 sq. ft.), floor space index 0.7.

An einer der schönsten Stellen der Costa Brava haben die Architekten auf einem Gelände von 3½ ha 300 Einfamilienhäuser und ein Hotel geplant. Elf Wohnzeilen unterschiedlicher Länge verlaufen ungefähr parallel zum Hang und etwa in Nordsüdrichtung. Alle Wohnräume haben daher Ostbesonnung; Westbesonnung würde in diesen Breitengraden unerträglich sein. Die etwa 4,5 m breiten Häuser sind in den Hang hineingebaut. Wohnraum und Balkon sind vorgezogen, so daß ein gedeckter Laubengang entsteht, in dem die Zugangstreppe liegt. Dieser Laubengang ist ein idealer Spielplatz für die Kinder bei Regen oder starker Sonneneinstrahlung. Da die Wohnzeilen stufenweise übereinander liegen und außerdem auch jede einzelne Wohnung den Hang »hinaufklettert«, haben in jeder Einheit der Wohnraum, ein Schlafzimmer und eine Terrasse Aussicht aufs Meer. Konstruktion: Ziegelwände und Betonbalkendecken, Abstützung der Wohnräume durch Pfeiler aus kreuzweise geschweißten Winkelprofilen. Bruttogeschoßfläche 63 qm–160 qm, GFZ 0,7.

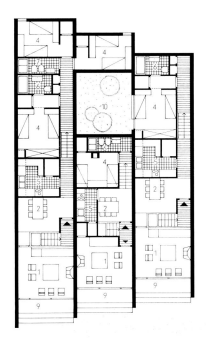

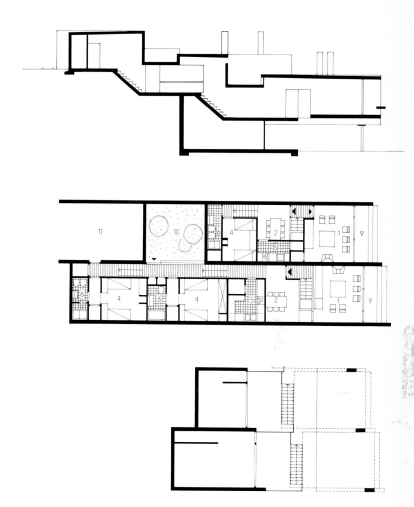

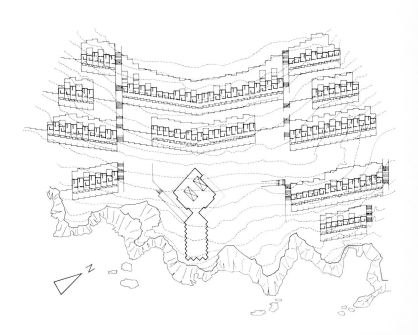

2. Plans and section, 1 in 300. The very well conceived basic type always contains a living room, dining area, kitchen, and a bedroom with bathroom and patio. Top lighting provides daylight access to the stairs and dining room. The architects have prepared 26 variants of this basic type, including dwellings with up to five bedrooms, three bathrooms and three patios, where the tree-clustered inner courtyard is assigned to the neighbour on the right-hand or left-hand side.

3. Site plan, 1 in 3000. The buildings are staggered so that the rooms of the different houses are not immediately adjacent to each other.

2. Grundrisse und Schnitt 1 : 300. Der sehr gut durchdachte Grundtyp enthält stets Wohnraum, Eßplatz, Küche und ein Schlafzimmer mit Bad und Patio. Ein Oberlicht dient der Beleuchtung der Zugangstreppe und des Eßraumes. Von diesem Typ wurden durch die Architekten 26 Varianten ausgearbeitet — Wohnungen mit bis zu fünf Schlafräumen, drei Bädern und drei Patios —, wobei der mit Bäumen bepflanzte Innenhof dem rechten oder dem linken Nachbarn zugeteilt ist.

3. Lageplan 1 : 3000. Damit die Räume der einzelnen Häuser nicht unmittelbar nebeneinander liegen, sind die Bauten gegeneinander versetzt.

4. A view of the living room.
5, 6. The living rooms are supported by columns. Below them are the access stairs.

4. Blick auf die Wohnräume.
5, 6. Die Wohnräume stehen auf Stützen. Darunter liegen die Zugangstreppen.

Page/Seite 147:

1. External view of Chermayeffs house. A high wooden fence separates the house from the road. Care has been taken to preserve the trees growing on the site.
2. Plans, 1 in 400, of the three house types developed by Chermayeff.

1. Außenansicht des Chermayeff'schen Hauses. Holzpalisaden schließen gegen die Straße ab. Die Bäume auf dem Grundstück konnten durch sorgfältige Planung erhalten werden.
2. Grundrisse 1:400 der drei von Chermayeff entwickelten Typen.

Patio house at New Haven, Connecticut, USA (1962)
Architects: Serge Chermayeff and P. Alexander, Menier, Reynolds, Christie

Atriumhaus in New Haven, Connecticut, USA (1962)
Architekten: Serge Chermayeff und P. Alexander, Menier, Reynolds, Christie

For years Serge Chermayeff has been preoccupied with the problems of high density, low-rise housing. Departing from the knowledge that deep plots are particularly economic, he developed inter alia a deep single-bay type of patio house as well as two double-bay types (cf. Fig. 2). The courts, ranging in size from 15 to 50 sq. metres (160 to 540 sq. ft.), are informally arranged within the house clusters. Type 3 has three courts; each of the other two types has four. In this way, clusters and groupings are created, each supplemented by open space so that, at the same time, privacy is ensured for each dwelling. Since each unit has, in principle, two entrances, the demand for variability and flexibility is also met to a high degree. On the basis of these ideas, Chermayeff has designed and built his own house as a prototype. The patios are, however, somewhat larger than usual. Construction: Load-bearing concrete block walls; flat timber roof decking. All the services, including heating, are grouped in accessible under-floor trenches. Gross floor area of the three types developed by Chermayeff (Fig. 2): 124 sq. metres (1340 sq. ft.), floor space index 0.6; 170 sq. metres (1830 sq. ft.), floor space index 0.7; 180 sq. metres (1940 sq. ft.), floor space index 0.6.

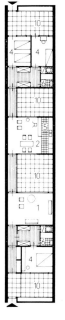

Der Architekt Chermayeff befaßt sich seit einigen Jahren mit dem Problem des urbanen Flachbaus. Von der Erkenntnis ausgehend, daß tiefe Grundstücke besonders wirtschaftlich sind, entwickelte er unter anderem auch einen tiefen, einschiffigen Typ eines Atriumhauses sowie zwei zweischiffige Typen (Abb. 2). Die Atrien mit Größen von 15 bis 50 qm werden nach Bedarf innerhalb der bebauten Flächen verteilt. Ein Typ hat drei Höfe, die beiden anderen je vier. Durch das Prinzip der Aufteilung in Raumgruppen mit jeweils dazugehörigem ergänzendem Freiraum wird gleichzeitig in jeder Gruppe störungsfreies Wohnen ermöglicht. Da die Häuser grundsätzlich zwei Eingänge haben, ist auch in hohem Grade der Forderung nach Variabilität und Flexibilität entsprochen. Als Demonstrativobjekt ist das eigene Haus Chermayeffs nach diesen Gedanken entworfen und gebaut. Die Atrien sind allerdings umfangreicher bemessen. Konstruktion: Die Wände bestehen aus Betonelementen, das Dach ist eine Holzkonstruktion mit vorfabrizierten Platten. Alle Installationen, einschließlich der Heizung, sind in zugänglichen, unter dem Fußboden liegenden Kanälen zusammengefaßt. Bruttogeschoßfläche der drei von Chermayeff entwickelten Typen (Abb. 2): 124 qm, GFZ 0,6; 170 qm, GFZ 0,7; 180 qm, GFZ 0,6.

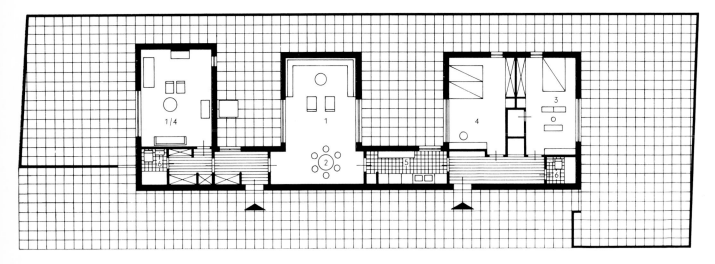

3. Plan of prototype house, 1 in 200.
4. Living court between main bedroom and living room.
5. Two-level living room.

3. Grundriß des Demonstrativhauses 1 : 200.
4. Wohnhof zwischen Elternschlafraum und Wohnraum.
5. Der zweigeschossige Wohnraum.

6. Living room, with view into the living court in front of the bedroom wing. Door and window openings from floor to ceiling.
7. Hall. On the left-hand side, facing the dining table, is the kitchen.
8. View from the husband's study and bedroom across the first living court to the living room wing and the second living court.

6. Wohnraum mit Blick auf das Atrium vor dem Schlafteil. Türen und Fenster sind geschoßhoch.
7. Blick in den Flur. Links vor dem Eßtisch die Küche.
8. Blick aus dem Arbeits- und Schlafzimmer des Hausherrn auf den ersten Wohnhof, den Wohnteil und den zweiten Wohnhof.

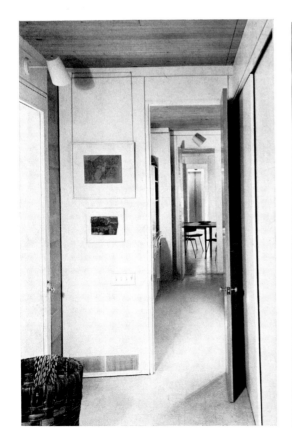

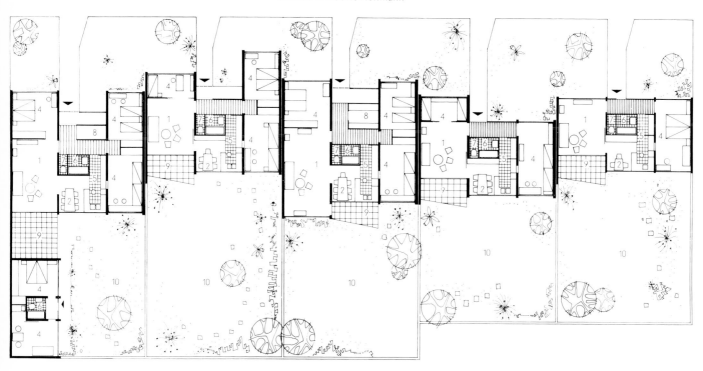

A typical suburban township with a population of 4 000, consisting of the remnants of an old village centre and newer detached houses scattered at random, is to be enlarged so as to accommodate a population of 24,000, with three twin school units, an industrial estate and a town centre. The specified increase in the floor space index from 0.1–0.2 to 0.5 is to be attained by a mixture of low-rise housing (60 per cent) and medium- to high-rise housing (40 per cent). As 20 per cent of all the residents already live in detached houses, it is envisaged to accommodate the further 40 per cent proposed in low-rise group housing. Two examples of expandible terrace houses, a single-storey type (A) and a two-storey type (B), are shown here. Type A may have south orientation or east-west orientation. In the final stage, the house is L-shaped, permitting the addition of further rooms. With the east-west orientated type B, the two bays of approx. 23 ft. width are staggered so that they can be used for a duplex unit or for the provision of a surgery on the east side. Both types are to be erected by panel construction methods, using prefabricated beams. Gross floor area: Type A, 53–120 sq.metres (570–1 280 sq.ft.), floor space index 0.3–0.7; Type B, 52–170 sq.metres (560–1 820 sq.ft.), floor space index 0.3–1.1.

Für eine typische Stadtrandgemeinde, bestehend aus Resten des alten Dorfkerns und neu hinzugekommener Streubebauung, wird eine planmäßige Verdichtung von 4 000 auf 24 000 Einwohner angestrebt, wobei drei Doppelschuleinheiten, ein Gewerbegebiet und ein urbanes Zentrum zu errichten sind. Die geforderte Steigerung der Ausnutzung von GFZ 0,1–0,2 auf 0,5 soll durch eine gemischte Bebauung in Flach- und Hochbau erreicht werden, das heißt 60% der Wohnungen sind in Flachbau und 40% in Mittel- und Hochbau vorgesehen. Da bereits 20% aller Einwohner in freistehenden Einfamilienhäusern wohnen, wurde für weitere 40% ein verdichteter Flachbau vorgeschlagen, von dem hier zwei Beispiele, ein eingeschossiges (A) und ein zweigeschossiges (B) erweiterungsfähiges Einfamilienreihenhaus gezeigt werden. Typ A ist süd- oder ost-westgerichtet. Die Endstufe des Ausbaus läßt einen L-Typ entstehen, der den Anschluß einer Ergänzungswohnung möglich macht. Beim ost-westorientierten Typ B sind die beiden rund 7 m breiten Schiffe gegeneinander verschoben und erlauben eine Duplex-Wohnung oder aber auch Praxisräume auf der Ostseite. Beide Typen sind in Scheibenbauweise mit vorgefertigten Balken zu erstellen. Bruttogeschoßfläche: Typ A 53–120 qm, GFZ 0,3–0,7; Typ B 52–170 qm, GFZ 0,3–1,1.

1. Plans, 1 in 300, showing Type A houses in different stages of development. The basic unit comprises a sitting room with dining recess, bedroom, hall, kitchen and W.C. Extensions may be added, in any desired sequence, on the garden side or on the entrance side. With increasing floor area, kitchen and ancillary rooms are likewise enlarged.
2. Model photograph of two groups of type A houses in different stages of development.
3. Part of the model of the whole area, showing the town centre, a number of tower blocks, and groups of low-rise houses placed among the pre-existing detached houses.
4. Plans, 1 in 400, showing Type B houses in different stages of development, with the basic unit on the left and the fully developed unit on the right. The variants are obtained by extending the bays. The two patios, permit a greater flexibility.

1. Typ A, Grundrisse der verschiedenen Ausbaustufen, 1:300. Die Grundstufe umfaßt Wohnraum mit Eßnische, Schlafraum, Flur und Naßzelle mit Küche und Bad. Anbauten können zur Garten- oder Eingangsseite hin in beliebiger Reihenfolge vorgenommen werden. Mit zunehmender Wohnfläche wachsen auch Küche und Nebengelaß.
2. Modellfoto zweier Hausgruppen mit verschiedenen Ausbaustufen des Typs A.
3. Ausschnitt aus dem Gesamtmodell mit dem Zentrum, einigen Punkthäusern und Flachbaugruppen, eingestreut in die vorhandene Einfamilienhaus-Bebauung.
4. Typ B, Grundrisse der verschiedenen Ausbaustufen, 1:400; links Grundstufe, rechts Endstufe. Die Varianten ergeben sich durch Verlängerung der Schiffe. Wohn- und Wirtschaftshof erleichtern die Flexibilität.

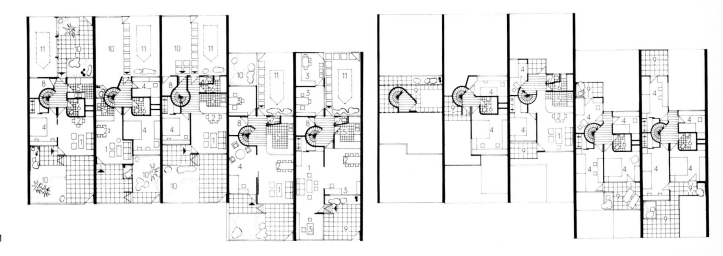

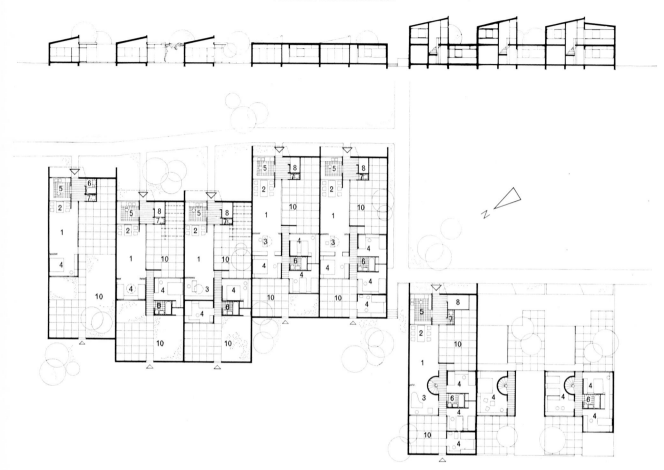

These expandible chain-type houses for one family have been developed by the architect from a combination of the principles underlying the narrow and deep type of terrace house with the Mediterranean concept of the house as a concatenation of buildings and patios. This has given rise to a basic single-storey model which can be converted, in six phases, into the ultimate two-storey model. This results not only in a high degree of flexibility—inasmuch as the plan can easily be adapted to the growth or shrinkage of the family—but also in highly efficient utilisation of the plot which has a net area of 200 sq.metres (2150 sq.ft.). If this type is used as part of an urban development scheme, groups of 46 units with a maximum of 92 dwellings are combined into a single housing unit (cf. Fig. 5). Sixteen of such units, with a population ranging from 3000 to 5000, form a school unit. Kindergarten and primary school are placed in the central, about 230 ft. wide open space within the school unit, and can be reached via residential roads, flanked by playgrounds for the youngest children. Secondary schools, shops and other common facilities are placed at the centre. Gross floor area 128–182 sq.metres (1380–1960 sq.ft.); floor space index 0.7–0.1.

1. Section and plans, showing the different development phases, 1 in 500. On the left the basic single-storey model, on the right the ultimate two-storey model. The two parts of the dwellings have separate entrances and halls. The larger part contains a sitting room, kitchen, W.C., store room and study. The adjacent bedrooms, surrounding the second patio, may be assigned to the larger or to the smaller part. The house can be further expanded by adding the upper floor.

1. Schnitt und Grundrisse der einzelnen Ausbaustufen 1:500; links die Grundform, rechts die zweigeschossige Endform. Beide Wohnteile haben getrennte Zugänge und eigene Atrien. Der größere enthält Wohnraum, Küche, WC, Abstellraum und ein Studio. Die anschließenden Schlafräume, gruppiert um den zweiten Hof, können der größeren oder kleineren Wohnung zugeordnet werden. Eine zusätzliche Erweiterungsmöglichkeit bietet der Obergeschoßausbau.

Der Architekt entwickelte dieses erweiterungsfähige Einfamilienreihenhaus, indem er die Prinzipien, die dem schmalen und tiefen Reihenhausgrundriß zugrunde liegen, mit der mediterranen Auffassung vom Haus als einer Folge von Baukörpern und Höfen verband. So entstand eine eingeschossige Grundform, die sich in sechs Ausbaustufen in die zweigeschossige Endform verwandeln läßt. Damit wird nicht nur Flexibilität – der Grundriß läßt sich vorteilhaft dem Wachsen und Schrumpfen der Familie anpassen –, sondern auch eine hohe Ausnutzung des 200 qm großen Nettogrundstückes erreicht. Bei einer städtebaulichen Anwendung werden jeweils 46 Wohneinheiten mit maximal 92 Wohnungen zu einer Gruppe zusammengefaßt (siehe Abb. 5). Sechzehn Gruppen mit 3000–5000 Einwohnern bilden eine Schuleinheit. Kindergarten und Grundschule liegen im zentralen, rund 70 m breiten Grünstreifen der Schuleinheit und sind über Wohnwege mit Spielplätzen für die Kleinsten zu erreichen. Weiterführende Schulen, Läden und andere Einrichtungen für die Allgemeinheit befinden sich im Zentrum. Bruttogeschoßfläche 128–182 qm, GFZ 0,7–0,1.

2, 3. Model photograph of the entrance side (top) and garden side (bottom) of a group of houses in different phases of development.
4. Layout plan of a school unit with main road (A) and residential road (B), 1 in 7 500. C Primary school, D Secondary school.
5. Site plan, longitudinal and cross section of a housing unit, 1 in 2 000. The joint garage is placed below the dwellings in the central part which are raised 1.2 metres (4 ft.) above ground level. To each housing unit belongs a club house (E) with sauna, (F) Footpath, (G) Playground, (H) Garage entrance.

2, 3. Eingangs- und Gartenseite (unten) einer Hausgruppe in den verschiedenen Ausbaustadien im Modell.
4. Planskizze einer Schuleinheit mit Hauptverkehrsstraße (A) und Aufschließungsstraße (B) 1:7500. C Grundschule, D weiterführende Schule.
5. Lageplan, Längs- und Querschnitt einer Wohneinheit 1:2000. Die Sammelgarage ist unter den um 1,2 m über Niveau angehobenen Wohnungen des Mittelteiles untergebracht. Zu jeder Wohneinheit gehört ein Klubhaus (E) mit Sauna. F Fußweg, G Spielplatz, H Garageneinfahrt.

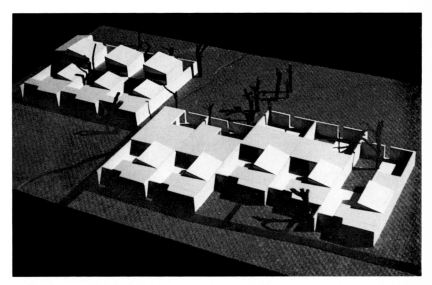

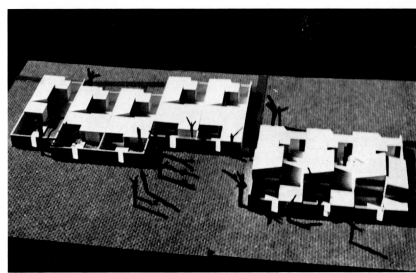

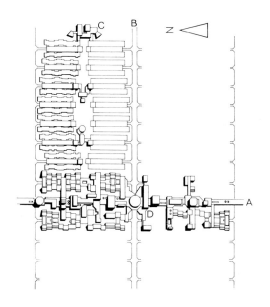

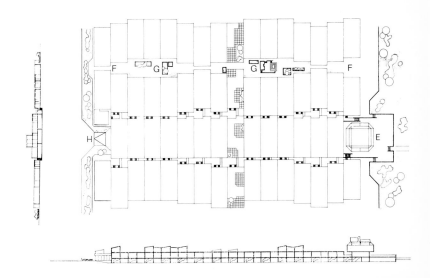

Terrace houses produced by the Neckermann Company, Frankfurt-on-Main (1965)
Architect: Egon Eiermann

Reihenhäuser der Firma Neckermann, Frankfurt am Main (1965)
Architekt: Egon Eiermann

The range of prefabricated houses produced by the Neckermann Company, which includes detached houses, has recently been extended to include single-storey terrace houses. From their production programme, three characteristic types have here been selected. All three have a frontage of 10 metres (approx. 33 ft.) and are provided with a cellar extending under part of the house. Type A, which is 6.5 metres (21′4″) deep, has an east-west orientation, with two patios. Type B is likewise designed for east-west orientation but has a greater depth (8 metres, i.e. 26′3″) and but one patio, measuring some 60 sq. metres (640 sq. ft.). Type C, 18 metres (59 ft.) deep, offers the largest floor area. Because of its L-shaped plan, the orientation of this type may vary over a range of 90° between east and south. The aggregate open space of the two patios is approx. 100 sq. metres (1080 sq. ft.). All three types are distinguished by a clearly conceived plan. With their economic construction they make a worthwhile contribution to the development of link-type prefabricated houses. Gross floor area: Type A 84 sq. metres (900 sq. ft.), Type B 82 sq. metres (880 sq. ft.), Type C 125 sq. metres (1340 sq. ft.); floor space index: Types A and B 0.5, Type C 0.6.

In ihrem Fertighausprogramm bietet die Firma Neckermann neben freistehenden Fertigbauten neuerdings auch eingeschossige Reihenhäuser an. Aus diesem Angebot sind hier drei charakteristische Typen ausgewählt. Alle drei haben eine Frontbreite von 10 m und sind teilunterkellert. Typ A, mit einer Haustiefe von 6,5 m, ist ostwestorientiert und besitzt zwei Höfe. Auch Typ B ist ostwestgerichtet, hat jedoch eine größere Tiefe von 8 m und nur einen Gartenhof mit rund 60 qm. Bei 18 m Tiefe bietet Typ C die größte Wohnfläche. Der L-förmige Grundriß erlaubt die Verwendung in einem Bereich von 90° zwischen Ost und Süd. Zwei Höfe ergeben zusammen eine Freifläche von etwa 100 qm. Alle drei Typen zeichnen sich durch klare Grundrißgestaltung aus. Sie stellen durch ihre ökonomische Konstruktion durchaus eine Bereicherung auf dem Gebiet des reihungsfähigen Fertighauses dar. Bruttogeschoßfläche: Typ A 84 qm, Typ B 82 qm, Typ C 125 qm; GFZ: Typ A und B 0,5, Typ C 0,6.

1, 2. The types lend themselves for loose grouping as well as firmly aligned arrangement.

3. Plans, Type A, 1 in 200. The rooms include living room, kitchen, main bedroom and another bedroom which can be used for a child or a relation or lodger.

4. Plans and section, Type B, 1 in 200. One of the two bays of the clearly conceived plan contains living room and kitchen, the other two bedrooms and a bathroom.

5. Plans, Type C, 1 in 200. On the entrance side are kitchen and ancillary rooms. The living room faces the garden court on the west side and serves as a link with the bedrooms facing south. Living court and entrance court have an area of 60 and 40 sq. metres (640 and 430 sq. ft.), respectively.

1, 2. Die Typen lassen sich in lockeren und streng geschlossenen Anlagen gruppieren.

3. Grundrisse Typ A 1:200. Das Raumprogramm umfaßt Wohnraum, Küche, Elternschlafraum und ein Kinderzimmer, das auch für einen Verwandten oder Einlieger verwendet werden kann.

4. Grundrisse und Schnitt Typ B 1:200. Der zweischiffige, klare Grundriß enthält in einem Schiff Wohnraum und Küche und im anderen zwei Schlafräume und Bad.

5. Grundrisse Typ C 1:200. Auf der Eingangsseite liegen Küche und Nebenräume. Der Wohnraum öffnet sich nach Westen zum Gartenhof. Er ist gleichzeitig Bindeglied zu den nach Süden gerichteten Schlafräumen. Wohnhof und Eingangshof sind 60 und 40 qm groß.

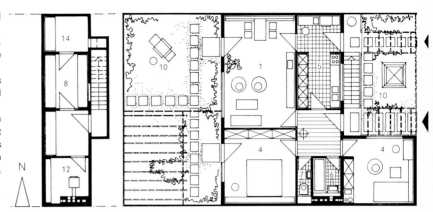

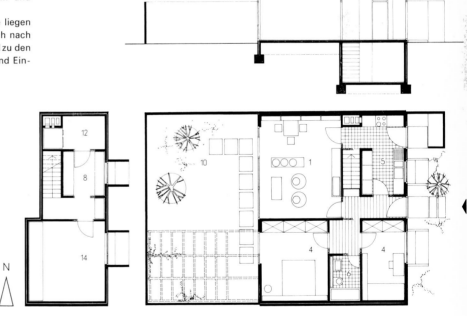

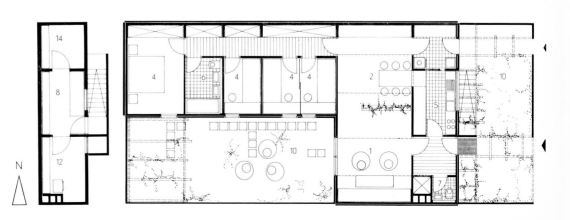

"Calder Homes" prefabricated houses, England (1964)
Architects: Peter Harding and Michael Horsman

Fertighaussystem Calder, England (1964)
Architekten: Peter Harding und Michael Horsman

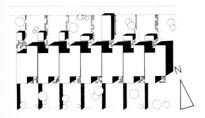

1. View from the south, garden side. The garden party walls have not yet been erected.
2. Site plan, 1 in 2000.

1. Ansicht von Süden, Gartenseite. Die Trennmauern zwischen den Gärten fehlen noch.
2. Lageplan 1 : 2000.

The architects made the interesting attempt to compose two-storey houses from four prefabricated "box units" of equal size. On the strength of this principle, they developed several types, the first of which, known as Type C 4, was erected at a housing estate at Washington, Co. Durham, early in 1964. The plan of this 23 ft. wide two-bay house is well conceived and offers the necessary flexibility. The frontages are enlivened through being alternately recessed and projected by 10 ft., a feature which also provides a protected sitting-out terrace on the garden side. Attractive features are the broken roof-line and the contrast between timber cladding and white Eternit panels. Construction: The walls and floors of the "box units" consist of a timber frame covered by glued plywood panels and clad on the inside with plasterboard. Insulation is provided by polysterene panels and aluminium foil. Gross floor area 104 sq. metres (1120 sq. ft.); floor space index 0.5.

Die Architekten unternehmen den interessanten Versuch, zweigeschossige Häuser aus vier gleich großen, vorgefertigten Raumeinheiten zusammenzusetzen. Sie entwickelten auf der Grundlage dieses Prinzips mehrere Typen, von denen als erster der Typ C 4, Anfang 1964, in Washington, Co. Durham, in einer Siedlung errichtet wurde. Der Grundriß des zweischiffigen, rund 7 m breiten Hauses mit ökonomischen Abmessungen ist gut durchdacht und bietet die notwendigen Variationsmöglichkeiten. Durch das Vor- und Zurückspringen der Fassade um etwa 3 m entsteht einmal eine lebendige Straßenfront und zum andern auch ein geschützter Sitzplatz auf der Gartenseite. Ansprechend sind die bewegte Dachlinie und der Kontrast zwischen Holzverschalung und weißer Eternit-Emaille. Konstruktion: Die Raumteile bestehen in den Wänden und Decken aus einem Holzskelett, das mit aufgeleimtem Sperrholz abgedeckt und innen mit Gipsplatten verkleidet ist. Isolierung durch Polystrol und Alu-Folien. Bruttogeschoßfläche 104 qm, GFZ 0,5.

3. Ground floor and upper floor plans and section, 1 in 200. On the ground floor, the entrance is flanked by a store room. In front of the house is a shed which can be extended and can also be used as a garage. Noteworthy features are the spacious kitchen and the possibility of partitioning living room and staircase to suit a number of different functions. On the upper floor are bedrooms and a bathroom.
4. Garden terrace. The door leads to the dining area. On the right, the living room window of the adjacent house.
5. North side with entrance and shed.
6. A "box unit" is being placed in position by a crane.

3. Grundrisse Erd- und Obergeschoß und Schnitt 1 : 200. Im Erdgeschoß befindet sich neben dem Eingang ein interner Abstellraum und vor dem Haus ein erweiterungsfähiger Schuppen, der auch als Garage genutzt werden kann. Bemerkenswert ist die geräumige Küche und die Möglichkeit, Wohnraum und Treppenhaus für verschiedene Funktionen abzuteilen. Das Obergeschoß enthält drei Schlafräume und ein Bad.
4. Gartensitzplatz. Die Tür führt zum Eßplatz. Rechts das Wohnraumfenster des nächsten Hauses.
5. Blick von Norden auf die Eingangsseite.
6. Eine Raumeinheit wird von einem Kran eingehoben.

"Formula" prefabricated houses, England (1963)
Architect: Formula Housing Research Ltd.

Fertighaussystem »Formula«, England (1963)
Architekt: Formula Housing Research Ltd.

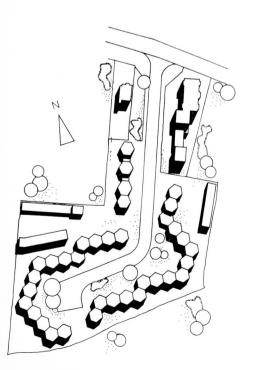

To counter the predominance of the "right angle," house designs have, in recent years, occasionally included hexagonal and octagonal plans (cf. Fig. 31, page 28). So far, however, the only buildings of such type actually realized have been public buildings, exhibition halls and the like. Now, for the first time, the English "Formula Housing Research Ltd." are producing a house with hexagonal plan (Patent No. 9065/63). A remarkable feature is that this prefabricated house can be built either as part of a concatenation, or else as a detached house with one or more storeys. Because of the reduction in external surfaces, the hexagonal shape has certain advantages in regard to thermal insulation. Externally, the houses are attractive; but their plan is still likely to undergo some modifications. Construction: Steel frame consisting of tubular columns, of 12 ft. 4 in. side length on a concrete foundation. The concrete walls of the warm air duct in the centre of the unit have a load-bearing function. Floors, roofs and walls consist of factory-made timber panels. External roof weathering: laminated boarding with aluminium faced felt, with drainage towards the centre. Gross floor area 100 sq. ft.; floor space index 0.4.

In dem Bestreben, die Vorherrschaft des »rechten Winkels« zu erschüttern, sind in Wohnungs-entwürfen der letzten Jahre gelegentlich auch hexagonale und oktogonale Grundrisse vorge-schlagen worden (siehe Abb. 31 Seite 28). Realisierungen fanden sich jedoch bislang nur bei öffentlichen oder Ausstellungsbauten. Die »Formula-Gesellschaft« produziert nun erstmalig ein Haus mit hexagonalem Grundriß, patentiert unter der Nr. 9065/63. Bemerkenswert ist dabei, daß dieses Fertighaus als Reihenhaus und auch als freistehendes ein- oder mehrge-schossiges Haus ausgeführt werden kann. Die hexagonale Form bringt durch die Verringerung der Außenflächen wärmetechnisch gewisse Vorteile. Die Häuser sind äußerlich ansprechend, doch dürfte die Raumaufteilung noch Änderungen erfahren. Für die Konstruktion werden einige wenige Elemente gleicher Abmessung verwendet. Den Kern des Hauses bildet eine konstruktiv genutzte Stahlstütze, in der Versorgungsleitungen untergebracht sind. Decken, Dach und Wände bestehen aus vorgefertigten Holzelementen. Dachhaut: Papplagen mit Alu-Innenentwässerung. Bruttogeschoßfläche 92 qm, GFZ 0,4.

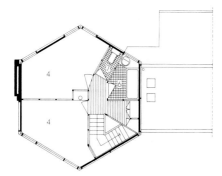

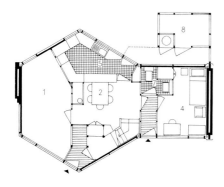

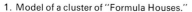

1. Model of a cluster of "Formula Houses."
2. Site plan, 1 in 3000.
3. Plan of ground floor and first floor of a variant of the type shown in the illustrations, 1 in 200. At ground floor level, one enters through a lobby into the dining hall which, together with the kitchen, occupies about one half of the ground floor, the other half comprising the living room. On the first floor are two bedrooms, bathroom and a storage room.
4. View of a cluster of houses already built, some of the houses are already in use.
5. Living room.
6. Breakfast bar with hatch from the kitchen.

1. Modell einer Hausgruppe.
2. Lageplan 1 : 3000.
3. Grundriß Erdgeschoß und Obergeschoß einer Variante des in den Abbildungen gezeigten Typs, 1 : 200. Im Erdgeschoß gelangt man über einen Windfang in die Eßdiele, die zusammen mit der Küche etwa die eine Hälfte des Grundrisses einnimmt. Die andere Hälfte umfaßt den Wohnraum. Im Obergeschoß befinden sich zwei Schlafräume, das Bad und ein Abstellraum.
4. Ansicht einer bereits erstellten und teilweise schon bezogenen Hauszeile.
5. Blick in einen Wohnraum.
6. Der Eßplatz mit Durchreiche zur Küche.

Vöpelswiese-Mixsiepen housing estate, Remscheid, Germany (1960–1963)
Architects: Walter Köngeter and Walter Arns

Siedlung Vöpelswiese-Mixsiepen, Remscheid, Deutschland (1960–1963)
Architekten: Walter Köngeter und Walter Arns

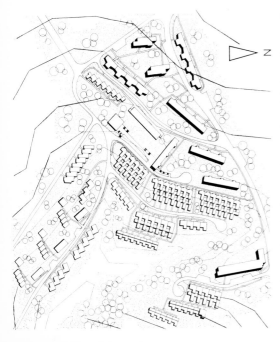

The plan for this housing scheme, comprising some 700 dwelling units, dates back to a competition in 1957. Köngeter and Arns were awarded the First and Second Prize, respectively, and were jointly entrusted with the realisation of the project. On an undulating site of about 50 acres nearly 2 miles from the centre of the city of Remscheid, the idea of optimum density hillside housing was realised as part of a composite housing programme. There are 525 flats in multistorey blocks and 173 dwellings in low-rise houses. The scheme also comprises a shopping parade with six shops and other services. Of particular interest are the patio type houses which, by skilful use of their hillside position, are stacked and terraced in such a way that, despite excellent sunlight and viewing conditions, the density reaches the maximum possible in low-rise housing. Construction: The houses are erected in hollow pumice concrete blocks, with floors and stairs of reinforced concrete. They have a built-up roof with wooden boarding and with drainage to the centre. All the houses have a cladding of silver-grey asbestos cement panels. Type A: Gross floor area 98 sq. metres (1050 sq. ft.); floor space index 0.75. Type B: Gross floor area 115 sq. metres (1240 sq. ft.); floor space index 0.9.

Für diese Siedlungseinheit mit rund 700 Wohnungen wurde 1957 ein Wettbewerb ausgeschrieben, bei dem die Architekten den 1. und 2. Preis erhielten. Daraufhin gemeinsam mit der Durchführung beauftragt, verwirklichten sie auf dem fast 20 ha umfassenden, stark bewegten Gelände, rund 3 km vom Stadtzentrum Remscheids entfernt, den Gedanken einer Hangbebauung mit optimaler Dichte bei gemischter Bebauungsweise. Es entstanden 525 Wohnungen in Mehrfamilienhäusern und 173 Wohnungen in Einfamilienhäusern. Zur Siedlung gehört außerdem ein Zentrum mit sechs Läden und weiteren Gemeinschaftseinrichtungen. Die ein- und zweigeschossigen Flachbauten lehnen sich an die stark fallenden Südosthänge an. Von besonderem Interesse sind die eingeschossigen Atriumhäuser, die terrassenartig, unter geschickter Ausnutzung der Hanglage, so über- und ineinandergeschachtelt sind, daß bei ausgezeichneter Besonnung eine Dichte entsteht, die an der Grenze der für den Flachbau möglichen Dichte liegt. Konstruktion: Die Wohnhäuser sind aus Bimshohlsteinen gemauert, Decken und Treppen in Stahlbeton erstellt. Für die Dachhaut wurden Kiespreßdächer auf Holzschalung mit Innenentwässerung gewählt. Sämtliche Häuser sind mit silbergrauen Asbestzementplatten verkleidet. Bruttogeschoßfläche: Typ A 98 qm, GFZ 0,75; Typ B 115 qm, GFZ 0,9.

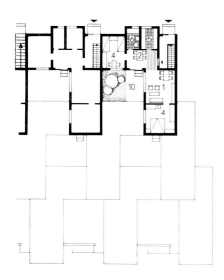

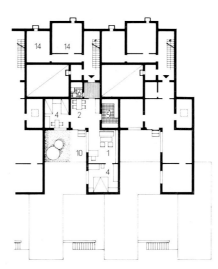

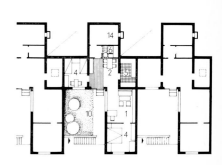

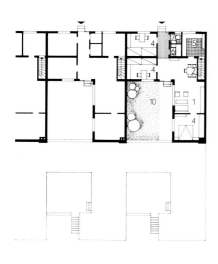

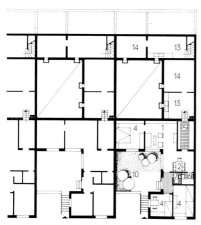

1. The estate seen from the east. Depending on the topographical conditions the houses are arranged in single, double or treble rows.
2. Site plan, 1 in 6000.
3. Plans and section, 1 in 500. Living rooms and bedrooms are grouped around a patio of 5×6 or 5×8 metres (16½×20 or 16½×26 ft.), open to the south-east. The entrance to the houses in the top row leads directly to a hall flanked by bathroom and W.C. In the lower houses, the entrance is through the patio which is reached via a flight of stairs. The three variants of the L-type house have two or three bedrooms. The kitchen has no direct connection with the patio.

1. Blick aus Osten auf die Siedlung. Je nach Geländeverhältnissen sind einfache, doppelte oder dreifache Zeilen entstanden.
2. Lageplan 1:6000.
3. Grundrisse und Schnitt 1:500. Um einen Hof von 5×6 oder 5×8 m, der sich nach Südosten öffnet, sind Wohn- und Schlafräume gruppiert. Bei den oberen Häusern erfolgt der Zugang unmittelbar in einen Flur, an dem Bad und WC liegen. Bei den unteren Häusern gelangt man über eine Treppe in das Atrium. Die drei Varianten des L-Typs haben zwei bis drei Schlafräume. Die Küche hat nur eine indirekte Verbindung mit dem Atrium.

4, 5. Staggered arrangement of the hillside houses.
6. Entrance side of the three bedrooms house. In the background is the multi-storey block.
7. One of the sitting-out terraces.

4, 5. Staffelung am Hang.
6. Zugangsseite des Typs mit drei Schlafzimmern. Im Hintergrund das Hochhaus.
7. Blick auf eine Wohnterrasse.

Page/Seite 163:

1. View of the Mauerberg estate from the south.
2. Model photograph.

1. Gesamtansicht von Süden.
2. Modellphoto.

Mauerberg housing estate, Vienna (1963/64)
Architect: Roland Rainer

Siedlung Mauerberg in Wien (1963/64)
Architekt: Roland Rainer

Architect Roland Rainer has consistently tried to prove and test his housing theories by practical examples. His earlier prototype estate at Veitingergasse, Vienna, was one of his courageous attempts to demonstrate the advantages of low-rise housing with prefabricated units. The Mauerberg estate represents a further noteworthy contribution towards assessing the potentialities of low-rise hillside housing. 43 houses, partly detached and partly combined in clusters or rows, are placed on a south-west slope offering a panorama of the Vienna Woods. At the very top are 18 dwellings in economically designed two-storey terrace houses. A particularly attractive feature of the estate is the network of stairs and footpaths providing access to the houses. The area is completely free from vehicular traffic. Construction: Durisol blocks with concrete core, timber-clad frontages. Floors supported by unconcealed glued timber beams with prefabricated panelling. Built-up roof with timber structure. Gross floor area: Type A 100 sq. metres (1080 sq. ft.), type B 92 sq. metres (990 sq. ft.), type C 114 sq. metres (1230 sq. ft.). Floor space index: 0.3–0.7.

Der Architekt Roland Rainer hat seine Theorien über Wohnformen und Bebauungsweisen stets in der Praxis durch Beispiele belegt und erprobt. Schon die Mustersiedlung Veitingergasse in Wien war einer seiner mutigen Versuche, die Vorzüge des Flachbaus mit vorgefertigten Elementen zu demonstrieren. Auch die Siedlung Mauerberg gibt einen weiteren beachtlichen Beitrag zur Frage nach den Möglichkeiten des Flachbaus am Hang. 43 ebenerdige, teils freistehende, teils in Gruppen und Reihen zusammengefaßte Häuser liegen auf einem Südwesthang mit Aussicht auf den Wienerwald. Den oberen Abschluß bilden 18 Einheiten sparsamer zweigeschossiger Reihenhäuser. Dabei gibt die Aufschließung durch Treppen und Wohnwege der Anlage ihren besonderen Reiz. Das Wohngebiet ist völlig frei vom Fahrverkehr. Konstruktion: Durisolstein mit Betonkern, an den Fronten Holzverschalung. Decke: Im Raum sichtbare verleimte Holzträger, mit Fertigelementen ausgefacht. Dach: Holzkonstruktion, eingedeckt mit Preßkiesbelag. Bruttogeschoßfläche: Typ A 100 qm, Typ B 92 qm, Typ C 114 qm. GFZ: Typ A, B und C 0,3–0,7.

3

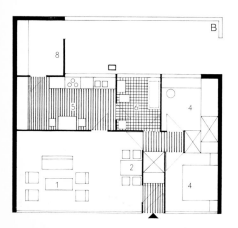

4

A

8

2

5

1

4

4

4

3, 5. Views of the estate.
4. Plans, 1 in 200. The three single-storey types represent modifications of a simple and consistent principle: entrance, kitchen, bathroom and dining recess, possibly also one of the bedrooms, are on the north side whilst the south side is reserved for the living room and two further bedrooms.
6. The entrance is flanked by a storage shed which serves as a substitute for a cellar.
7. The large living room window is protected by an awning against excessive sunlight.
8. Living room with dining area.

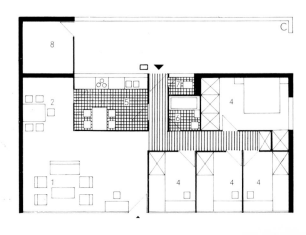

B

8

5

6

4

1

2

4

C

8

2

5

7

4

6

1

4

4

4

5

6

7

3, 5. Verschiedene Ansichten der Siedlung.

4. Grundrisse 1:200. Die drei eingeschossigen Typen sind Abwandlungen eines einfachen und klaren Prinzips: Eingang, Naßräume und Eßnische, eventuell auch ein Schlafraum, liegen auf der Nordseite. Die Südseite ist dem Wohnraum und zwei weiteren Schlafräumen vorbehalten.

6. Neben dem Eingang befindet sich als Ersatz für den Keller ein Abstellraum.

7. Das große Wohnraumfenster ist durch eine Sonnenblende gegen allzu starke Einstrahlung geschützt.

8. Wohnraum mit Eßplatz.

8

Terraced houses at Ullernaasen, Oslo (1962)
Architects: Anne-Tinne and Mogens Friis

Terrassenhäuser in Oslo-Ullernaasen (1962)
Architekten: Anne-Tinne und Mogens Friis

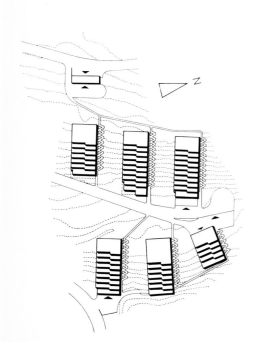

This group of terraced houses provides an example for the highest possible density of a low-rise housing estate on a slope as steep as 45°. Owing to this concentration, it was possible to preserve the surrounding landscape with its birch trees, firs and pines. On the eastward slope stand six groups with a total of 54 terraced houses. Each house has a frontage of 20 metres (66 ft.). The terrace steps are governed by a horizontal module of 4 metres (approx. 13 ft.). Three of the groups are above and three below an approach road from which the individual houses can be reached by stairs. As the angle of the slope varies, the size of the different "steps" ranges from 190 to 400 sq. metres (2050 to 4300 sq. ft.), resulting in 22 variations of the basic plan. The flues of all the fireplaces are connected to a main chimney which is built into the rock behind the houses. The houses are electrically heated; the outdoor terraces are provided with infra-red heating. The estate is generously laid out, well designed, and carefully conceived in its technical details. Unfortunately, the plans do not quite conform to this high standard—the bedrooms are facing north, and the planning of the rooms is not very economic. Construction: Bearing parts of reinforced concrete, facade units of timber. Gross floor area 200–400 sq. metres (2150–4300 sq. ft.); floor space index 1.2.

Die Terrassensiedlung der Architekten Friis ist ein Beispiel für stärkste Verdichtung an einem Hang mit Gefälle bis zu 45°. Durch die Konzentration konnte erreicht werden, daß die Landschaft der Umgebung mit ihren Birken, Rottannen und Kiefern erhalten blieb. Auf dem nach Osten geneigten Hang wurden sechs Gruppen mit insgesamt 54 Terrassenhäusern angelegt. Die Frontbreite der Häuser beträgt 20 m. – Die Terrassen wurden nach einem horizontalen Modul von 4 m gestuft. Je drei Gruppen liegen oberhalb und unterhalb einer Erschließungsstraße, von der Treppen zu den einzelnen Häusern führen. Entsprechend der ungleichen Neigung des Hanges differiert die Größe der einzelnen Typen zwischen 190 und 400 qm, wodurch sich 22 Grundrißvarianten ergeben. Alle offenen Kamine münden in einen Hauptschornstein, der hinter den Häusern in den Fels eingelassen ist. Die Wohnungen werden elektrisch beheizt; die Außenterrassen sind mit Infrarotheizung ausgestattet. Die Siedlung ist großzügig angelegt, formal gut gestaltet und technisch sorgfältig durchdacht. Leider entsprechen die Grundrisse nicht ganz der übrigen Qualität – Schlafräume nach Norden und mangelhafte Raumökonomie. Konstruktion: Tragende Teile aus Stahlbeton, Fassadenelemente aus Holz. Bruttogeschoßfläche 200–400 qm, GFZ 1,2.

1. View of the estate from south-east.
2. Site plan, 1 in 3000.
3. Plan, 1 in 500, and section. The size of the standard type is 215 sq. metres (2310 sq. ft.) to which must be added the ancillary rooms built into the rock which are on the same level as the main premises. Adjacent to them are kitchen and bathroom, followed by dining room and nursery on the east side, and living room and main bedroom on the south side. The partially covered terrace of 80 sq. metres (860 sq. ft.) surrounds the house on the east and south sides.
4. The steps leading to the houses are equipped with electric heating to prevent ice formation during the winter.
5. A view of the terraces on the south-west side.

1. Südostansicht der Siedlung.
2. Lageplan 1 : 3000.
3. Grundriß 1 : 500 und Schnitt. Der Normaltyp hat eine Größe von 215 qm, wozu noch die in den Fels getriebenen Nebenräume kommen. Sie liegen auf einer Ebene mit den Haupträumen. Daran schließt sich die Zone der Naßräume an. Es folgen Eßraum und Kinderzimmer, nach Osten, und Wohnraum und Elternschlafzimmer, nach Süden gerichtet. Die teilweise überdeckte Terrasse von 80 qm umfaßt die Hauseinheit auf der Ost- und Südseite.
4. Die Zugangstreppen. Sie lassen sich, um im Winter Eisbildung zu verhindern, elektrisch beheizen.
5. Blick auf die Terrassen der Südwestseite.

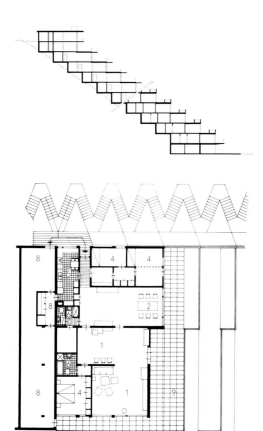

6. View from the south.
7. Living room.
8. All the houses have a magnificent view of the valley and Oslo.

6. Ansicht von Süden.
7. Ein Wohnraum.
8. Von allen Wohnungen hat man eine wunderbare Aussicht auf das Tal und Oslo.

Terraced houses for a residential area at Neugereut, Stuttgart (1963)
Architects: Roland Frey, Hermann Schröder, Claus Schmidt

Terrassenhäuser für ein Wohngebiet in Stuttgart-Neugereut (1963)
Architekten: Roland Frey, Hermann Schröder, Claus Schmidt

The architects had their first success with a proposal for a "hill" of terraced houses in a competition for "Weststadt," Frankfurt-on-Main. The first practical application, in a slightly modified form, is at present coming to fruition at Marl. Their design for Neugereut, Stuttgart, awarded the First Prize, has also been adopted. In principle, a "housing hill" of this type combines a number of different housing types in a single unit which, in its core, also provides space for parked cars, community premises, and shops. In their north-south orientation, the five-storey "housing hills" have the special advantage that all the dwellings enjoy ample sunlight, thus avoiding a major drawback of conventional blocks of flats. On an average, each "hill" contains 95 dwelling units, viz. 30 single-family houses, 16 flats with four or five rooms, 38 flats with three rooms and 12 flats with two rooms. The floor areas are relatively ample; this applies not only to the spacious rooms but also to the outdoor terraces which must serve as a substitute for the garden and provide a glimpse of the open sky. Construction: A module of 3.37 metres (approx. 11 ft.) has been adopted. Party walls, floors and flower boxes can be installed as prefabricated units. The load is transmitted through the girder framework of the garage roof so that stanchion-free construction is possible. The stairs are so arranged that lifts are unnecessary.

Erfolg mit einem Vorschlag für »Wohnhügel« hatte das Architektenteam bei dem Wettbewerb für die »Weststadt« Frankfurt/Main. Die erste Realisierung jedoch, in etwas abgewandelter Form, erfolgt zur Zeit in Marl. Auch die mit dem 1. Preis ausgezeichnete Arbeit für Stuttgart-Neugereut soll verwirklicht werden. Im Prinzip handelt es sich beim Wohnhügel um eine gemischte Bebauungsweise in einem Baukörper, der außerdem in seinem Kern Raum für ruhenden Verkehr, Gemeinschaftsräume und Läden schafft. Bei Nordsüdstellung haben die fünfgeschossigen Wohnhügel den besonderen Vorzug einer einwandfreien Besonnung und vermeiden somit einen wesentlichen Nachteil des üblichen Hochhauses. Jeder Wohnhügel enthält im Schnitt 95 Wohneinheiten: 30 Einfamilienhäuser, 16 Vier- bis Fünfzimmerwohnungen, 38 Drei- und 12 Zweizimmerwohnungen. Die Wohnflächen sind verhältnismäßig reichlich bemessen, sowohl hinsichtlich der geräumigen Zimmer als auch der Terrassen, die den Garten ersetzen sollen und den freien Himmel zum Teil sichtbar machen. Konstruktion: Das Achsmaß beträgt 3,37 m; Wohnungstrennwände, Decken und Blumentröge sind als fertige Elemente einsetzbar. Der Rahmenträger der Garagendecke nimmt die Lasten auf, so daß eine stützenfreie Konstruktion möglich ist. Durch die Anordnung der Treppen erübrigen sich Aufzüge.

1. Model of the entire estate, seen from south-west.

1. Modellphoto der gesamten Anlage. Blick aus Südwest.

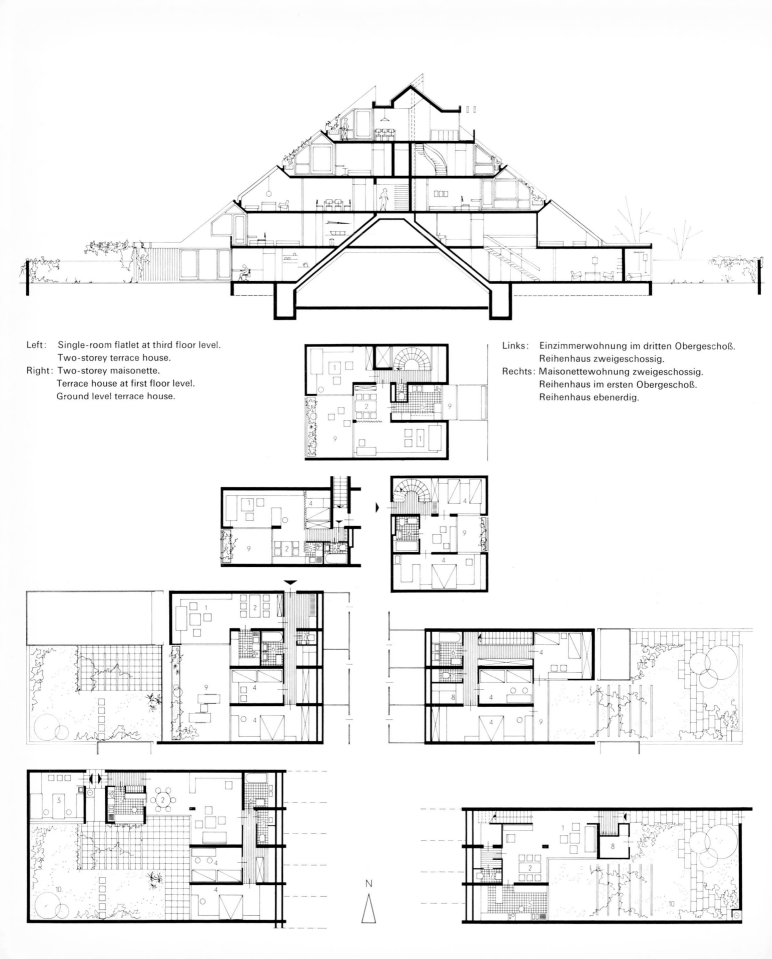

Left: Single-room flatlet at third floor level.
      Two-storey terrace house.
Right: Two-storey maisonette.
      Terrace house at first floor level.
      Ground level terrace house.

Links: Einzimmerwohnung im dritten Obergeschoß.
       Reihenhaus zweigeschossig.
Rechts: Maisonettewohnung zweigeschossig.
        Reihenhaus im ersten Obergeschoß.
        Reihenhaus ebenerdig.

2. Plans and section, 1 in 300. The two lower levels are occupied by single-storey and two-storey terrace houses with three to six rooms and private garden. On the three upper floors are angle-type houses which are grouped around a large terrace with flower boxes so that they convey the impression of detached houses. The second floor is mainly used for three-room flats accessible from a passageway placed in the centre. The two top floors are combined to provide maisonettes, alternately facing east or west. The internal passageway receives daylight not only through the stairwells but also through toplight shafts.

3. The "housing hills" are also suited for hillside construction.

4–6. View from south-west, with entrance for cars (top); terrace and living room of a four-room dwelling, and view of the private gardens of the ground level terrace houses (bottom).

2. Grundrisse und Schnitt 1:300. Ein- und zweigeschossige Einfamilienreihenhäuser mit drei bis sechs Zimmern und eigenem Garten nehmen die beiden unteren Geschosse ein. Das zweite bis vierte Obergeschoß enthält Winkeltypen, die sich um einen großen Balkon mit Blumentrog gliedern und so Einfamilienhäusern ähneln. Auf der Ebene des zweiten Obergeschosses liegen vorzugsweise eingeschossige Etagenwohnungen mit drei Zimmern am innenliegenden Erschließungsgang. Die beiden obersten Geschosse sind zu Maisonettewohnungen vereinigt, die im Westen verschränkt und je nach Osten und Westen orientiert sind. Der Innengang wird nicht nur über die Treppenhäuser belichtet, sondern auch über das Dach durch Schächte.

3. Die Wohnhügel eignen sich auch für eine Hangbebauung.

4–6. Ansicht von Südwest mit Autoeinfahrt (oben); Terrasse und Wohnraum einer Vierzimmerwohnung und Blick in die Wohngärten der ebenerdigen Einfamilienreihenhäuser (unten).

171

Terraced houses at Zug, Switzerland (1957–1962)
Architects: Fritz Stucky and Rudolf Meuli

Terrassenhäuser in Zug, Schweiz (1957–1962)
Architekten: Fritz Stucky und Rudolf Meuli

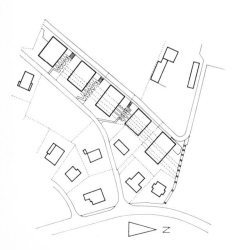

This estate comprises 25 terraced houses in five units, each with its own garage. The architects had to overcome numerous legal and technical difficulties before they were able to build these houses on the steep, irregular slope. The design is reminiscent of a flight of stairs, leading up the slope and secured at its foot by a heavy concrete block. The legal requirements for the super-position of the houses were met by dividing the slope into long and narrow plots of a width corresponding to the stagger of the different floors. Thus, although each owner owns no more than 50 sq. metres (540 sq. ft.) of ground, he has the use of a gross floor area of, say, 150 sq. metres (1620 sq. ft.) and of a terrace of 60 sq. metres (640 sq. ft.). Each dwelling unit in the terraced block has its own service connections and its own oil heating so that it offers the advantages of a detached house, especially also in regard to sound proofing. Gross floor area: type A 110 sq. metres (1180 sq. ft.), type B 112 sq. metres (1200 sq. ft.); floor space index 1.3.

Die Siedlung umfaßt 25 Terrassenhäuser in fünf Blöcken mit den dazugehörigen Garagen. Die Architekten mußten zahlreiche rechtliche und technische Probleme lösen, um die Bebauung des ungleich geneigten, außerordentlich steilen Hanggeländes durchführen zu können. Die Konstruktion entspricht in etwa der einer Treppe, die sich an den Hang anlehnt und der ein schwerer Betonklotz am Fuß als Abrutschsicherung dient. Die rechtlich vorhandene Möglichkeit der Überbauung wurde dadurch ausgenützt, daß man den Hang in Streifenparzellen aufteilte, deren Tiefe der Versetzung der einzelnen Stockwerke entspricht. Bei nur 50 qm Grund stehen dem Eigentümer zum Beispiel 150 qm Bruttogeschoßfläche und 60 qm Terrasse zur Verfügung. Jede Wohnung im Terrassenhaus hat eigene Installationsanschlüsse und eine eigene Ölheizung. Sie besitzt also die Vorzüge eines Einfamilienhauses, insbesondere auch in Hinblick auf den Schallschutz. Bruttogeschoßfläche: Typ A 110 qm, Typ B 112 qm, GFZ 1,3.

1. View from the west.
2. Site plan, 1 in 3000.
3. The spacious terraces are bordered by 80 cm (2′7½′′) wide built-in flower boxes which prevent a view on to the floor below. These artificially created "hanging gardens" are to be planted with grass, and even with trees.
4. Plans, 1 in 300. Twelve different types of dwellings have been developed, ranging from four to eight rooms. In principle, all the living rooms and bedrooms face south, and all the ancillary rooms north. The civil defence shelter below the houses is utilised as storage room. The size of the terraces exceeds the minimum specified for privately owned open space per person. Adequate sunlighting is also ensured.

1. Ansicht von Westen.
2. Lageplan 1 : 3000.
3. 80 cm breite Tröge am Rande der umfangreichen Terrassen verhindern die Einsicht in das darunterliegende Stockwerk. Rasen und auch Bäume sollen auf diesen künstlichen Freiflächen wachsen.
4. Grundrisse 1 : 300. Zwölf verschiedene Wohnungstypen wurden entwickelt. Die Variationsbreite reicht von Vier- bis zu Achtzimmerwohnungen. Grundsätzlich sind alle Wohn- und Schlafräume nach Süden orientiert, die Nebenräume liegen nach Norden. Der darunter befindliche Luftschutzkeller wird als Abstellraum genutzt. Die Terrassen überschreiten das Mindestmaß der privaten Freifläche/Person. Auch ausreichende Besonnung ist gesichert.

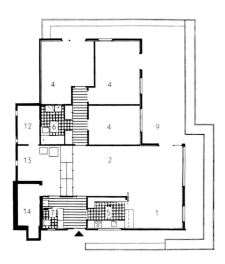

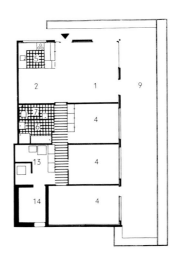

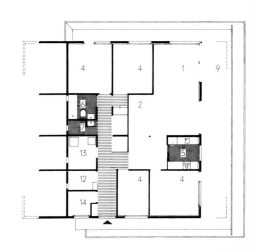

1   Living room

2   Dining room, dining area

3   Working room, study

4   Bedroom, parents' bedroom, nursery

5   Kitchen

6   Bathroom, shower bath

7   W. C.

8   Multi-purpose room, store room, hobby room

9   Terrace, balcony, loggia

10   Patio, garden court, utility court

11   Garage

12   Boiler room

13   Utility room, laundry, drying room

14   Basement, cellar

The entrance is marked by an arrow, the hall by parallel hatching, kitchen, bathroom and W. C. by cross-hatching.

1   Wohnraum

2   Eßzimmer, Eßplatz

3   Arbeitsraum, Studio

4   Schlafraum, Elternschlafraum, Kinderzimmer

5   Küche

6   Bad, Dusche

7   WC

8   Mehrzweckraum, Abstellraum, Hobbyraum

9   Terrasse, Balkon, Loggia

10   Atrium, Gartenhof, Wirtschaftshof

11   Garage

12   Heizraum

13   Hauswirtschaftsraum, Waschküche, Trockenraum

14   Keller

Der Eingang ist jeweils durch einen Pfeil bezeichnet, die Diele durch Parallelschraffur, die Naßräume (Küche, Bad, Toilette) durch Kreuzschraffur.

Photo Credits · Fotonachweis